MUSTANG

A Documentary History of the P-51

MUSTANG

A Documentary History of the P-51

For

Ervin C. Ethell, Colonel, USAF (Ret)
My Dad
who put me on the wing of his Mustang
when I was barely old enough to walk,
who instilled in me the love of flying.
Nothing has been quite the same since.

by Jeffrey Ethell

JANE'S
LONDON · NEW YORK · SYDNEY

During 6 June 1944 most pilots flew several missions in support of the invasion. As this pilot steps out of his P-51, fuel is already going into the port wing tank and the 0·50-caliber guns are being rearmed. *(USAF)*

First published in the United Kingdom in 1981 by
Jane's Publishing Company Limited
238 City Road, London EC1V 2PU

ISBN 0 7106 0070 4

Published in the United States of America by
Jane's Publishing Incorporated
730 Fifth Avenue
New York
N.Y. 10019

ISBN 0 531 03736 3

Designed by Geoffrey Wadsley

Printed in Great Britain by
Netherwood Dalton & Co Ltd, Huddersfield

Contents

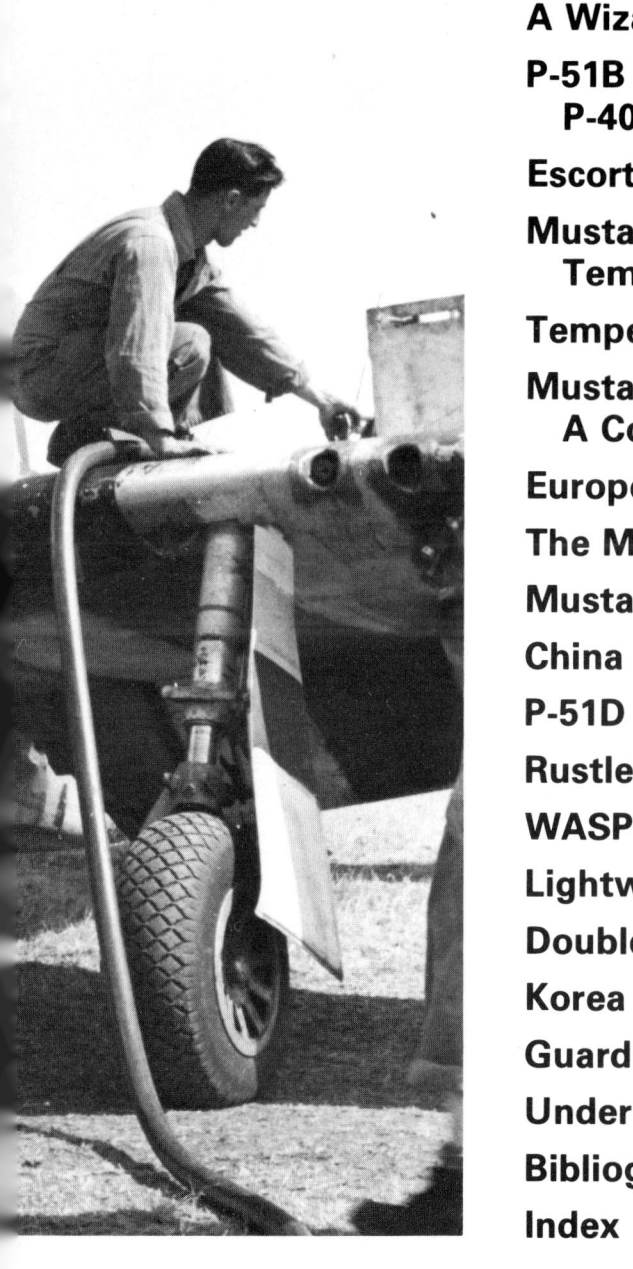

Acknowledgements

In spending over two years researching *Mustang,* I have come to owe a debt of gratitude to a great number of aviation historians and collectors. Most were incredulous that I was going to try to write something new about the "ole '51": hadn't it all been said? Nevertheless, each dug into their areas for me, producing sometimes a little, sometimes a great deal. Added to my records and pictures from official and personal sources, the material began to multiply until there was enough for several new books on the aircraft.

All the agencies connected with the US Air Force gave me great support in my quest for material: Maj Paul Kahl Jr, Magazine & Book Division; the entire staff of the Albert F. Simpson Historical Research Center, Maxwell AFB, Alabama; Dana Bell of the AAVS in Arlington, Virginia; Chuck Worman and Royal Frey at the Air Force Museum; Bill Heimdahl, Jacob Neufeld and Don Rightmyer at the Office of Air Force History, Bolling AFB, Maryland; Robert J. Smith, Office of History, Air Force Logistics Command.

Jay Spenser, Phil Edwards and Claudia Oakes at the National Air and Space Museum, Smithsonian Institution, helped whenever asked, often beyond the call of duty. Earl Blount, Ralph J. "Doc" Watson, Bob Hoover and Gene Boswell at Rockwell International pitched in, as did Cindee Gracyalny at the Experimental Aircraft Association.

My fellow historians and enthusiasts made much of this possible: Paul Coggan of Mustang International, the new Association of P-51 Historians, Alfred Price, Christopher Shores, Bill Hess, Jerry Vernon, Dick Phillips, John Dienst, Dave McLaren, Dusty Carter, Roger Freeman, Mike Bailey, Kenn Rust, Yasuho Izawa, Osamu Tagaya, Henry Sakaida, Yoji Matsumura, David Glover, Frank F. Smith, Bruce Hoy, Thomas Hitchcock, Norm Malayney, Roger Besecker, Ron Witt, Arno Abendroth, Dave Menard, Dave Knight, Daniel T. Williams of Tuskegee Institute, Tom Ivie, John Horne, J. Watson Noah, Garry Fry, J. Andrew White, John Lambert, Preben Bajlum, F. Kovacs, Rainer Niedree, Paul Hermsen, George Punka, Dave Anderton, R. D. Crookham, T. R. Bennett, Sally Van W. Kiel, Elmer Ward and George Enhorning (both P-51 owners), Fred E. Robinson of the North Dakota ANG, John Stanaway, Lillian Moore of the AIAA, Florian Davatz, Robert Esposito, Norman Avery, Norman Taylor, Ken Bokelman, AAHS Negative Lending Library.

Then there were those who actually took part in the Mustang's history as engineers, pilots, ground crews and technicians: Ben Kelsey, Don Maggert, Glenn Eagleston, Kenneth Martin, Edward "Buddy" Haydon, Don Lopez, Jack Ilfrey, Horace Q. Waggoner, Jerry Brown, Tony Chardella of the 369th FS Assn, George Gosney and Dave Mayor of the BAD 2 Assn, Lee Archer, Lou Purnell, Roscoe Brown, Barrie Davis, Cass Hough, Wayne Rutherford, Parke Smith, Jerome Jacobs, James H. Doolittle, David Hudson, Milt Miller of the 14th AF Assn, John Woolnough of the 8th AF Historical Society, Jean Landis, Barbara Erickson London, Louis J. Walkover, Donovan Berlin, Alexander R. Ogston, Alexander H. Flax, Frank Compton, Frank Erny, Walter Tydon, R. M. Bascom, Bill Burchard, Gorden H. Hunsberger of the 355th FG Assn, Larry Horras, Lars Olausson, Edward J. Steiner, Elmer W. Odell, James H. Howard, James A. Gasser, Daniel Zoerb, Jim Carter, Joseph M. Fiedler, W. Bruce Overstreet, Arval J. Roberson, Thomas Hayes, Budd J. Peaslee, Hubert Zemke, Bill Cullerton, Bill Dumas, Ben Williams, John A. Kirk, Ed Bollen, Günther Rall, Yohei Hinoki, Duxford 78th FG Assn, Merle Olmsted, George Meacham Jr, Thomas Glasgow and Erv Ethell.

Introduction

When Michael Stevens of Jane's first approached me through my good friend and fellow writer Alfred Price about doing a new book on the P-51 Mustang, I was surprised that anyone would still consider publishing yet another work on such a well covered subject. Only the Spitfire could possibly exceed North American's spirited pony in the number of books on a single aircraft. To come up with any new material—much less enough for a major book—would be a challenge.

However, I had an ace up my sleeve that gave a hint not only of new material, but information that would literally change the history that has been written. It came in the form of Benjamin S. Kelsey, former Pursuit Projects Officer for the Army Air Corps during the genesis of the Mustang. I had interviewed Ben on numerous occasions concerning the beginnings of such aircraft as the P-35, P-36, P-38, P-39, P-40, P-47 and P-51. His recollections of the Mustang were revealing to say the least.

Subsequent research into the original British and American records began to turn up contradictions to earlier accounts of the Mustang's career. As I interviewed the people behind the records, confirmation of many controversial points was almost unanimous. The documents reproduced here have never been printed before, and rarely have they even been consulted. I have remained faithful to the actual record, injecting nothing that could not be substantiated. There were several other controversial areas of the aircraft's history that I did not include, simply because they could not be substantiated with documents from the period concerned.

From the original NA-73X to the P-82 Twin Mustang, this history will make stimulating reading for all students of the P-51. The beginnings of the Mustang, as related here, contradict the previously accepted story. The attitude of the US Army Air Force to the XP-51 has never been accurately stated, particularly in relation to Wright Field and the origins of the A-36. The Merlin Mustang was not considered the answer to the AAF's escort-fighter dilemma by some, and in spite of its performance advantage it was almost removed from AAF service due to its severe reliability problems.

For the most part the photographs in this book have never been published before. I was surprised and delighted that so much could be unearthed.

The story of the Mustang, told here by those who lived with it, by their documents and by the pictures, is even more fascinating than the legend that has grown up around the aircraft.

Jeffrey Ethell
November 1980

The Curtiss XP-40, originally fitted with an aft belly scoop radiator, first flew on 14 October 1938. Designer Donovan Berlin's innovative cooling system was later removed, though it was subsequently incorporated into the follow-on XP-46. *(Walter Tydon)*

Ordered in September 1939, the Curtiss XP-46 was Don Berlin's attempt to incorporate the latest aerodynamic advances into a fighter. Due to the difficulties of stopping the P-40 production line to introduce the new fighter, the wind-tunnel data on this aircraft were sold to North American Aviation in April 1940 for $56,000 to form the basis for a new fighter to be built for the Anglo-French Purchasing Commission. The XP-46 first flew in February 1941. *(NASM)*

Foaling of a Mustang

The 1930s found the nations of the world rearming for conflict or isolating themselves from the possibility, depending upon the prevailing philosophy. As Europe headed towards the inevitable, the United States attempted to avoid involvement, and its military posture reflected this desire for isolation. But behind the scenes US officers and men were fully aware of the eventual outcome of such a posture: lack of military preparedness for global war. That the US armed forces had enough men and equipment to survive, let alone prevail, in the war that came was a tribute to these men and their behind-the-scenes maneuvering.

Nothing illustrates this better than the state of American military aviation, particularly the US Army Air Corps, during those years. When Gen Henry H. "Hap" Arnold took control of this underfunded arm, aviation was still a stepchild of the ground forces. Aircraft would either defend the coastal areas of the USA (a mission which the US Navy was determined not to relinquish) or support ground forces as "flying artillery". Arnold and his subordinates were forced to use any subterfuge in order to build up the Air Corps.

The breath that kept the Air Corps' experimental sections alive in the mid-1930s was their considerable freedom in the procurement of experimental and test aircraft. This came under the direction of Col Oliver Echols, and it is due to his work that the Air Corps had as much as it did when war finally came. Echols ruthlessly made use of experimental and trials aircraft to push forward the state of the art. Once the project had been agreed, up to 14 examples could be built before the Air Corps had to go to Congress for more money. Cash was always limited, however, so even this procedure could not be over-exploited.

The experimental and production types were controlled from Wright Field, Ohio. Benjamin Kelsey headed the office which controlled pursuit types, Leonard Harmon had bombers, and attack aircraft came under Patrick Timberlake. The relative importance of these project offices within the Air Corps is reflected by the ranks of those in charge of them: all were first lieutenants, and their total staffs consisted of one civilian engineer and one secretary for each office. Everything else the Air Corps required in the way of aircraft came under the office for transports and trainers.

During the mid-1930s there was a distinct lack of urgency about the development of new fighters. In spite of this, however, Oliver Echols was able to get money and push the development of the XP-38, XP-39 and XP-40 designs, as well as other less successful types. The XP-38 and XP-39 were both born as "interceptors," a term with enough ambiguity to allow the Pursuit Projects Office to go for the highest performance without having to adhere to any rigid philosophy.

The Curtiss XP-40 deserves to be considered in some

detail, for it was to have an important influence on the evolution of the P-51. In fact the XP-40 was not a new design, but merely a re-engined P-36. Ben Kelsey had pushed for the construction of the next-generation Curtiss fighter, which was already on the drawing boards in 1938. But the Air Corps could not allow the time needed to build the "follow-on development of the XP-40". That would have meant running another fighter competition, with additional time to allow other competitors to alter their designs also.

The XP-40 flew for the first time on 14 October 1938 with its radiator mounted far aft of the nose, under the belly. Three months later it won the 1939 fighter competition at Wright Field, leading to the largest airframe and engine contract let by the War Department since 1918. The production aircraft, however, had the radiator mounted forward under the nose because, according to designer Donovan R. Berlin: "The Curtiss-Wright management thought it looked better that way." Berlin hoped to take his advanced wind-tunnel studies for a more advanced belly-scooped fighter and apply them to his next-generation fighter.

Following the German invasion of Poland in September 1939, the British and the French purchasing teams were in the US within days, seeking new fighters. The British settled on the P-40 as the best of the American fighters and by early 1940 both they and the French had placed orders for as many as they could get.

Kelsey and Echols regretted the push to build the aircraft. When Arnold came to Wright Field during this period, Kelsey recalls, "Echols told him that if the US could just hold off building these P-40s for a while and not try to increase production, we could rush through [what had become known as the XP-46, which had been ordered on 29 September 1939] and substitute the P-46 for the P-40 in the build-up. Then we'd have the airplane we should have and not the one that was locked, essentially, into the 1936 P-36 procurement. Echols and Arnold walked down the hall together. Arnold was impressed and he said he would check it out in Washington and let us know. The next day or day after he called back and said: 'We're committed to a training programme with a great many pilots and to a deployment programme that involves the creation and commissioning of new groups. We just can't afford to lose the P-40s.'"

Not only did the British and French want fighters quickly, but the Air Corps saw the significance of building up its own pitifully poor force into a fighting machine; numbers were of paramount importance, and rightly so. Every P-40 was already committed.

In the late fall of 1939 the British Purchasing Commission, working with the French, began to scout around for other companies that might build P-40s under license. Sir Henry Self, in charge of the Commission's New York office, had particularly good relations with North American Aviation of Inglewood, California. NAA was building sturdy Harvard advanced training aircraft for both the British and French, who were well pleased with the product. A 1939 proposal from the Commission, for NAA to build P-40s, was not taken very seriously.

Then in January 1940, recalls Ben Kelsey, "Echols made a suggestion to the British Purchasing Commission that they find a manufacturer who wasn't already bogged down in high-priority stuff. Then Curtiss-Wright and the Air Corps would make available all the data we had on the XP-46, to help them build a new fighter."

Self again approached James H. "Dutch" Kindelberger of North American about the possibility of building P-40s under license, or of designing a new fighter using the Curtiss wind-tunnel data and the results obtained when the belly scoop was flown on the original XP-40. The latter course was chosen. From January to April 1940 J. Leeland Atwood, vice-president and assistant general manager of North American, was ordered by Kindelberger, president and general manager, to deal with both the British and with Curtiss-Wright.

Since Don Berlin had spent the better part of the past two years developing the more advanced XP-46 he was approached by Burdett Wright, general manager at Curtiss-Wright at Buffalo, about the possibility of selling the data to North American. Berlin gave the go-ahead, and North American bought the XP-46 data for $56,000. It must be stressed that these were not, as has been so often reported, the P-40 data.

In his letter to Sir Henry Self on 1 May 1940 (reproduced as Appendix B), Atwood reported: "We have reached an extremely satisfactory agreement with the Curtiss Aeroplane Company of Buffalo whereby they are furnishing to us data covering a comprehensive series of wind tunnel, cooling, and performance tests of a *similar airplane* [author's italics], which data will assist us in the design and manufacture of these airplanes."

The previous month, after he had outlined the concept for a new fighter, Atwood accepted a letter contract from Self (reproduced as Appendix A) to get the project started. Initially it was designated the NA-50B. More significantly, on 4 May 1940 North American signed a Foreign Release Agreement with the Air Corps for the foreign sale of the Model NA-73 (as the new fighter was now known) that gave the Air Corps two aircraft of the type intended for sale. The release specifically requested the fourth and tenth production examples.

On 23 May a formal contract was signed between the Anglo-French Purchasing Commission and North American Aviation Inc for 400 examples of the Model NA-73. NAA chief engineer Raymond Rice and his team, under chief designer Edgar Schmued, began working seven days a week to get the job done.

"The original concept did not include the laminar flow wing," says Lee Atwood. The design of the wing was placed under the aerodynamics engineering group headed by Larry Waite. Engineering concepts developed during the 1930s were to have a profound effect on the Mustang. At the National Advisory Committee for Aeronautics (NACA) research offices at Langley Field, Virginia, serious work had been done on new airfoil shapes. In the full-scale wind tunnel there the first airfoil to display "laminar flow" had been tested in June 1938. The wing section had a drag coefficient of only 0.003, far better than any previous airfoil of similar thickness. True laminar flow can be achieved only under ideal conditions: a perfectly smooth surface of perfect contour, without any disturbances to the airflow caused by dirt, rivets, servicing doors, dents, vibration, wing distortion or manufacturing flaws. Anything that breaks up the sheet of air passing nearest the wing makes it impossible to achieve the desired effect of having layers of air "laminated" on top of each other to produce a perfectly smooth flow. Although a great deal has been said about the NA-73's laminar-flow wing as one of the keys to its success, the contribution of what is now known as a "No 66 section" airfoil lay in the fact

The prototype NA-73X was never expected to fly within 120 days of go-ahead. When it did fly on 26 October 1940 in the hands of Vance Breese, it was evident to NAA personnel that the aircraft was a superb blend of the latest innovations in American aviation. *(AAHS)*

that the maximum thickness of the wing was around two-thirds of the distance from the leading edge, thus delaying the turbulence that tends to disturb airflow. In fact true laminar flow could never be achieved, but the wing section finally incorporated into the NA-73 certainly enhanced its performance.

In June 1939 the Langley wing section research was released under a confidential classification for use by the aircraft industry. Edward Horkey, working for Waite on the aerodynamics of the NA-73, became convinced that this wing section should be used on the new fighter.

Still behind the scenes, but well aware of what was happening, Echols sent Ben Kelsey down to Langley to make sure North American received as much data as possible from Curtiss and from the NACA tests. "The records show all this happened," recalls Kelsey, "without anybody at Wright Field having the foggiest notion of what was going on. We had to stay out of it, because it was a British procurement."

Work on the new fighter advanced rapidly. When Eastman Jacobs of NACA came out to visit the California office he was "pressganged" into temporary service to mate the new airfoil section with the NA-73 design. The North American team was now working 16 hours a day, seven days a week on the project. The famous air-racing pilot Art Chester was put to work designing the powerplant installation as far back as the firewall. The only practical high-powered liquid-cooled engine available in the USA, the Allison V-1710, was selected for the prototype and Chester's installation was both clean and efficient.

In retrospect, it is clear that the true genius of the North American team at this time lay in its ability to take several years' of aerodynamic research from others and incorporate it into their own design. In striving for the cleanest possible configuration, they had used the basic XP-46 data and incorporated them in an aircraft with a laminar-flow wing. In the interests of mass production, the design team decided on square-cut wings and tail rather than the rounded shapes then in vogue in the USA.

Contrary to the legend that has grown up around the Mustang, the British set no 120-day time limit for completion of the prototype. The only dates mentioned in the contract were January 1941 for the initial delivery and 30 September 1941 for completion.

Using as much as possible in the way of existing internal systems from the AT-6 (hydraulics, wheels, brakes and electrics), the men at North American pushed the NA-73X out of the shop in a remarkable 102 days. The engine arrived 20 days later, and on 26 October 1940 Vance Breese, the noted freelance test pilot, took NX19998 into the air for its maiden flight from Mines Field, California.

As Curtiss later found when they finally flew the XP-46, there were some problems with the ventral cooling scoop (in fact the majority of the problems would not be solved until the P-51B appeared in 1943 and the scoop was lowered out of the boundary-layer turbulence under the fuselage). Contrary to what some accounts have stated, the initial Mustang radiators did not produce thrust by virtue of the so-called "Meredith Effect".

It would have been impossible to create a design as well balanced as the NA-73 from scratch in just 120 days, but the legend has been repeated so many times that it has taken on the air of fact. Those outside North American who were concerned with the innovations incorporated into the NA-73X received little credit, such was the urgency of the drive to build as many aircraft as quickly as possible. The chief engineer at Curtiss-Wright reflected on this, shortly before

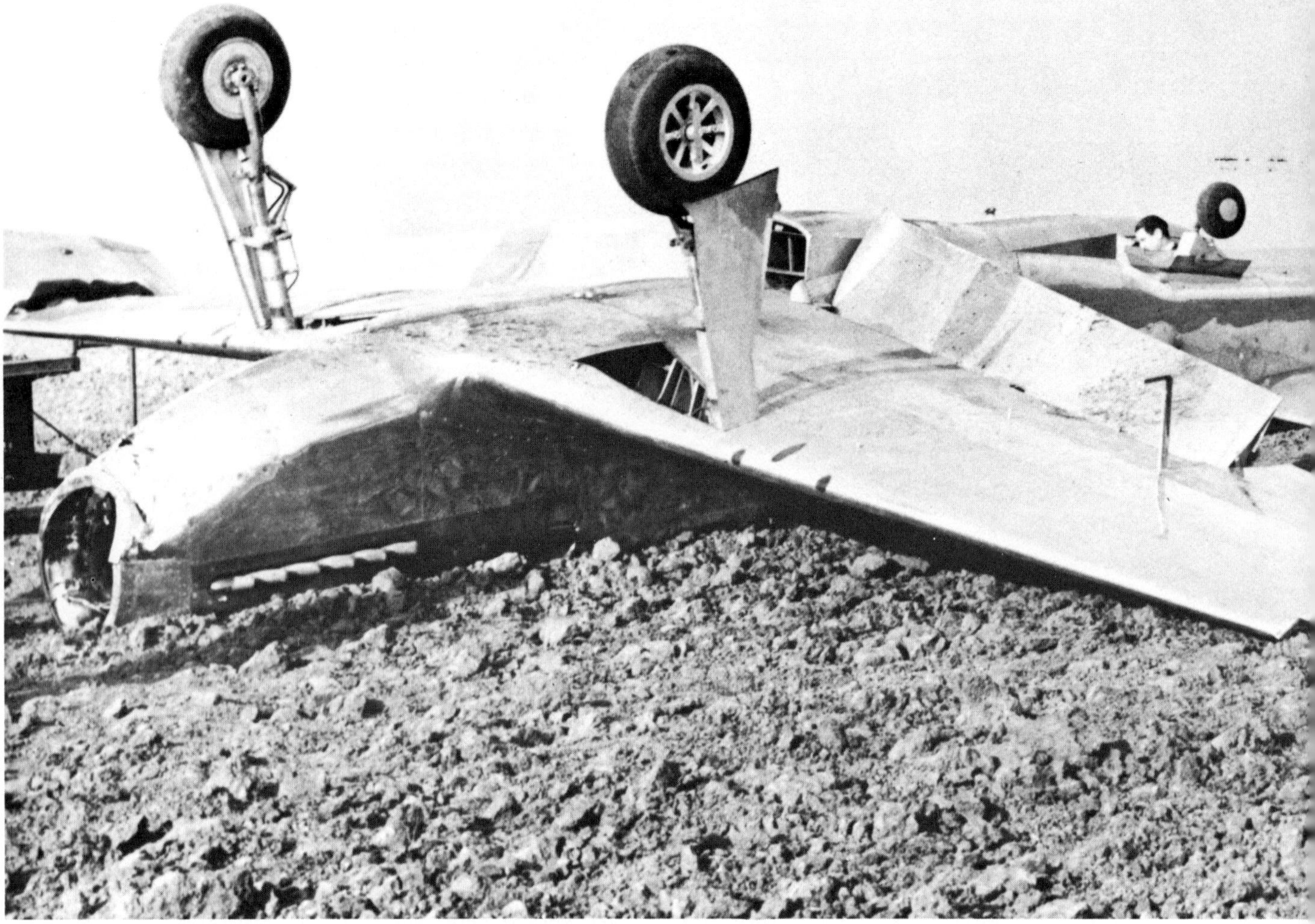

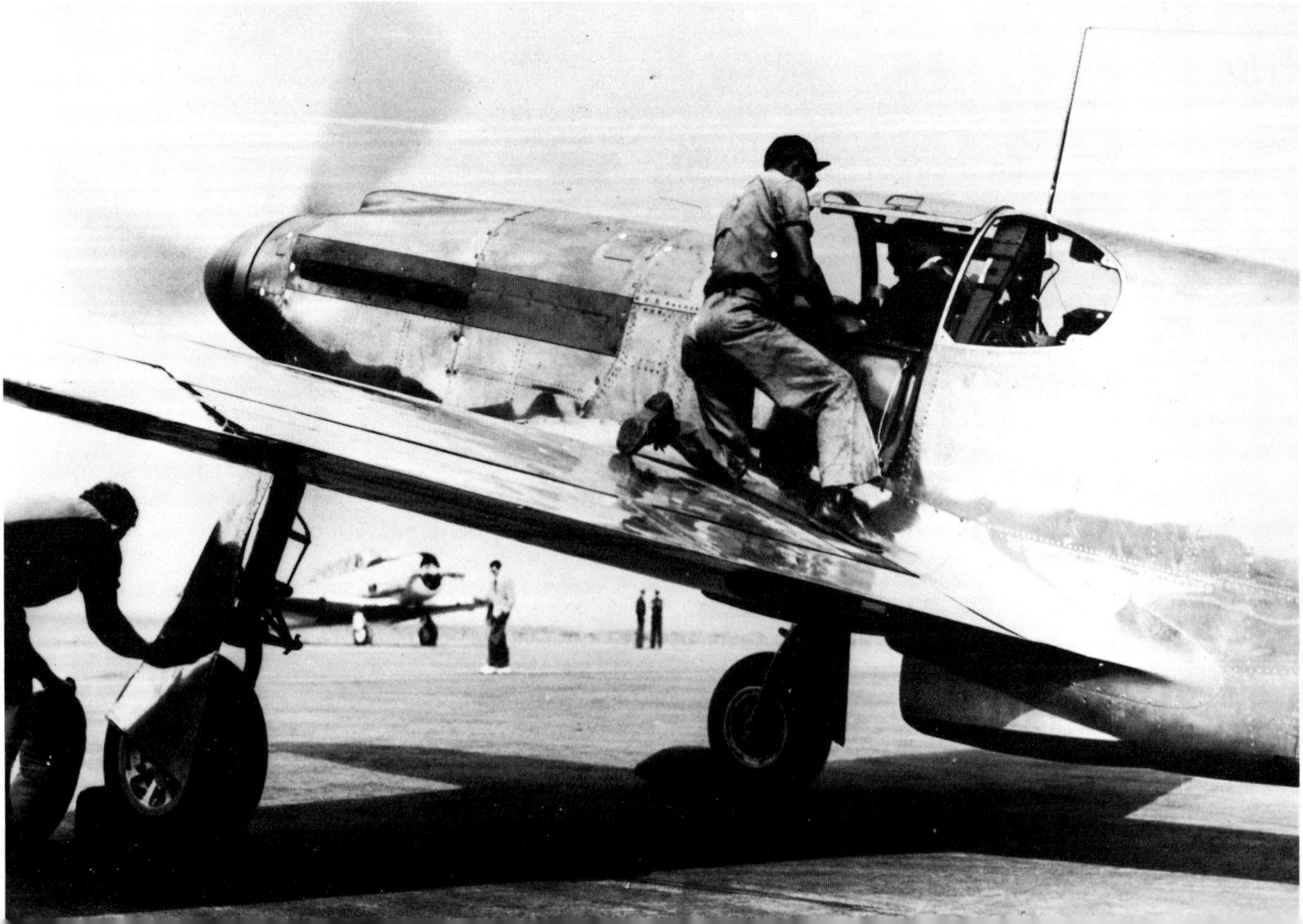

Above: **On 20 November 1940 Paul Balfour made his first (the aircraft's fifth) test flight in the NA-73X. The engine stopped and Balfour was forced to put the aircraft down in a plowed field, severely damaging the prototype.** *(NAA via Roger Freeman) Left:* **The NA-73X was rebuilt after the crash. Here test pilot Vance Breese runs up the Allison engine before the first post-crash flight, on 11 January 1941.** *(NAA via Norm Avery)*

One of the most influential designers to work on the NA-73X and subsequent Mustangs was Edgar Schmued, seen here getting out of the third production P-51. *(Frank Compton)*

the Mustang reached the peak of its fame in World War II. In a letter dated 28 October 1943, Fredric Flader told Curtiss-Wright employees: "While the first 525 P-40s were being produced, a brand new pursuit was developed. This was the XP-46. It was completely new in external shape and internal construction. It was the result of extensive wind-tunnel research at the NACA and was considerably faster than the original P-40s. It handled well but had certain minor troubles in cooling, etc, which could have been solved, if it had been decided to produce it.... It seemed certain that before it would be desirable to take a chance on slowing up [P-40] production by introducing a new model, we would have available an airplane far superior to the XP-46. Therefore, the wind tunnel data and design data of the XP-46 were sold to the North American Company for development into a pursuit for Britain. A comparison of the outlines and construction of the XP-46 with those of the highly successful Mustang will show that Curtiss Engineers have contributed substantially to this aspect of winning the war. This fact, while unknown to

the general public, is well known to responsible military personnel. Incidentally, the performance of the XP-46 and the original Mustang were strikingly similar, even to certain difficulties with cooling; and recent great improvements are due primarily to greatly superior engine performance."

On 24 September 1940, before the NA-73X flew, the British were confident enough to place an order for an additional 300 examples of the new fighter. Someone in the British Air Ministry displayed the English talent for coming up with the proper appellation. A popular tune of the time contained the line: "Saddle your blues to a wild mustang, and gallop your troubles away, away." The free-spirited mustang of America's Western plains certainly seemed an apt namesake, and on 9 December 1940 the British Purchasing Commission wrote to North American concerning the NA-73: "We are to inform you that the above mentioned aeroplanes are to be given the official designation 'Mustang' and this name shall be used in all correspondence."

The new colt was off and running.

Appendix A

N. A. A.   11.4.40

I am directed by His Majesty's Government to inform you that it is their intention to purchase from you 400 single-seat fighter aeroplanes, plus spare parts therefor in the amount of 20% of the value of the aeroplanes.

Material Ordered

(a)   400 North American model N.A.-50B single-seat fighter aeroplanes fitted with Allison CV-1710 engines and three bladed metal propellers all in accordance with North American specification No. -1592 as finally altered and amended and agreed upon.

(b)   It is agreed that the price of each aeroplane ready for conditional delivery at your factory and fitted with Government-furnished engine, propeller and governor, radio, machine guns, gun sights, oxygen equipment and any other armament or special military equipment items which may be furnished by the Government will not exceed $40,000. The final price will be agreed upon at the time of final approval of the specification as provided hereunder.

(c)   Spare parts to be selected from a list you will submit providing spares for all units furnished by you in the manufacture and supply of these aeroplanes in an amount of 20% of the total money value of the aeroplanes.

(d)   Export crating of the completed aeroplanes shall not exceed the amount of $800 per aeroplane additional.

(e)   Crating for the export of the spare parts referred to in (c) above amounting to 4% of the purchase price of the spare parts.

Delivery

You agree that subject to final agreement on all the terms and provision of Specification 1592 as amended by mutual consent, and subject to the payment of the initial payment specified hereunder within 30 days of the date of this letter, to effect conditional delivery of the first completed aeroplane in January 1941 and to effect conditional delivery of the 400 aeroplanes by September 30th, 1941. You further agree to deliver at least 50% of the spare parts called for herein by September 30th, 1941 and to complete delivery of all the spare parts by December 31st, 1941.

Payments

The Government agrees that within 30 days of the date hereof and upon mutual agreement on the final terms of the specification and the price of the aeroplanes to pay to you 10% of the total contract amount. The Government further agrees to pay you an additional 2½% of the total contract amount each thirty days after the payment of the initial 10% until a total amount of 25% of the contract amount has been paid.

Immediately upon receipt of your acceptance and acknowledgement of this letter the Government will transfer to your account the sum of $100,000, which sum shall be considered a part of the initial payment of 10% specified above.

Sir Henry Self
Anglo-French Purchasing Commission

Appendix B

Sir Henry Self,   May 1, 1940.
Anglo-French Purchasing Commission,
15 Broad St.,
New York, N. Y.

Dear Sir:

In accordance with our understanding, we are proceeding with the design of a single-seat fighter airplane, our Model NA-73, incorporating an Allison engine and fitted with provisions for equipment and armament as detailed more completely hereunder.

We have reached an extremely satisfactory agreement with the Curtiss Aeroplane Company of Buffalo wherein they are furnishing to us data covering a comprehensive series of wind tunnel, cooling, and performance tests of a similar airplane, which data will assist us in the design and manufacture of these airplanes. We have also received release from the United States Army for the manufacture and export of these airplanes and wish to assure you that all arrangements are entirely satisfactory.

We are prepared to construct and deliver to you 320 of these airplanes before September 30th, 1941, and guarantee to effect deliveries in accordance with the following delivery schedule:

1941	JAN	FEB	MAR	APR	MAY	JUN	JUL	AUG	SEP	OCT	NOV
Airplanes	1	5	20	40	50	50	53	51	50		
Spares (Equivalent Airplanes)			1	3	5	5	5	5	10	15	15

We further offer to continue the manufacture of these planes at the rate of fifty airplanes per month until at least the end of the year 1941, should you desire to incorporate and exercise an option for these additional airplanes prior to April 30, 1941.

We have constructed a mockup and have completed the initial phase of the detail design and are submitting to you herewith certain data and information regarding the characteristics of the airplane. You will note that we have provided for armor protection for the pilot and a sealing arrangement for the fuel tanks. Provisions are being made for the installation of four .50 cal. machine guns, two of which are in the fuselage and the other two in the wing. As a normal load we are specifying 200 rounds of ammunition per .50 cal. gun, but are making additional provisions for more ammunition as a special load. Provisions are being made for four British Type 303 machine guns with ammunition boxes to accomodate 500 rounds of ammunition per gun as normal load.

Strictly for comparative purposes, we are including results of a study showing the difference in size and performance between the airplane offered and one which might be offered with a minimum of armament and without protective armor. This second design (P-509) incorporates only four machine guns and is not fitted with protective armor, but is otherwise the same. It will be noted that the high-speed in this condition is 400 mph with a wing area of 190 sq ft. With a full complement of armament and armor plate protection front and rear, the weight is increased from 6,450 lbs to 7,765 lbs and the wing area is increased from 190 sq ft to 230 sq ft in order to maintain the same landing speed. The resulting performance is materially reduced and the high-speed is 384 mph under the same conditions.

The speeds quoted above are based on a power of 1,030 hp at 16,000 feet altitude, using 90-octane fuel. Since we do not have precise and final information on the power rating of the engines to be furnished for these airplanes, this rating is still somewhat of an estimate. We believe the Anglo-French Commission has or will shortly have accurate information on this matter. When we receive the exact figures, the performance guarantees will be arithmetically adjusted.

The general provisions for armament have been discussed with Air Commodore Baker and Mr. Thomas and it is believed that the arrangement offered is the most practical possible at this time, consistent with the general instructions we have received. It is possible to increase the fire power through the installation of additional guns if absolutely necessary but the performance will suffer a proportionate loss. We feel there will be no difficulty in making any changes or modifications which you may feel are essential or desirable and are prepared to cooperate with your Technical Staff to the fullest extent. We do feel, however, that the design as presented is close to an optimum condition, all things considered. Details of equipment and installation are yet to be covered but our previous experience with Harvard aircraft, which incorporate much British equipment, leads us to believe that we will have no difficulty whatever in arriving at satisfactory agreements in all these matters.

We have made a careful estimate of the price, including sufficient structural tests to guarantee the structural integrity of all parts, wind tunnel testing and flight testing. We have included a price breakdown, separating and pricing all items of equipment to be installed and supposedly furnished by us. We have not considered the price of engine, propeller, radio, oxygen, machine guns or other items of armament or military equipment, and it is assumed that these items will be furnished to us free-of-charge for installation in the airplanes. The price summary for airplanes, exclusive of crating or transportation, but covering all other charges, is as follows.

(A) Power Plant, Engine Accessories	$ 983.95	
(B) Instruments	1,787.35	
(C) Electrical Equipment	890.75	
(D) Miscellaneous Equipment	528.40	
(E) Radio Equipment	Customer Furnished	
(F) Armament	Customer Furnished	
Total equipment to be furnished by Contractor	$ 4,190.45	
Base Airplane	33,400.00	
Total per Airplane	$37,590.45	
Total for 320 Airplanes		$12,028,944.00
Spare Parts (20%)		2,405,788.80
Crating, per Airplane $675.00, Total		216,000.00
Crating for Spare Parts (4%)		96,231.35
Total Contract Amount		$14,746,964.35

Within sixty (60) days after the contract has been executed we will furnish a complete percentage breakdown and a recommended list of spare parts to approximate 20% of the contract price of the airplanes. Spares will be delivered in accordance with the delivery schedule attached hereto provided a spare parts list is approved and agreed upon within sixty (60) days after submission of such a proposed list by us.

We are prepared to proceed immediately upon receipt of a letter from you accepting this proposal and receipt of down-payment. We desire a down-payment of 10% of the contract amount upon approval of this proposal and a subsequent monthly payment of 2.5% of the contract amount each month until 25% of the contract has been paid. Details of final payments and acceptance will be as mutually agreed upon and in general accordance with our previous contracts with the British Government. We feel there will be no difficulty in the preparation of the final contract at your convenience inasmuch as we have reached agreements with your staff concerning all principal points involved in a contract of this type.

The prices quoted above are intended to include all normal and reasonable modifications and changes which you may require, provided that such changes are agreed upon within three months of the date of the agreement and provided there is no considerable additional expense to us as might be involved in the purchase of additional material or equipment. Changes initiated after this time may involve a delay in delivery or an increase in cost.

May we request that you give this matter your early attention as we are prepared to proceed on receipt of a letter of approval from you and receipt of down-payment as requested above. We will consider the date of receipt of this payment as the date of the contract.

If there are any matters not properly covered in this letter or the enclosed data and it is necessary to withhold the letter until such matters are clarified, we will greatly appreciate it if you will notify us of these matters by telegram or telephone at our expense in order that there will be no delay.

Very truly yours,
NORTH AMERICAN
AVIATION, INC.

J. L. Atwood,
Vice President

British Yearling

Vance Breese made three further flights in the NA-73X before turning over flight-test work to North American's Paul Balfour, who made his first flight in the prototype on 20 November 1940. Fuel starvation caused the engine to cut out, however, and Balfour crash-landed into a plowed field short of the runway, seriously damaging the aircraft.

Even though the aircraft was rebuilt, the flight-test schedule had to be completed with the first production Mustang I, AG345, which was flown for the first time on 23 April 1941 by Louis Wait. The aircraft was subsequently retained by North American for project testing. AG346 was the first Mustang shipped to Britain; it arrived at Speke Aerodrome in October for assembly and initial flight testing. Deliveries had been delayed by a number of things that did not show up until AG345 was under full test. Initial results revealed that at one particular throttle setting the engine ran very rough because of a lack of effective ram air for the carburetor. When this was found to be the cause of the NA-73X crash, the carburetor air scoop on top of the cowling was lengthened.

The Mustang displayed indifferent high-altitude performance with the Allison engine, and the Royal Air Force assigned the new fighter to Army Co-Operation Command for low-altitude attack and tactical reconnaissance. In this role it was a marked improvement over the Lysanders and Tomahawks which it replaced.

The first Mustang Is were issued to No 26 Squadron in February 1942 and the first sorties over France were flown on 5 May.

On 28 January 1942 two Mustang Is, AG360 and AG365, were sent to the Air Fighting Development Unit at Duxford for tactical and armament trials. The resulting report, the first evaluation of the Mustang as a combat type, is given below:

TACTICAL AND ARMAMENT TRIALS—MUSTANG I AIRCRAFT

Pilot's Cockpit

The cockpit is fully enclosed and although a trifle cramped for a tall pilot [it] is otherwise roomy and comfortable. The positioning of the instruments and controls, apart from the undercarriage lever which is difficult to reach, is reasonably good. The top of the cockpit and the port side panel are hinged in order to facilitate entry and exit. Sliding clear vision panels are fitted on either side similar to those used in the Defiant. It is possible to jettison the whole enclosure in emergency.

The cockpit, although fitted with a cold air duct, is excessively hot, even whilst flying at high altitude under freezing conditions. In addition, there is a warm air duct which it has never been necessary to use. Tests are being carried out at A.S.T. Hamble with a modification prepared in conjunction with this Unit which should overcome this trouble.

TACTICAL TRIALS

General

The Mustang is considered an excellent low and medium altitude fighter and certainly the best American fighter that has so far reached this country. It is faster than the Spitfire VB at all heights up to 25,000 feet and compares favourably in manoeuvrability. It can out-dive the Spitfire with ease, but has an inferior rate of climb.

Flying Characteristics

The aircraft is pleasant to fly, being extremely stable in all planes. The take-off is rather long but with little tendency to swing, and as the engine is not fitted with an automatic boost control, care must be taken not to overboost. The landing is easy though the run is longer than that taken by a Hurricane or Spitfire. The controls are well balanced and can be made light or heavy as required by adjustment of the servo-tabs fitted to ailerons and elevators. There is little tendency to heavy-up at high speeds. With the controls lightened by the tabs, the Mustang is as light as the Spitfire but far smoother in all manoeuvres. The aircraft handles extremely well in aerobatics and gives ample warning of the stall. In particular, it was found far more difficult to effect a high speed stall than in a Spitfire.

Performance

The Mustang was compared with a Spitfire VB, both aircraft carrying full war load, and up to a height of 25,000 feet was found to be faster. Its maximum true speed is developed at a height of about 15,000 feet and is between 375 mph and 380 mph. The approximate speed advantages of the Mustang at various heights are as follows:

At 5,000 feet—30 mph faster than the Spitfire VB
At 15,000 feet—35 mph faster than the Spitfire VB
At 25,000 feet—1-2 mph faster than the Spitfire VB

Climb

The rate of climb of the Mustang at all heights is not so good as that of the Spitfire VB. At low altitudes the difference is only slight, but more marked as height is increased, and from 20,000 feet it takes one minute longer than the Spitfire to climb to 25,000 feet. It is considered that the operational ceiling of the aircraft is approximately 25,000 feet, where although the level speed is slightly faster than the Spitfire VB, the rate of climb has fallen off to about 1,000 feet per minute. The Mustang was climbed on from 25,000 feet up to 30,000 feet, the climb being very slow and uncomfortable and the controls sloppy. In level flight at 30,000 feet, however, the aircraft handled quite well though accurate flying was necessary to prevent losing height in turns.

Dive

The Mustang dives very fast, its initial acceleration being particularly good, and in comparative trials was always able to dive away from the Spitfire; when diving, recovery was found to be easy even at an indicated speed of 500 mph. Instructions contained in the Pilot's Notes state that during dives it is necessary to turn to the reserve tank to avoid starvation and to lower the deflector plate in front of the radiator to prevent the glycol temperature becoming too low, but diving tests showed that this was unnecessary. During prolonged dives, however, particularly at altitude when the radiator temperature was inclined to fall, the lowering of the deflector plate was found to be necessary. This plate, when in use, affects the trim considerably and causes vibration.

Search

The all-round view from the Mustang is fairly good in its present form, but when the proposed armour plate is fitted behind the pilot, the view directly astern will be very poor. The frames running level with the pilot's eyes hinder the view considerably, though he can see round them by moving his head. The view is improved by opening the side panels but these cannot be opened at speeds above 250 mph, IAS, and even when open are sucked shut at higher speeds. A rear view mirror is fitted inside the cockpit and is the best internal one that this Unit has seen. It covers a wide field though it does not extend very far downwards. The field can be increased upwards by moving the mirror, which is hinged at the top of its mounting. The clarity of images in the mirror is especially good considering the very small angle at which the line of sight passes through the top perspex of the hood.

Endurance

The total fuel capacity is 140 gallons, which allows an endurance of approximately 4 hours at economical cruising (1,800 rpm and 25″ mercury). At maximum continuous cruising (2,600 rpm and 37″ mercury) the endurance is reduced to about 1 hour 40 minutes.

Instrument Flying

The aircraft, being extremely stable, is very easy to fly on instruments and it can be trimmed to fly "hands and feet off" in level flight or when climbing or diving.

Low Flying

The pilot's view forwards and downwards is better than from a Spitfire and this makes it far better for low flying and ground strafing. As the cockpit hood cannot be opened in flight, however, and there is no forward clear vision panel, low flying in bad visibility is unpleasant.

Formation Flying

The aircraft is pleasant to fly in formation. It has a wide speed range, but owing to its clean lines, deceleration is slow.

Engine Starting and Quick Take-Offs

The Allison engine is very easy to start even under the severest winter conditions, but some minutes are necessary for warming up after a cold start, as the minimum oil temperature that is safe for take-off is far higher than for Merlin engines. A warm engine offers no difficulty and a quick take-off was effected in six minutes from time of the order being given to the aircraft being airborne.

Manoeuvrability

The Mustang was compared with a Spitfire VB, both aircraft carrying full war load, for turning circles and dog-fighting at all heights up to 25,000 feet. At that height there was nothing to choose between the aircraft, but at lower altitudes the Spitfire had the advantage over the Mustang, being able to turn a little tighter.

The use of flap for tightening the Mustang's turn was tried and found to be quite effective but even so it could not out-manoeuvre the Spitfire. Up to 15° of flap can be used and usually results in a gain of height when applied but the advantage is only momentary and can become a serious disadvantage if the Mustang wants to break away in a fast dive.

The Mustang can easily out-dive the Spitfire and owing to the cleanness of its design and its weight can retain the high speed obtained in a dive for a long time after levelling out. Its superior speed below about 25,000 feet and the ability to dive with full power from straight and level flight by applying negative 'G', ie like the Me 109, allow it to break off combat or re-engage at any time.

The rate of climb being inferior to that of the Spitfire, it cannot make use of climbing turns to obtain an advantage unless it has already dived down from a superior height, its best tactics being to attempt to engage from above and then to use the speed gained in the dive to zoom up out of range for a second attack.

One difficulty encountered during dog-fighting and diving is that having no automatic boost fitted, the pilot must constantly check his boost gauge below 15,000 feet, as the limitations can easily be exceeded during the heat of combat.

Short trials were also carried out against the Typhoon between 10,000 and 15,000 feet, in which the Mustang proved to be the more manoeuvrable though outclimbed by the Typhoon. When either attempted to break off the engagement by diving away it was found that the Mustang could accelerate away at the beginning of the dive but was soon caught up by the Typhoon and conversely the Mustang might get a chance of a shot at the beginning of the Typhoon's dive but in the end the latter drew away.

ARMAMENT CHARACTERISTICS

Gun Installation

The armament consists of two ·5's and four ·30's in the wings, and two ·5's in the lower part of the fuselage below the engine. The guns are fired by electric solenoids operated by a trigger on the front of the control column, and a switch is fitted on the port side of the dashboard allowing the pilot to select as follows:- "Wings", "Fuselage", "All" . . .. The absence of vibration during the firing trials was remarked upon by all pilots.

EQUIPMENT REQUIRED AT FORWARD BASES

It is thought that little extra equipment would be required for operating the Mustang from a forward base. The radiator, however, picks up mud easily on a muddy aerodrome and water under pressure is required for removing it successfully . . .. It has the benefit of having three good methods of starting—by external battery, by internal battery, and by hand inertia. It must be noted that the size of the forward base must be greater than the minimum necessary for contemporary types.

(signed)
Ian Campbell-Orde
Wing Commander,
Commanding, A.F.D.U.

AFDU/3/20
5th May 1942

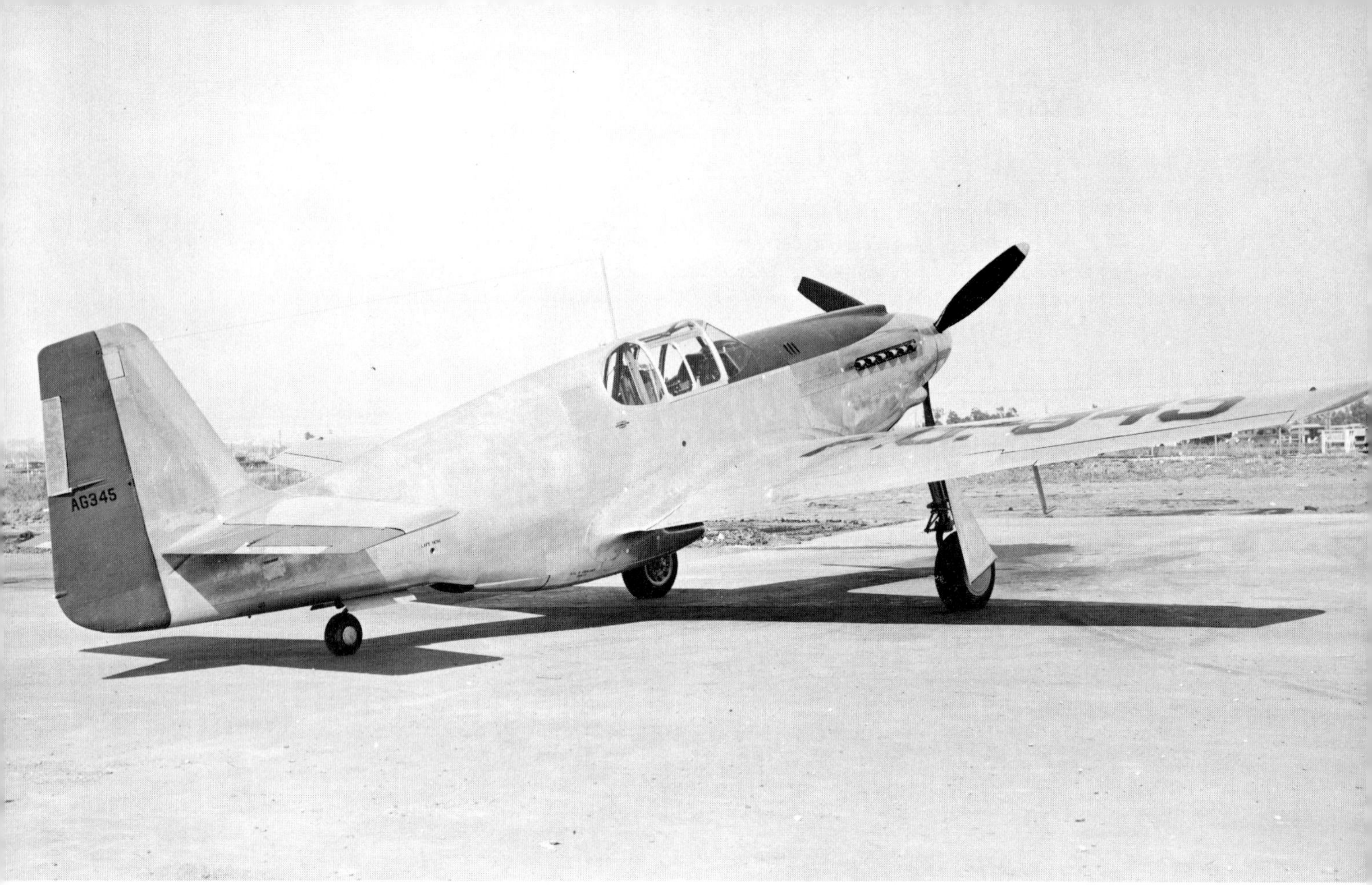
AG345

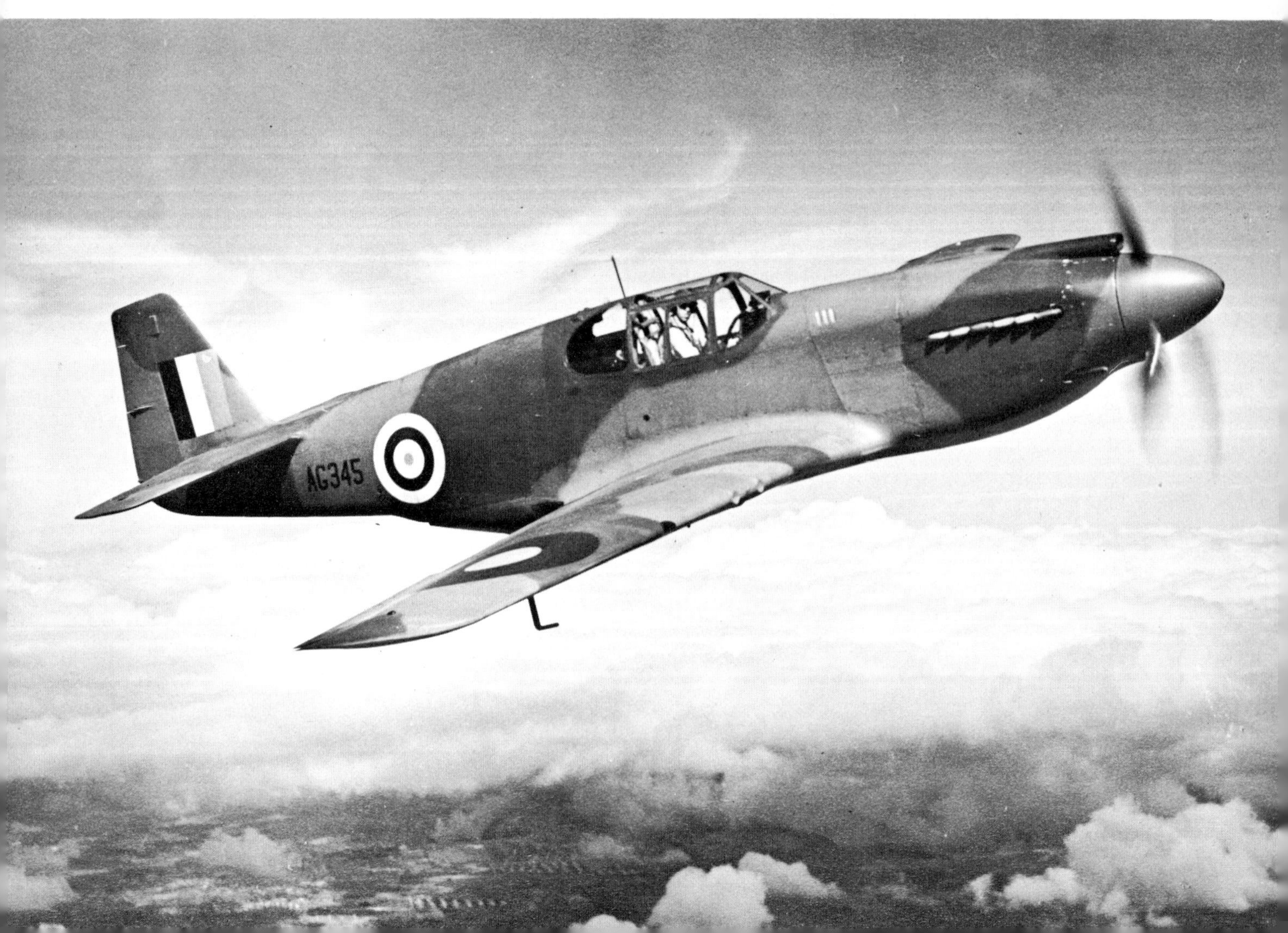
AG345

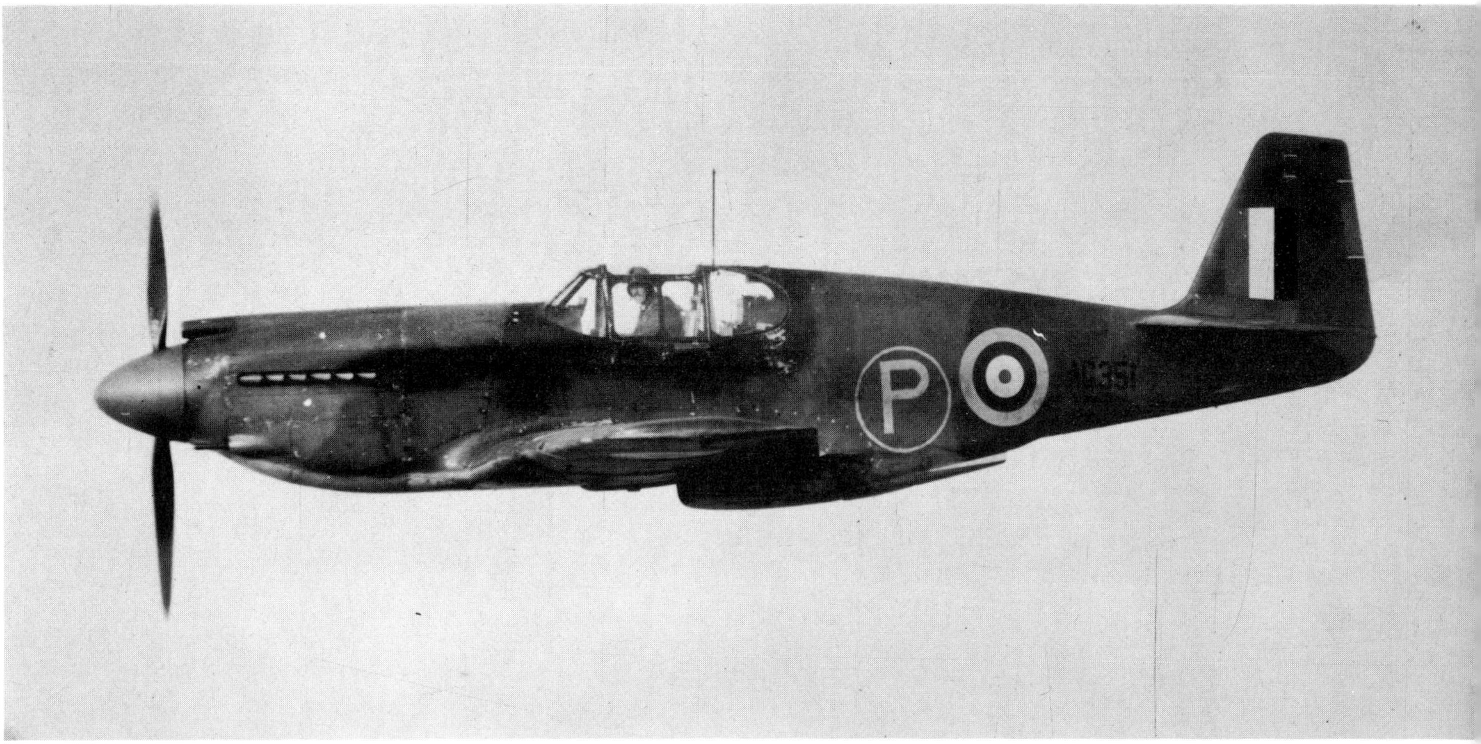

Above left: **AG345, the first production Mustang, flew for the first time on 23 April 1941 in the hands of Louis Wait. Note the original short carburetor air scoop on top of the cowling.** *(NAA via Roger Freeman)*

Below left: **Although the first Mustang was retained in California by North American for flight testing, it was painted in RAF camouflage and the carburetor scoop was lengthened to production standard.** *(NAA via Roger Freeman)*

Above: **The seventh production Mustang I was one of the few to have the circled P (for prototype) painted on during Air Fighting Development Unit trials.**

Right: **No 2 Squadron RAF Mustangs in flight on 26 July 1942. Due to the altitude limitations of the Allison engine, the Mustang was given to Army Co-Operation Command for low-level strafing and tactical reconnaissance.** *(Keystone Press via Mike Bailey)*

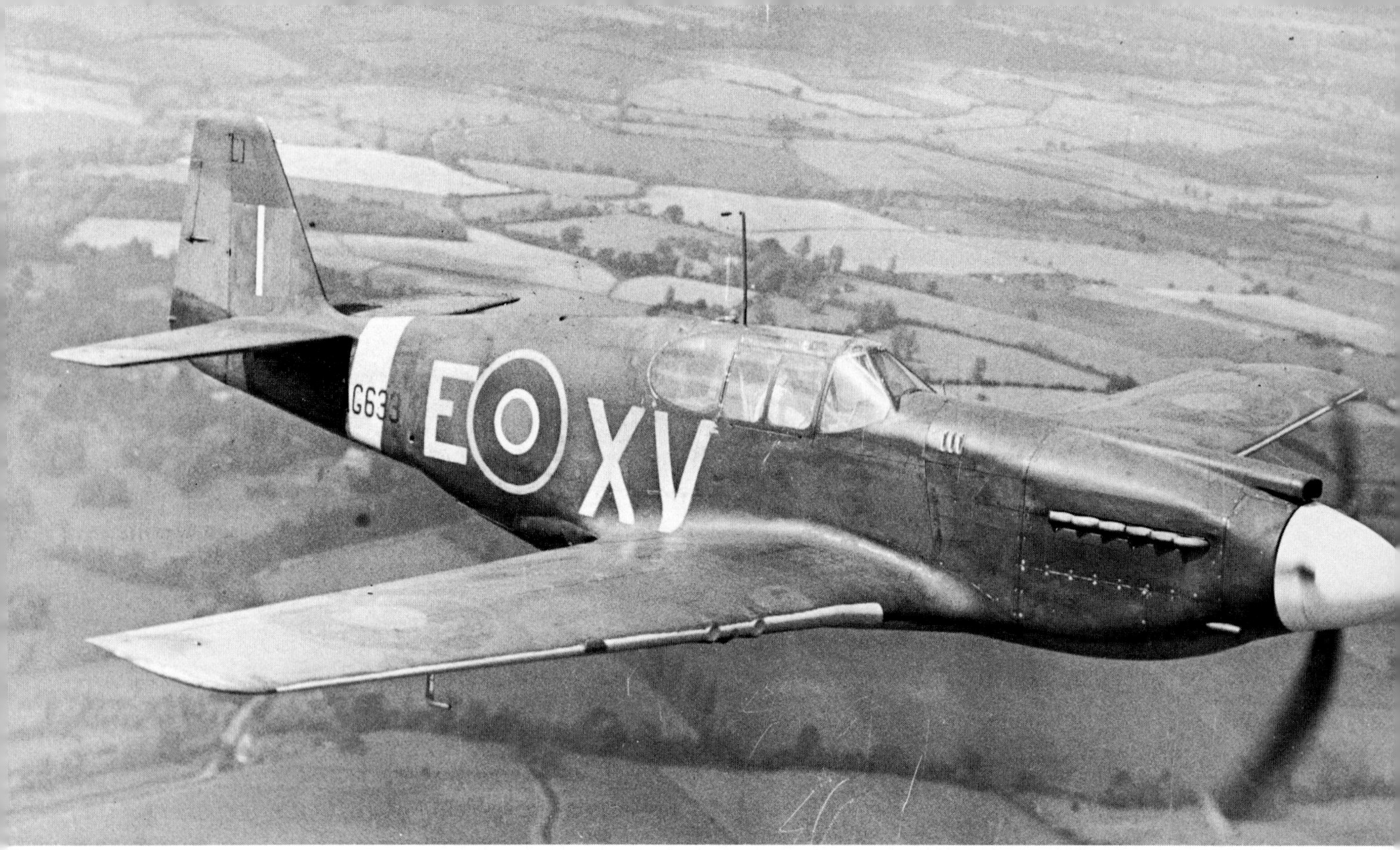
G633
E
XV

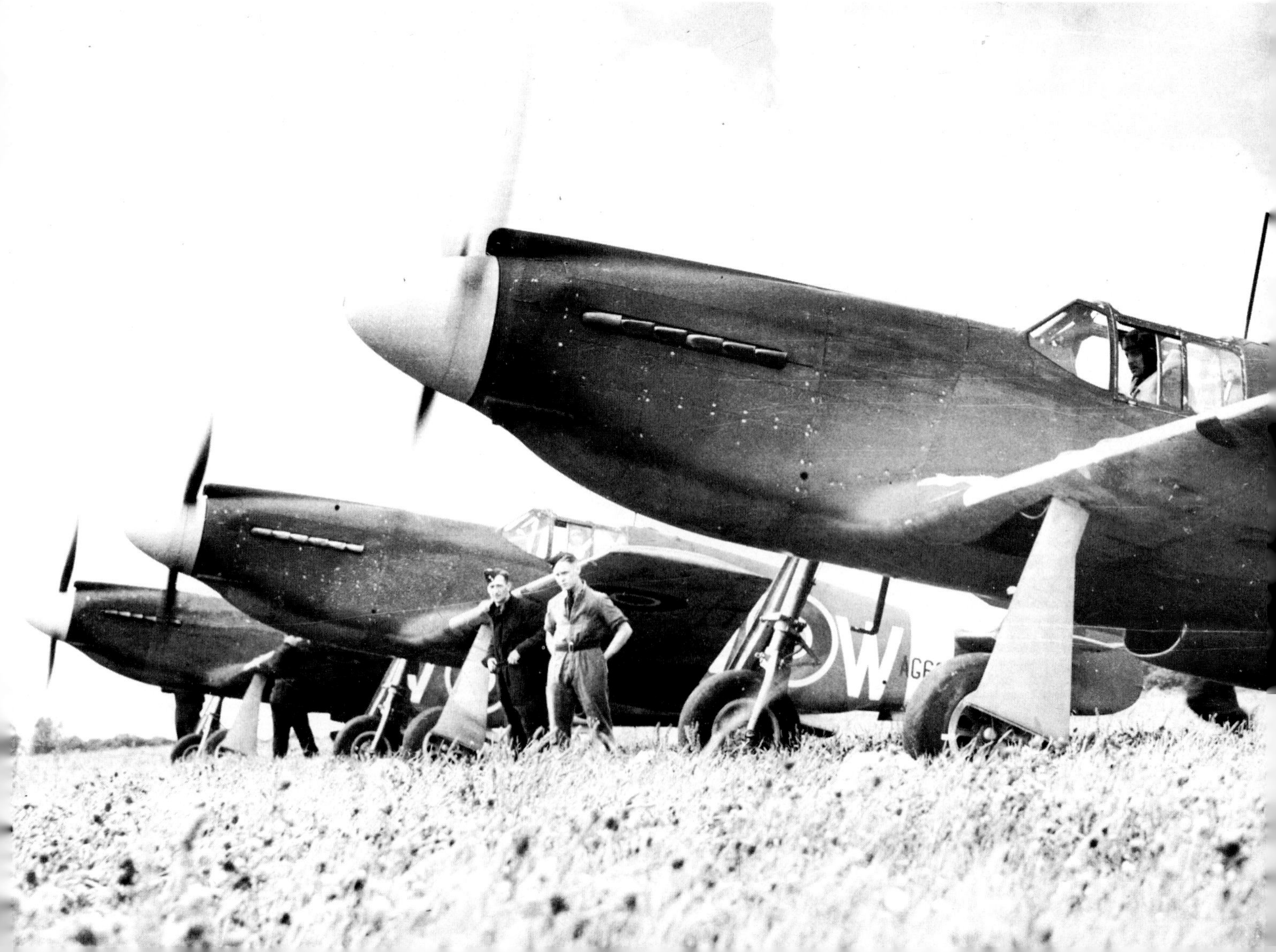
W

Above left: **An early No 2 Squadron Mustang I in July 1942.** *Keystone Press via Mike Bailey)*

Above: **The RAF gave newly arrived Yanks a chance to work on their country's product at Burtonwood. Taken on 1 April 1943, this picture shows (from left to right) Flt Sgt R. A. Wellersman, Margate, England; SSgt Arthur Cunningham, Minnesota, USA; TSgt F. L. Resnak, Washington DC, USA; LAC S. H. Cooke, London; and TSgt Robert Root, Kentucky, USA.**

Left: **One of the early Mustang units, No 2 Squadron, warming up their Allisons in mid-1942. Although several units were transitioning to the aircraft, there were none at full strength for the 19 August 1942 mission over Dieppe, in which the aircraft saw its first intensive action.** *(Mike Bailey)*

In April 1942 No 16 Squadron traded in their Lysanders for Mark Is and No 613 Squadron got rid of their Tomahawks for the new fighter, followed in May by No 239 Squadron (previously Tomahawks) and No 4 Squadron (Tomahawks, Lysanders and other types). By late summer Nos 2, 63, 169, 241, 268, 400 and 414 squadrons (the latter two RCAF units) were flying Mustangs.

Initially the Army Co-Operation Mustang squadrons stretched their muscles with low-altitude recce missions, using an F24 camera mounted behind the pilot's seat. Even though enemy territory was being crossed, the Mustangs did not see much action until "Operation Jubilee" over Dieppe on 19 August 1942. A composite unit of Mustangs and operational pilots was drawn from several of the squadrons to fly reconnaissance sorties over the raid area. Flying Officer Hollis H. Hills, a US citizen from California, claimed an FW190 to draw first blood for the Mustang.

After Dieppe some of the squadrons began to fly "Rhubarb" missions, nuisance raids on which two or four aircraft flew at low level and strafed targets of opportunity. Even though the Army missions were not aimed at hunting enemy aircraft, the Mustang pilots began to appreciate what the aircraft could do in combat below 15,000 feet. Confidence grew.

One of those who had the opportunity to transition into Mustang Is found the aircraft quite a step forward. Pilot Officer Parke F. Smith had joined the RAF from his native Virginia in the hope of flying with one of the Eagle squadrons. At the end of 1942 he graduated to fighters and in February 1943 he reported to 41 OTU at Hawarden, Wales, to fly the Mustang with Army Co-Operation Command.

Smith's checkout in the fighter on 18 February consisted of his being told the following: "Here's how to start the bloody thing; read this manual; make sure the temp gauges don't go into the red . . .. That's a good chap, have a good flight." He had never before flown a high-performance fighter, and he recalls rocketing down the field at a horrifying rate and then being off the ground before he knew what was happening.

Three out of five pilots in Smith's class were killed converting to the Mustang. Seagulls inhabited the area and it was not unusual to hit one or more when coming in to land. They would batter the leading edge of the wings or get stuck in the carburetor air scoop. When trying to go around pilots found much of the lift on the wings destroyed, and with landing gear and flaps either down or on the way up, there was not enough power to stay in the air.

There were cooling problems too. When taxiing the engine would overheat; Smith remembers the Allison boiling over quite often. In flight the oil would freeze in the radiator, causing the temperature to go up due to lack of circulation, while the glycol temperature would go down. The procedure, which was not mentioned in the manual, was to shut the radiator exit gate and retract the forward portion of the scoop to warm the oil—the reverse of what was normally done when oil temperatures went into the red.

The Mustang I was much heavier that other British fighters and Smith did not think it a great aerobatic machine. Visibility out of the cockpit was not very good, particularly on take-off and landing, but interior comfort was excellent and the cockpit was quiet.

The Mustang's shining attribute, in Smith's opinion, was speed. The fighter could gain airspeed rapidly and once at speed it would stay there easily. Smith enjoyed pulling up to the Spitfires and Hurricanes based at Hawarden, waving and then shoving the throttle forward to leave them behind.

Early in 1943 Army Co-Operation Command was disbanded and its Mustangs given to Fighter Command pending formation of the tactical air force designed to support the invasion of France. By 31 May the transition was complete. Soon afterwards US officers wrote the following report on the employment of the Mustang by the Royal Air Force:

BRITISH ARMY CO-OPERATION TACTICAL EMPLOYMENT OF THE MUSTANG I (P-51)

26 August, 1943

Introduction

Wing Commander Peter Dudjeen, a former squadron commander of one of the Army Co-Operation units, was contacted on 31 May, 1943, the day Army Co-Operation activities were being taken over by the RAF Fighter Command.

General

The long range of this aircraft (180 US gallons) made it an excellent tactical reconnaissance aircraft and its armament made it effective against most ground targets. As their operation progressed, they swung more and more to offensive reconnaissance and began to take advantage of targets of opportunity until the operation finally developed into a strategic effort against ground objectives such as railway locomotives, canal barges, heavy motor transport vehicles and aircraft on the ground.

These daylight intrusion raids (Rhubarbs) were very successful, largely due to the care and effort which went into the planning and operation of the missions. The theme was the destruction of those targets designated with the minimum number of casualties. That this was achieved is attested by the record of this squadron, which in 18 months of operation destroyed or damaged severely 200 locomotives, over 200 barges and an undetermined number of enemy aircraft on the ground. This was accomplished with only one ship being shot down by enemy fighters, five ships lost by enemy flak and two ships vanished without any record or information as to what happened to them.

During this period of operation they were never once intercepted over enemy territory. This included raids over Holland, occupied France, Belgium and Germany, the longest one having been a flight of over 1,000 miles. Their furthermost victory was a locomotive shot up just outside Wilhelmshaven, an airline distance of approximately 350 miles from their base.

The results of a typical raid are as follows: two ships were gone from the base 3:40 (90 miles was flown over Germany), each ship used approximately 118 US gallons of fuel. The two Mustangs destroyed or damaged 5 locomotives, 5 loaded goods barges, and one ''R'' boat. The Mustangs were unharmed.

It is felt that with the present load on the enemy shops and the possible shortage of the high quality steel necessary for the boiler tubes, a locomotive which has been holed by ·50 caliber machine gun fire will be out of service from 3 weeks to 6 months depending on the location with reference to repair facilities. In some cases the locomotive explodes; if it does not explode, often the escaping steam blows the fire out of the fire box into the cab. The repetition of these attacks has definitely made the profession of locomotive engineer unpopular in that part of Europe within the range of the Mustangs.

In general their tactics consist of sending into a given target area a sufficient number of ships to ''saturate'' the enemy air defense warning system and to cause the maximum confusion through a multiplicity of plots and through pre-determined zig-zag courses laid out in short legs (6 min each) arranged so as to carry them parallel to their objectives (canals and railways). The most usual formation employed is a pair line abreast, although four line abreast, or two and sometimes three flights of four abreast have been used. It was found that the smallest unit of two abreast worked out better in most cases. The formation proceeds to a given point off the enemy coast, at which time it breaks up into the smaller units, who then fly their respective pre-determined courses so as to cover the particular section to be attacked. All crossings of the enemy coast are at as nearly the same time as possible.

The flight from the home base to within 40 miles of the point of crossing the enemy coast is made at 200 IAS, 1100 rpm and 30·0″ Hg at between 25 to 50 feet altitude. Upon reaching the above mentioned point, the power is increased to maximum cruising (250-275 mph—2,600 rpm—34·5″ Hg) and left there during the entire time over enemy territory and until 40 miles away from enemy coast on the return trip. If a landfall is not made within 5 miles of the predetermined point at which the enemy coast was to be crossed, then the flight should return home immediately because the entire flight plan will be thrown off too much, and also, since the entry point is chosen with careful regard for the flak map, there is apt to be serious trouble from this cause.

Just at the point of crossing the coast, an attempt should be made to ''flash'' in as quickly as possible—pulling up slightly and then diving with a burst of gun fire in the direction of any gun locations that may be firing—once across the coast, going back to tree top height, taking advantage of all the natural cover possible. Attacks on locomotives should never be made near stations or other locations where flak defenses are apt to be concentrated, but should be made between the stations out in the country where there is usually only single track; in which case the damaged locomotive holds up traffic until a wrecker or another engine can be brought in to tow the disabled engine to a siding. It often happens that the locomotive explodes, which usually causes damage to the track and roadbed, further disrupting traffic. Attacks should be alternated between the two members of the flight, one covering while the other makes the attack. Each pilot of the pair should be constantly searching for enemy aircraft so as to avoid a surprise attack by enemy pursuit. Attacks should be made from one side of the railway, canal or roadway to the other—never along. An attack should never be repeated even though the objective has been missed, because the protecting element of surprise is no longer present. At a speed of 270 mph and at zero altitude, the search area is comparatively limited and targets appear quickly. Experience and alertness are required to pick out these targets in time to make an attack. It has been found necessary for inexperienced pilots to fly at not over 250 mph until they acquire the necessary skill and experience. It has also been found that depressing the flaps 5° will have little effect on the speed, but it will change the attitude of the aircraft so that targets can be more easily seen over the nose.

The route in enemy territory usually involves about 90 miles following the predetermined zig-zag course which has been laid out with reference to the latest flak map and with maximum target possibilities in mind. The six-minute legs of the courses just about give the enemy time to pick out a plot, determine the speed and course, and dispatch interception. The course is then changed and the interception is always about 6 minutes behind time or out of phase. Strict adherence to the original flight plan must be maintained for many reasons, one [of] which is so that the rendezvous after the enemy coast is left will not be prevented, thereby depriving the entire flight of the protection offered by supporting numbers during the trip home, when interception is more likely.

At the point of leaving the coast, flash out as fast as possible, weaving and changing place in the flight. Make use of cloud cover if possible. After 40 miles from the coast throttle back to 200 mph (1,100 rpm and 30·0″ Hg) and proceed to the home base.

It has been found that speed is not protection or at least not sufficient protection from ground fire and weaving must be employed for the maximum protection.

The use of cloud cover is an important feature of these operations. 10/10 clouds at 500 ft to 1,000 ft would represent an almost ideal condition. For operations deep into Germany 10/10 clouds at not over 1,500 ft is required while 6/10 to 7/10 clouds at 1,500 ft is allowable for operations into Holland, Belgium and France. Since the only interception has been at sea every effort is made to take advantage of such cloud cover during the over-water portions of the return trip. On the outgoing trip low flying and proper selection of the approach course give comparative security from detection by radar until a landfall is made. Absolute radio silence must be observed on the outgoing trip and if for any reason this silence is broken, the flight must return to the home base immediately since the enemy will have been alerted. Once the coast is crossed, there is no longer any great necessity for radio silence, since security and complete concealment are no longer possible; however, even then it is desirable to use the utmost discretion in the use of the radio, preserving silence unless an emergency warrants the use of the radio.

Training

Specialized pilot training is a very important phase in this operation. New pilots coming with the unit are not allowed to go on an operational flight for several months. They must have become familiar with every phase of the operation before going out on their own. They are thoroughly instructed in radio procedure and discipline. They must know their airplane completely and have the responsibility for keeping their own ground crew on their toes. They are allowed to make changes in their own aircraft for their personal comfort and are encouraged to keep the wings polished and free from scratches. In fact, no one is allowed to climb up on the wings without a pad in place. The pilots enter from the front, stepping on the wing at only two designated spots. They must run slow-speed fuel consumption tests so that they are convinced that it is possible to operate at 200 mph and approximately 20 gal per [hour] if they keep the rpm down to 1,100. They must supervise the swinging and checking of their own compass in order to increase their confidence in their equipment. Blind flying practice is carried on at all times. Each pilot is so trained that he can "lay on" a complete mission in all details.

Each day there is range estimation and gunnery practice. They are encouraged to go out in pairs and practice "shadow shooting" over the water in addition to the carefully scored aerial gunnery practice. Competition is introduced in all phases of the training, with the possibilities of becoming a flight leader as a reward.

Formation flying is practised continually by twos and fours until the pilots are automatic in their ability to handle themselves in a formation of either type. After they have been paired off, they are usually not separated but continue to fly with same partner, developing their own system of signals for target designation, etc. The four plane, line abreast formation is very maneuverable but is difficult to fly. Proficiency is acquired only through constant practice. The two place line abreast formation is most usually used as it is the more flexible.

They are briefed constantly on enemy tactics and the capabilities of their own aircraft compared to the enemy opposition.

It has been found that the Mustang is faster than the ME 109 and the FW 190, and that 4,000 to 8,000 ft is a good altitude at which to catch the enemy. At sea level, the Mustang can run away from any enemy aircraft they have encountered to date. The pilots are schooled to run rather than fight because their main object is the destruction of ground targets, not to fight enemy aircraft. They are instructed in the use of the flaps in combat to reduce their turning radius (which with flaps is shorter than the ME 109 or FW 190). At least one FW 190 has been made to spin in through the use of a small amount of flap by the Mustang when engaged in a turning contest at low altitude; the 190 tried to tighten his turn to keep the Mustang in his sights after the pilot had dropped his flaps slightly, but spun out of the turn. They practice combat, evasion, flak evasion, low altitude flying continually.

They are taught the importance of the proper flying equipment. Goggles must be worn at all time while over enemy territory to protect their eyes from windshield and hood splinters. They must wear escape boots, flying suits (so as to provide two or more layers of clothing), helmets and gloves at all times for the protection those give in case of a fire in the air. In short, they are taught to know their aircraft and equipment and how to use both to the maximum advantage.

A considerable amount of time is spent in training for emergency situations. They practice forced landings under all conditions—particularly the condition following an engine failure at low altitude over land. It has been found that if the Mustang must be "ditched" it will go under like a shot and that "ditching" must be avoided. If the engine fails at 200 mph and 25 ft altitude, the aircraft can be pulled straight up to about 500 ft, at which point the pilot jumps, but this must be practised in order to convince the pilots that it is possible if everything is done without any delay. In case of such a failure over water, the I.F.F. should immediately be shifted to switch position #3, which is an emergency position giving a wide emergency plot on any radar screen which happens to be following the aircraft at the time. All stations will drop all operational plots and follow an emergency plot giving the location immediately to the nearest Air Sea Rescue Unit. If the aircraft must be "ditched" they are told to use coarse pitch, no flaps, radiator shutters closed, slow up as much as possible and stall onto the water along the swell regardless of wind. The hood should be off, parachute harness off, safety belt and Sutton harness taut, one hand on the instrument panel, and the head slightly forward and rigid. They are cautioned that as long as the engine will run enough to fly, they should keep the aircraft headed for home and endeavour to reach home even if the engine is ruined. They are taught how to handle their engines in such emergencies; if the oil temperature goes up, reduce rpm and increase boost; if the glycol temperature goes up, increase rpm and reduce boost. During their period of operation the squadron did not have any complete engine failures, nor did they have any internal glycol leaks.

They are continually lectured by intelligence officers concerning the general situation in the countries or territories over which they are flying. Particular emphasis is placed on the problems of escape and the changes in the escape situation from time to time. The customs and dress of the people are studied; stories of escapes are discussed and wherever possible people who have escaped discuss their experiences with the pilots. Everything is done to make them more escape-conscious. They are encouraged to have personal weapons with them in the aircraft (knife or black jack rather than a gun) and to exercise their own ingenuity in concealing compasses, small saws, etc, in their clothes. They have many types of such compasses; a few are made more or less obvious so that they will be taken, leaving the concealed ones for later use. Battle dress should consist of clothing which will not look out of place or strange in the locality where a pilot is apt to be forced down.

During their training period, the pilots are first sent on shipping reconnaissance missions to allow them to get familiar with the aeroplane and navigation and to check their fuel consumption, while doing something which they feel is operationally important. They are next required to simulate three practice Rhubarbs over friendly country; then they are sent out to sea, out of sight of land, and required to fly a predetermined 3 leg course and simulate an approach to the coast and an attack on a land objective. When they are proficient at the above, they are then ready for their first operational Rhubarb.

Performance of the Mustang I and IA

The record of the Mustang I is excellent. The pilots all like to fly it and its success has been due to its reliability, simplicity and the fact that it is faster than any contemporary aircraft at low and medium altitudes.

This aircraft is powered with the Allison 1710-39 engine having a rated power of 1,150 hp at 3,000 rpm and 44″ Hg at 12,000 ft. The engine was originally equipped with an automatic boost control limiting the manifold pressure at the lower altitudes to 44″. The British remove this so as to get the vastly increased performance at lower altitudes through the judicious use of over-boost. As has been mentioned before, they have had exceptionally good service out of these engines and due to its smoothness at low rpm's they are able to operate it so as to obtain a remarkably low fuel consumption giving them an operational range greater than any single-engine fighter they possess (the fact that the Merlin engine will not run well below 1,600 prevents them from obtaining an equivalent low fuel consumption and therefore limits its usefulness for similar operations).

Actual combat has proved that the aircraft can run away from anything the Germans have. Its only inferior points are that it can't climb as well as the ME 109 and FW 190 and that at the lower speeds of close combat it loses effectiveness of aileron control and therefore has a poor rate of roll—but its turning radius with a slight amount of flap is shorter than either of the German aircraft.

In view of the British experience, it is felt that we have a plane excellently fitted and suited for long range, low altitude daylight intrusion and for a medium altitude escort fighter to accompany our medium bombers. It must be realized that an aircraft which will fulfill the conditions for a medium bombardment escort fighter might not be completely suitable as a long range intruder due to an inability on the part of the engine to run at the exceptionally low rpm necessary for such long range operation. This is also assuming an operation which will allow a major portion of such missions to be made over waters where interception would be unlikely, such as from North Africa or the Mediterranean Islands to the mainland.

In view of the British operation and the fact that we have an approved war emergency rating on the 1710-39 engine of 56″, it is suggested that immediate steps be taken to remove the automatic boost controls from our P-51 airplanes in this theatre and that the instrument dials be marked with the proper lights. The British have operated at full throttle at sea level (72″ Hg) for as much as 20 min at a time without hurting the engines. According to them, the Allison is averaging 1500 hrs between bearing failures as compared to 500 to 600 hrs for the Merlin. The Allison, they have found, will drag them home even with the bearings ruined.

It is suggested that the Allison-powered P-51A may lend itself better to a combination low altitude fighter-intruder and a medium bombardment escorter than will the Merlin-powered P-51B due to the inherent difficulty of operating the Merlin engine at the low rpm's necessary for a low fuel consumption. It is felt that definite engineering and flight information should be secured in these two aircraft immediately.

HEADQUARTERS
NORTHWEST AFRICAN STRATEGIC AIR FORCE

CHARLES F. HORN
Brigadier General, GSC,
Asst Chief of Staff, A-3

This excellent report gave the US Army Air Force a solid idea of what their new aircraft could do. The F-6 and A-36 had already been in action in the Mediterranean, fully demonstrating the performance capabilities of the Allison-powered Mustang. However, reaching this point had been a long process.

Right: **Several Royal Canadian Air Force squadrons were equipped with Mustang Is. Here an all-Canadian crew work on one of their aircraft.** *(Public Archives of Canada via Roger Freeman)*

Below: **A Mustang of No 400 Squadron RCAF in the environment for which it was best suited: low level. Note the flame-damping exhausts, installed for the unit's night Ranger operations.** *(RCAF)*

Above: **AG365 of No 400 Squadron RCAF. Note the early-style underwing roundels and the flame-damping exhausts.** *(Chris Shores)*

Below: **AM251 in service with the RCAF. Mustang units went on to serve with the 2nd Tactical Air Force after Army Co-Operation Command was disbanded in June 1943. By the end of the war fewer than 100 Allison Mustangs were still in service with the RAF, equipping for the most part No 26 Squadron (the first Mustang unit) and No 268 Squadron. The RAF found no aircraft to better the Allison Mustang at tactical recce.** *(Public Archives of Canada via Roger Freeman)*

An Allison Mustang in company with an RAF Liberator, Typhoon and Tempest and a 78th Fighter Group P-47 at Duxford. *(Duke Morrison, 78th FG Assn)*

XP-51

Above: **The first of the two XP-51s, 41-038, was the fourth production Mustang I. Painted initially in RAF camouflage and markings, the aircraft was flown for the first time on 20 May 1941 by Robert Chilton.** *(AAHS)*

Below: **Several delays meant that 038 was not delivered to Wright Field, Ohio, where this picture was taken, until 24 August 1942, and 039 did not arrive until 16 December. Since the final test report on the XP-51 was made in July 1942, there seems to be little truth in the story that the aircraft was totally neglected.** *(NASM)*

41-038 during flight-test work at Wright Field in late 1941. In the strict sense of the word the two XP-51s were not prototypes in the way that the NA-73X was. They were random examples of a production aircraft that required little modification for US military use. *(USAF)*

On 4 May 1940, when the Air Corps approved construction of the NA-73 for the British, it asked for the fourth and tenth production aircraft for testing. Few in the AAC fighter development community were then aware of the new aircraft's potential. Authority for Purchase No 165265, dated 24 July 1940, asked for the two aircraft under the designation XP-51, and on 20 September the official contract was approved by the Assistant Secretary of War.

On 20 May 1941 Robert Chilton made the first flight in Air Corps 41-038 (AG348 in the British production run), the first XP-51. Subsequent delays meant that the aircraft was not flown to Wright Field, Ohio, for official performance tests until 24 August 1941. The second aircraft, 41-039, did not get to Wright until 16 December.

The old story of official neglect of the XP-51 being responsible for the delay to its acceptance by the US Army Air Forces is not confimed by the documents. The two XP-51s did not sit on the ground at Wright due to lack of interest; there were in fact some geniune problems. The two aircraft

038 at Freeman Field, Indiana, in 1945 after the USAAF had finished with it. Hap Arnold had the foresight to keep the XP-51 from being scrapped, preserving the aircraft along with many other World War II types for the National Air (now Air and Space) Museum. Its sibling was not so fortunate: 41-039 spent most of its wartime career with NACA at Langley Field, Virginia, where it was used for high-speed flight testing, but it was ultimately scrapped. *(Haney Collection)*

were to have been delivered for testing in February and March of 1941, but they actually arrived much later than that. Even then problems kept cropping up, and most of the tests at Wright were carried out without the second aircraft.

The document reproduced below reveals the events which delayed the entry of the P-51 into the Army Air Force inventory.

DATE July 15, 1942

WAR DEPARTMENT
AIR CORPS, MATERIEL DIVISION
WRIGHT FIELD, DAYTON, OHIO
AIR CORPS TECHNICAL REPORT No. 4801
FINAL REPORT OF INSPECTION
PERFORMANCE AND ACCEPTANCE OF NORTH
AMERICAN AIRPLANE MODEL XP-51
by
Captain W. G. Logan, A. C.

Approved:
  H. Z. Bogert, Colonel, Army Air Forces Chief, Technical Staff   Branch Chief
By direction of the Chief of the Materiel Division.
  F. L. Carroll, Colonel, Army Air Forces   Chief Experimental Engineering Section

OBJECT
  The object of this report is to present a brief resumé of the development of the XP-51 airplane including the procurement, inspection and performance of the airplanes.

SUMMARY

Model XP-51, which is the designation for N.A.A. Model NA-73, airplane is a low wing, single engine, single place, all metal monoplane with an Allison V-1710-P, 3 R engine with a three blade tractor propeller. The wing and tail surfaces are of full cantilever construction. The airfoil is a modified laminar flow, and was at the time of construction the closest approximation to a true laminar flow yet built. The armament consists of two synchronized caliber ·50 machine guns and two caliber ·50 and four caliber ·30 wing guns. In order to expedite delivery of the first airplane for performance testing, no gun charging was provided. The second airplane was equipped with fully automatic gun chargers as developed by the Bendix Corporation. Passive armament consists of self-sealing fuel tanks and lines, bullet-proof glass and armor plates in front of the pilot where the engine does not offer adequate protection. Provisions only were made for the installation of armor plate behind the pilot.

OBJECT OF DEVELOPMENT

This airplane was developed by the contractor primarily for sale to the the British Government.

PROCUREMENT

On May 4, 1940, the North American Aviation, Inc. signed a Foreign Release Agreement with the Army Air Forces for the foreign sale of the Model NA-73 airplane that entitled the Army Air Forces to two airplanes of the type contemplated for sale. The release specifically set forth that the Army Air Forces would receive the fourth and tenth articles from the production line. The engines, propellers and other normal items of regular Government furnished equipment specified for Army Air Forces Airplanes were specified as Government furnished equipment for these two airplanes. There were no provisions made for mock-up or 689 inspection of these two airplanes although arrangements were made for process inspection and flight testing of the first airplane by Army Air Forces personnel. Following the completion of negotiations between the North American Aviation Corporation and the Anglo-French Purchasing Commission, Authority for Purchase No. 165265 for two XP-51 airplanes was initiated on July 24, 1940 and followed by a contract which was approved by the Assistant Secretary of War on September 20, 1940. The airplanes were built in accordance with the British Model Specification except that certain modifications were made to accommodate standard Army Air Forces equipment.

Except for minor incidental changes the project progressed at a normal rate. On February 24, 1942 an Engineering Order was issued to remove the original hydraulic gun chargers out of both airplanes and install in lieu thereof fully automatic gun charger equipment which was being developed by the Bendix Corporation in the second airplane. This was done so that the new charging equipment could be flight tested at an early date. Since the delivery date of the automatic hydraulic chargers was such that a delay in delivery of the airplane would result from the installation, it was decided that provision only would be made for the installation of this equipment.

Preliminary flight testing was conducted on the first airplane at the contractor's plant by the contractor's personnel and Government pilots in accordance with the terms of the contract. Considerable trouble was incurred with the Allison engine installation in the early stages of the airplane development. At one particular throttle setting the engine was found to be extremely rough and in one instance the engine completely cut out resulting in a forced landing in a plowed field. This landing was made by the contractor's pilot without damage to property or personal injury although considerable damage was done to the airplane.

Although no mock-up or 689 inspection was made, a preliminary flutter and vibration survey was made by Army Air Forces personnel prior to any flights by Army Air Forces pilots.

Under the terms of the contract the Army Air Forces were supposed to receive the fourth and tenth production articles. These airplanes were scheduled for delivery in February and March of 1941. The production of the NA-73 airplanes was delayed both by the crash landing of the experimental model and the delay of engines for the British airplanes. To facilitate the delivery of the XP-51 models it was decided to take the fourth and tenth articles from their place in the assembly line and install the Army Air Forces engines in them for delivery to Wright Field. This procedure was followed and the first airplane was accepted at the plant of the contractor and flown to Wright Field on August 24, 1941, for the purpose of conducting official performance tests. The second airplane was accepted and flown to Wright Field on December 16, 1941.

Upon arrival of the first airplane at Wright Field, a safety inspection was conducted. The airplane was next weighed and balanced and an actual weight and balance report prepared. Before flight testing could be conducted, it was necessary to install backfire screens to prevent damage to the airplane due to engine backfire. This work took considerably longer than was anticipated due to the breaking off of studs. It was also necessary to install new aileron and flap bracket bolts to correct an unsatisfactory condition found by N.A.A. in other airplanes. The replacement parts were furnished by the contractor and installed by Army Air Forces personnel under the supervision of the contractor's representative.

MOCK-UP AND ENGINEERING INSPECTION OF THE XP-51 AIRPLANE

Because of the nature of procurement no mock-up or Engineering Inspection was made on these two airplanes. However, Army Air Forces personnel were granted an opportunity to visit the plant of the contractor to study design details and observe construction.

CONTRACTOR'S TESTING

The contractor conducted thorough and complete testing of the airplane and parts during construction and conducted complete flight tests on the first airplane. It was during these flight tests that the airplane was damaged in a forced landing due to the cutting out of the engine. Additional flight tests were conducted on the two airplanes delivered to the Army Air Forces. It was during flight testing of the first Army Air Forces airplane that it was discovered that engine difficulties previously encountered could be overcome by increasing the length of the ramming air intake scoop. It was only after the contractor considered the airplanes to be satisfactory that they were turned over to the Army Air Forces.

FLIGHT TESTING

Preliminary performance tests were conducted at the contractor's plant by personnel on the contractor's first article during March, 1941. Final official performance flight tests were conducted at Wright Field between October 8 and December 22, 1941. The reason for the long period of flight testing was due to the higher priority of other airplanes to be tested, bad weather and malfunctioning of the coolant scoop control and landing gear retracting mechanism during the cold weather. These difficulties and others of a minor nature were corrected by Army Air Forces personnel and the contractor's representatives.

The second airplane was thoroughly inspected by the Flying Branch after delivery and was then turned over to the Armament Laboratory for firing tests. The installation and testing of the automatic hydraulic gun chargers will be covered by another report.

OFFICIAL SUMMARY OF CHARACTERISTICS
AIRPLANE

Manufacturer *North American* Type *Interceptor Fighter* Model *XP-51* Mfr. Model Spec. No. *1620* Contract No. *15471* Crew *1* Wing Loading *33.7* lb/sq ft Power Loading *6.90* lb/bhp Design Altitude *15,000* ft Wing Area *233·19* sq ft Span *37·03* ft Aspect Ratio *5·815* Airfoil *NAA NACA* Weight Empty *6,275* lb Design Gross Weight *7,967* lb Take-off Power at S. L. *1,150* bhp

OFFICIAL PERFORMANCE SUMMARY

1. Level Flight Speed at Design Altitude of *13,000* ft with Design Gross Weight of *7,934* lb.
   Maximum Speed *382* mph at *3,000* rpm with *1,110* bhp (MAX % rated)
   High Speed *370* mph at *3,000* rpm with *1,110* bhp (MAX % rated)
   Cruising Speed *325·5* mph at *2,280* rpm with *750* bhp (75·2 % rated)
2. Optimum Range and Endurance with *170* gal fuel and *None* lb bombs, *750* bhp
   At Cruising Speed *780* miles at *4·6* mi/gal or *2·4* hr at *71* gal/hr
3. Climb Data with Gross Weight of *7,934* lb

Standard Altitude ft	0	5,000	10,000	15,000	20,000	25,000	30,800
Climbing Speed mph	178	194	208	222	236	248·5	262
Engine Speed rpm	3,000	3,000	3,000	2,600	2,600	2,600	2,600
Total Power bhp	1,050	1,095	1,140	820	680	550	—
Maximum Rate fpm	2,200	2,270	2,345	1,570	1,070	610	100
Minimum Time min	0	2·24	4·41	7·06	10·91	17·03	38·96

4. Ceiling: Normal Engine Operation: Service Ceiling *30,800* ft
   Absolute Ceiling *31,900* ft Supercharger Blower Ratio *8·8:1*
5. Take-off and Landing Distances—To Clear 50 ft. Obstacle at Sea Level (no wind)
   Take-off *1,780* ft at *92* mph *15* deg flap Gr. Wt *7,934* lb. Ground run *1,030* ft
   Land *2,000* ft at *94* mph *50* deg flap Gr Wt *7,934* lb. Ground run *1,495* ft

41-038 displays its extremely clean lines . . . in 1980. After being stored for over 30 years at Silver Hill, Maryland, the first XP-51 was handed over to the Experimental Aircraft Association and restored by Darrell Skurich. Faithful in every detail, except for silver paint instead of natural metal to preserve the airframe, the aircraft flies as a part of EAA's Warbirds of America. EAA Museum director Gene Chase is flying the aircraft in this shot. *(EAA)*

Even though this report clears up much of the uncertainty about the Mustang's tardiness in getting into service, there were also some delay caused by the people running things at Wright Field. As General Hap Arnold later commented: "That we did not have it sooner was the Air Force's own fault."

One document that reveals this prejudice against the North American product is a letter from Col Homer L. Sanders, commanding officer of the 51st Fighter Group in Karachi, India, written on 26 August 1942. Frustrated by his unit's lack of superiority over the Japanese, he made the following comments to the Commanding General, US Army Air Forces in India and China: "Reports originating with our forces in China lead to but one conclusion, namely, the small margin of superiority in combat possible with P-40 equipment by skillful pilotage is dwindling away with improvements in Japanese equipment . . . . We must face the fact that the P-40, as a modern combat airplane, is out of the picture . . . . Were it true that it is the best available, that our technical minds were incapable of anything better, then there would be nothing to do but accept them without question. This is not the case [since there is] an American fighter plane the equal of anything in any Air Force in the world . . . . This is not a new airplane. Many pilots of this Group flew it and tested it before the end of 1941 and all these pilots have been preaching it ever since. We tested it against all available fighter planes; it was faster than the P-38 at altitudes up to and including 15,000 feet; it would almost hold a tight circle with a P-36, would easily outmaneuver a P-40, P-38, and P-66. It is an extremely simple airplane and has such perfect handling qualities as to put a smile of joy on the face of any fighter pilot. Control is perfect even at indicated airspeeds of 500 mph. It has a low landing speed, no ground looping tendency, good armament (British model has four ·50 caliber and four ·303 guns), good armor protection, self sealing tanks, and a range greater than any of the above tested airplanes. This sounds a little like flights of fancy, but I can assure you it is the consensus of opinion of all the pilots who tested the three P-51 airplanes loaned to us by North American.

"At the time of the tests (Dec. 1941) officials at North American said they had an order for only 400 of these planes from the British Purchasing Commission and consequently were building only 3½ per day, but could raise the production rate to 10 per day within three weeks after being given the go-ahead signal by the Air Corps. Apparently the go-ahead signal was not given or there would certainly be some available for combat duty by this time. It appeared there was a tendency by the Materiel Division to hinder the development of this airplane, which can only be accounted for by the fact that it was strictly a North American project and Materiel Division could claim no credit for it.

"During the first few days of January I had the occasion to inquire about the P-51 from a senior officer of the Flight Test Section. At first he did not know which plane I was talking about, but after a moment or so remarked 'Oh yes, there have been a couple of those setting around up there, but they didn't look like much so we haven't bothered much with them.' An answer like this helps a little in trying to understand why we haven't received modern fighter planes.

"It is requested that this Group be equipped with P-51 airplanes as expeditiously as possible . . . in preference to the P-47."

The 51st Fighter Group was eventually equipped with Mustangs, but not until almost two years later.

Behind this curious combination of enthusiasm and indifference lay a struggle between a few members of the inner circle of AAF fighter development who were working feverishly to get the P-51 into production, and others who were grossly neglecting what they saw as an unwanted stepchild. Many proponents of the P-51 were now overseas, flying with front-line units. Ben Kelsey, for example, had gone with the 1st Fighter Group to England, flying P-38s in the summer of 1942.

Fortunately, enough responsible people kept pushing for development and acceptance, although the road to these objectives took some odd detours.

Apache, Invader, Mustang: Into the Army Air Force and Combat

On 7 July 1941, long before the XP-51 had completed its flight tests at Wright Field, the USAAF placed an order for 150 P-51s for the RAF. These aircraft, while primarily for British use, carried US as well as RAF serial numbers and had four 20 mm cannon in place of the 0·30 and 0·50-caliber machine guns.

Far from being neglected, the Mustang was still the subject of much maneuvering on the part of Echols and a few others who had been pushing for an AAF version. Through some skilful negotiation, only 93 of these "Plain Vanilla" (there was

no letter designation for this model; it was known only as the "P-51") Mustangs went to the RAF as Mustang IAs, and 55 were kept by the AAF. Most of the AAF machines eventually became F-6A tactical reconnaissance fighters. But, significantly, two were set aside for the XP-78 project, to be fitted with a Packard-built Rolls-Royce Merlin engine.

On 29 May 1942 Louis Wait made the first flight in a P-51, taking off in Air Corps (now Air Forces) 41-37320 (RAF FD418). But by then the money had run out; no more was available in Fiscal Year 1942 for fighter aircraft. There was however money left in the budget for an "attack aircraft." No time was lost by the men at Echols' Pentagon office, the Pursuit Projects Office at Wright and Dutch Kindelberger's cubbyhole at Inglewood. Talking over what might be done to keep the P-51 in production, they decided to add bomb racks and dive brakes to the airframe, calling it an "attack bomber". Before the first P-51 even flew, an order had been placed for 500 A-36s on 16 April 1942. As Ben Kelsey later

The A-36A went into combat with the 27th and 86th Bomb Groups over Sicily in July 1943. It did not take long to prove the effectiveness of the aircraft in dive bombing and strafing, though these were not its designed missions. *(USAF)*

recalled, the birth of the A-36 had nothing to do with a need for a new dive bomber or attack aircraft: it was merely a device to get the Mustang into production for the USAAF.

When the P-51 was first assigned to the AAF the name "Apache" was chosen, but by July 1942 this had been dropped in favor of the British "Mustang". To add to the confusion, the A-36 was known as the "Invader" for a period, though the name never stuck.

Bob Chilton took the first A-36 (42-83663) into the air on 21 September 1942. On 3 February 1943 he flew the first P-51A (43-6003) fighter, which was part of an order for 310 aircraft contracted on 23 June 1942 (right at the beginning of a new fiscal year). A total of 50 P-51As, fitted with four 0·50-caliber guns in place of the cannon, were shipped to England under Lend-Lease as Mustang IIs.

By March 1943 the first operational F-6As were in North Africa, flying with the 68th Observation Group's 111th and 154th squadrons. The first A-36A unit, the 86th Bomb Group, was formed in late 1942 and was shipped to North Africa. The 27th Bomb Group was the first A-36 unit to enter combat, however, encountering the enemy over Sicily on 6 June 1943.

After these two groups had left for the Mediterranean the AAF released its final report on the operational suitability of the A-36. The following excerpts make it clear that the AAF realized that it had the makings of a fine fighter:

PROOF DEPARTMENT
ARMY AIR FORCES PROVING GROUND COMMAND
EGLIN FIELD, FLORIDA

FINAL REPORT
ON
TEST OF THE OPERATIONAL SUITABILITY
OF THE A-36 TYPE AIRPLANE

Serial No.: *4-42-14* Date: *15 April 1943*

Description. Three (3) A-36 type aircraft were received at this station on 23 November 1942. One (1) A-36 airplane was lost as the result of the wings pulling off in a vertical dive. Complete tests on dive bombing were not carried out due to restrictions placed on diving speeds and pull-outs by the Materiel Center, Wright Field, Dayton, Ohio.

Conclusions:

It is concluded that:

a. The A-36 airplane is an excellent minimum altitude bombing and attack aircraft.

b. The A-36 airplane is an inferior dive bomber due to the fast diving speeds at angles of dive greater than seventy (70) degrees.

c. The A-36 airplane, after jettisoning its bombs, is an excellent fighter aircraft at low altitudes.

Recommendations:

It is recommended that:

a. The A-36 airplane be utilized as a minimum altitude attack bomber.

b. All A-36 type aircraft be equipped with the A-1 variable reflector sight.

c. The dive brakes be eliminated.

d. Flame dampers be installed for night operation.

Performance:

(1) Maximum speed without bombs at the critical engine altitude of five-thousand (5,000) feet is approximately three-hundred-twenty-four (324) miles per hour at war emergency power.

(2) Maximum speed with two (2) five-hundred (500) pound bombs at the critical engine altitude of five-thousand (5,000) feet is approximately two-hundred-ninety-eight (298) miles per hour at war emergency power.

Diving Characteristics:

The A-36 has excellent diving characteristics from the standpoint of a fighter, but it dives too fast for a dive bomber, the dive brakes slowing the airplane down approximately eight-three (83) miles per hour. This is insufficient from the dive bomber standpoint, as the airplane will still dive with the dive brakes open to speeds in excess of four-hundred-fifty (450) miles per hour, necessitating bomb release at approximately four-thousand (4,000) feet in order to pull out of the dive. The best diving angle is approximately seventy (70) degrees.

Flying Characteristics:

The A-36 is very pleasant to fly, being extremely stable on each axis. The controls are well balanced with little tendency to tighten up at high speeds. The airplane handles well in acrobatics and gives ample warning of a stall.

Prepared by: (signed)
M. A. McKenzie
Captain, Air Corps,
Project Officer

When the A-36 actually had some combat time behind it, the pilots found they could handle dives up to the near-vertical without damaging the aircraft. The resulting accuracy made it useful for both dive bombing and glide bombing; the A-36 also offered the best range of any single-engined aircraft in the theater. Initial combat results were summarized in Tactical Bulletin No 23 *The A-36 (Mustang fighter/bomber) in North Africa,* from the Northwest African Air Force, dated 1 July 1943:

"It became an excellent fighter-bomber, capable of delivering its bomb load with extreme accuracy . . . Its high speed and good maneuverability make it an excellent aircraft for either [glide or dive] bombing, but it must be noted that the accuracy obtained by glide bombing is much less than that obtained by using the dive brakes to secure vertical dives on the target.

Because of the excellent range characteristics, the A-36 may be used to good advantage against strategic pin-point targets, and could complement the work of the strategic bombers very effectively within a reasonable range . . . Dive bombing accuracy greatly increases the accuracy now realised by our other fighter-bombers. With its high speed, fighter-bomber support calls can be answered more quickly . . . The A-36 carries a greater bomb load than any other

An A-36A of the 526th Squadron, 86th Fighter Bomber Group, in Italy. The obscured serial number is 42-84007. By 1944 the Invaders were becoming quite ragged, with painted-out markings and non-standard markings applied to all portions of the airframe. Note the mission tally over the star and down the fuselage. Most Mediterranean-based Apaches, Invaders and Mustangs had yellow bands painted around the wings just inboard of the national markings. *(Chuck Olmsted)*

An 86th FBG A-36 in typical Italian conditions. Even though the primary mission of the Invaders was air-to-ground, combat with enemy fighters was inevitable: this aircraft carries two kill marks just behind the spinner. *(USAF)*

After 63 missions this A-36 came to grief in Italy when it flew through the explosion of an ammunition truck and hit trees. Damage from ground fire was a constant thorn in the side of the 27th and 86th Groups, which often had to fly through enemy fire to land at their forward operating bases, particularly on the Salerno beachhead. *(USAF)*

The 10th P-51A off the line (a-1) with the newly installed four 0.50-caliber guns in place of the four 20mm cannon fitted to the "Plain Vanilla" P-51. These aircraft were allocated to the 154th and 111th Observation (later Tactical Reconnaissance) Squadrons, the first American units to take the Mustang into action. *(USAF)*

tactical fighter-bomber in use at present. It is exceeded only by the P-38 fighter which is now used only strategically.

Technique of Attack The essential element in a successful dive bomb attack is a vertical dive. Accuracy of the bombing varies directly with the steepness of the dive and any dive of less than 72 degrees is considered as glide bombing. The best possibilities for a successful attack [result from] a twelve ship formation, close line abreast, with the leader on the flank toward the target and into the sun . . ., the leader rolling

over and diving as soon as he comes directly over the target, followed as closely as possible during the dive by the other ships and then reforming in a normal fighter defensive formation. The second formation used is an echelon of flights back and away from the target . . .. For well defended targets, an altitude of about twelve thousand feet is obtained before the bomb run. The formation loses altitude to ten thousand feet for the beginning of the dive and recovery is made between four and five thousand feet. For lightly defended targets, the altitude at the start of the dive is from six to eight thousand feet with recovery on the deck. A higher degree of accuracy is obtained by the latter but at the expense of greater danger to the flight from ground fire. The roll-over method is much preferred to the push-over method for obtaining a vertical dive. The dive brakes are opened immediately before the roll-over on signal from the flight leader. Strafing with all guns is possible with individuals of the flight during the dive.

Loading and Range Characteristics (conservative estimate)

Load	Type of Mission	Radius of Action
2×500 lb bombs	To target, bomb, patrol ½ hour, return to base.	150 miles
2×500 lb bombs	To target, bomb, return to base.	225 miles
1×500 lb bomb 1×75 gal tank	To target, bomb, patrol ½ hour, return to base.	250 miles
1×500 lb bomb 1×75 gal tank	To target, bomb, return to base.	300 miles

"

When the 86th Bomb Group was forming up on A-36s at Key Field, Mississippi, in late 1942, one excited young lieutenant in the AAF reported to begin his service career in the A-36. Wayne R. Rutherford stayed in the group until after the main action over the Salerno beaches. Recalling those days, he provides a rare glimpse of what it was like to fly the A-36 in combat: "We felt very lucky to be flying the A-36—it was a 'hot ship'. The two groups' [27th and 86th Bomb Groups] planes were shipped by aircraft carrier in the same convoy and we landed in North Africa, where the planes were serviced. All of the squadron commanders, of which I was one, flew a few missions with a P-40 group to gain experience. These missions were a little difficult because our cruising speed was at least 25 mph faster. We then started flying missions on the island of Sicily. Most of these missions were in flights of twelve planes. We were dive-bombing selected targets such as gun emplacements and shipping; we also carried out strafing missions against enemy troops. We would fly two or three missions a day since our base was in North Africa on the coast; we could reach most target areas in 45 minutes to one hour. We experienced heavy anti-aircraft fire but very few enemy fighters during these particular missions. We flew cover, along with other aircraft, for our ships during the invasion of Sicily on 10 July 1943 [hitting railroads, road junctions, trains and vehicles while P-40s flew cover for the amphibious landings].

"Immediately after the invasion our group was stationed on Sicily close to the southern coast (our airstrip was on dirt runways with no facilities such as housing, etc). We slept on the ground or on cots all through the Sicilian campaign. We were again flying three or four missions a day in direct support of our ground troops. Some missions were as short as 15 minutes, others were as long as 3½ hours.

"Most of our navigation was at low level to stay under the enemy's radar. When we reached the target area we would climb to about 10,000 feet as rapidly as possible and then go into vertical dives straight down to deliver the two 500lb bombs we carried on most missions. The speed of the dive with dive brakes was around 300 mph. We would endeavor to deliver these as low as possible and come out on the deck. Then we would either head back to base or go back over the target area after the bombs exploded to do some strafing.

"The terrain in Sicily and Italy was very rough and mountainous. We lost some pilots and aircraft on low-level strikes when they flew into the rough terrain, [sometimes while trying to avoid] enemy ground fire.

Later our base was moved to the northern coast of Sicily, where we flew a great number of missions during the mopping-up phase of the Sicilian campaign.

Our most dangerous flights were down the Straits between the toe of Italy and the island of Sicily, when we were assigned the task of bombing enemy barges which were being used to get troops out of Sicily. The anti-aircraft fire was intense during these missions, which were successful but costly in terms of pilots and planes. We were very successful in hitting the barges during dive bombing. I have no idea how many enemy guns were mounted on the barges; we were too busy concentrating on our dive bombing and strafing runs to count guns. We then flew a lot of missions up the boot of Italy chasing the German and Italian troops; most of these were strafing missions.

"We flew four or five escort missions for some bombing raids by B-24s and B-17s on Naples, but these were difficult since we had poor superchargers on the Allison engines. We were at a distinct disadvantage because at altitude our speed and maneuverability were greatly decreased. We were assigned the escort job because ours were the only fighter

A P-51 (redesignated F-6A) with the 111th Tactical Reconnaissance Squadron in its revetment at Anzio in April 1944. By July these aircraft were "weary," with no new examples to take their places. Pilots were generally unanimous in their appreciation of their F-6As as they let them go to fly P-47s and Merlin Mustangs. *(Chris Shores)*

groups within the area with the range to get to the target area. We did meet a great number of enemy fighters on these missions, plus intense anti-aircraft fire; we had some confirmed kills, but we also lost some bombers and fighters.

"The invasion of Italy at Salerno was a big operation involving quite a large naval force with landing craft, troop carriers, etc. The two groups of A-36s based in Sicily flew cover over part of the Salerno beach-head. A few days after the invasion we moved to a base right on the Salerno beach-head, flying dive-bombing and strafing missions on enemy troops and gun emplacements. The missions were very hazardous: we would encounter enemy fire during take-off and landing, which was quite an experience.

"I came home shortly after this invasion. I can't say enough about our mechanics and ground personnel, who did a wonderful job under difficult circumstances. The A-36 was a super airplane, reliable and sturdy with excellent stability."

The F-6As of the 111th Tactical Reconnaissance Squadron and the A-36As bore much of the task of close support in Italy into 1944. But by March 1944 more than half of the A-36s built had been lost. This forced the 27th Group to re-equip with P-40s. In July the 86th Group gave up its last A-36s for P-47s, and the 111th converted to Merlin Mustangs.

An F-6B, 43-6163, of the 107th Squadron, 67th Tactical Reconnaissance Group, 9th Air Force. From December 1943 to June 1944 this unit operated about two dozen of these converted P-51As from the UK, working within the 2nd Tactical Air Force in preparation for the invasion of the Continent. Many were fitted with the bulged Malcolm hood. *(T. R. Bennett)*

A Wizard for the Yanks

On 29 April 1942 Wing Commander Ian Campbell-Orde, CO of the Air Fighting Development Unit at Duxford, Cambridgeshire, was in the process of completing the AFDU Report on the Mustang I trials (see Chapter 2). Considering the aircraft the best American type he had flown, he invited Rolls-Royce test pilot Ronald W. Harker to fly AG422, one of the two test aircraft. After 30 minutes' flying Harker knew that the airframe had great potential, and was particularly impressed with its light ailerons and high top speed.

Dr Albert J. Warner, an American aeronautical engineer, had come to England during this period to study the Mustang, prompted by British reports of the aircraft's high speed at low level. Warner's findings confirmed that its airframe had very low drag compared with that of the Spitfire.

After returning to Rolls-Royce at Hucknall, Harker asked Witold Challier to mate the new Merlin 61 to the low-drag airframe of the Mustang. Initial calculations promised a boost in rate of climb and a whopping 441 mph top speed at 25,600 feet. Harker believed that the combination could result in the best fighter of the war.

To his amazement, however, his proposal to modify the Mustang in this way met with opposition even though Rolls-Royce had obtained Mustang AG518 for testing to confirm the performance data. Harker's note to the general

manager at Derby, Lord Hives, was circulated among the senior executives; it spawned the reply (as Harker recalled in his book *Rolls-Royce From The Wings*) "that my proposal was unrealistic, that the Air Ministry would not approve and that there would not be any engines available anyhow as they were all required for the Spitfires—and why waste time on an untried, American-built aeroplane!"

However, Ray Dorey, manager at Hucknall, had Harker speak to Hives about a trial installation; in this conversation Harker's most convincing point was the possibility of an airplane superior to the FW190. Hives thought the idea had merit and spoke to Air Marshal Sir Wilfrid Freeman at the Air Ministry; as a result three aircraft were approved for transfer to Hucknall for conversion to the Merlin. In the meantime, Challier completed the specifications for Merlin XX and Merlin 61 conversions, using flight-test data from AG518.

At the same time Rolls-Royce let North American Aviation

know what they were doing, and a friendly competition developed to see who would be the first to fly a Merlin Mustang.

The assistant air attaché at the US Embassy in London, Maj Thomas Hitchcock, wrote of the conversion programs on both sides of the Atlantic in a memorandum dated 8 October 1942: "The reasons for the remarkably low drag of the Mustang are not fully understood on this side of the ocean. The English think it is only partly due to the laminar flow wing.

"The Rolls people became very much interested in the possibilities of the Mustang airframe with the Merlin engine. Estimates were made as to the speeds that could be obtained with the installation of the 61 and 20 Merlin. The Air Ministry instructed the Rolls people to install five Merlin 61 engines in Mustang airplanes. Simultaneously with this development it was arranged to have the North American Company install a Packard version of the Merlin 61 in the Mustang airframe.

Rolls-Royce converted five Mustang I airframes to take the Merlin 65 engine, the first three arriving at Hucknall for preliminary work in June 1942. AL963, the fourth conversion, is shown here after installation of a dorsal fin in February 1943, the result of pilot complaints about lack of directional stability. *(Cliff Glidewell, 78th FG Assn)*

Requests were sent to the United States to have the Packard Company start manufacturing Merlin 61s as promptly as possible.

"The interesting qualities of the Mustang airframe were brought to the attention of General Arnold and Admiral Towers when they were in London in June last, by the American Ambassador [John C. Winant], Air Chief Marshal Sir Charles Portal, Chief of the Air Staff, Air Chief Marshal Sir Sholto Douglas, Commander in Chief Fighter Command, and Air Marshal F. J. Linnell, Ministry of Aircraft Production Research and Development. Robert Lovett, Assistant Secretary of War for Air, was also advised by letter dated June 5, 1942, of the importance which English and various American representatives attach to the Mustang airframe and the desirability of energetically pushing the Merlin development.

"Mr [Phil] Legarra, North American representative, reported when he came back from the United States in the early part of September that the Mustang had the lowest priority that could be granted to an airplane.

"The Mustang is one of the best, if not the best, fighter airframes that has been developed in the war up to date . . . Its development and use in this theater has suffered for various reasons. Sired by the English out of an American mother, the Mustang has had no parent in the Army Air Corps or at Wright Field to appreciate and push its good points . . .

"Important people on both sides of the Atlantic . . . seem more interested in pointing with pride to the development of a 100% national product than they are concerned with the very difficult problem of rapidly developing a fighter plane that will be superior to anything the Germans have."

Hitchcock's wrath was not entirely justified, but then he had no idea what was going on behind closed doors. Arnold had been very impressed with the Merlin Mustang's potential. Echols, now a brigadier-general and Arnold's Chief, Materiel Division, was ready to run with the ball.

Since 1940 Echols had been responsible for getting the license-built versions of the Merlin engine on to the Packard Motor Car assembly lines. Now that the Merlin 61 was being built as the V-1650-3, Echols made sure that two examples found their way to North American for the XP-78 project, later redesignated XP-51B.

On 26 August 1942, well over two months before the first Merlin Mustang flew, the USAAF placed an order for 400 P-51B-1NA fighters. By 8 October, still before any flight testing on either side of the Atlantic, another order was placed, for 1,350 Merlin Mustangs (designated P-51C) to be built in the North American plant at Dallas, Texas. When the program finally gathered momentum, Arnold wrote to President Roosevelt: "The RAF is very keen about the P-51, and we have installed Rolls-Royce engines into two of them—one in England and one in the US. Tests indicate that they will be a highly satisfactory pursuit plane for 1943. We think so much of them we have already given orders for 2,200."

On 7 June 1942 AM121 arrived at Hucknall from Speke for conversion to the Merlin, followed by the end of the month by AL963 and AL975. After preliminary performance tests on the stock aircraft in July the Rolls-Royce installation design department went to work, with North American not far behind on two conversions of its own.

In August two more machines, AM203 and AM208, were added to the conversion program at the request of the USAAF in Britain. Lt Col Cass S. Hough, one of the technical officers at HQ VIII Fighter Command, saw the potential of the aircraft in talks with Rolls-Royce liaison officer William Lappin. Joining forces with Hitchcock, he maintained a keen interest in the program.

In early October AL975 was rolled out as Merlin Mustang AL975/G. The Mark X designation was applied, although the aircraft were never known as anything but "Merlin Mustangs" at Hucknall. On 13 October chief test pilot Ronnie Shepherd took the aircraft up for a 30-minute maiden flight, attaining a speed of 376 mph with the Merlin 65 installed. As the program turned out, all five test Mustangs were powered by Merlin 65s rather than 61s.

After over 45 hours' flying time 963 was re-engined with another Merlin 65 for intercooler development. Placing the small intercooler radiator in the belly scoop with the glycol radiator streamlined the nose, making the aircraft the sleekest of the Mustang Xs. Note that the dorsal fin has been removed, the vertical stabilizer having been enlarged by an extra three square feet. *(Rolls-Royce via Roger Freeman)*

On 30 November 1942 Bob Chilton took the first XP-51B up for 45 minutes at Inglewood. The Merlin Mustang program was now off in earnest, enjoying official support from two countries.

Cass Hough was invited by Bill Lappin to come out to Hucknall and fly the new conversion, providing General Hunter would give permission. Hough recalls: "Hunter was reluctant to give me the okay because it was an experimental aircraft; but he did it, with the admonition, 'If you break your neck don't blame me!' I took my P-47 there for all the hands to see and fly while I was to have a go at the 'new' Mustang.

"I just assumed it would be a conventional airplane because nobody told me anything. The only information I got from Bill Lappin was that the first flights that had been made up at Hucknall resulted in the pilots being just delighted with the airplane.

"Flying a new airplane I always put the power on easily at the start to get the feel of the airplane on the ground, then gradually gave it power. When I got airborne, a couple of

41-37352 was the first of two P-51s converted to take the Packard-built Merlin V-1650. As development began in England, information was freely supplied to allow NAA to undertake similar work on a Merlin Mustang. The aircraft flew for the first time on 30 November 1942. *(USAF)*

hundred feet off the ground, I pulled up the gear and decided then I'd see how it would climb from scratch. I poured the coal to it and the aircraft snap rolled! Rolls-Royce hadn't provided enough vertical fin area, and not enough offset.

"I was eager to get it to altitude and see how it performed because that was the critical thing then. I studied the fuel curves of the Merlin in several other airframes so I knew what the range of the airplane would be on internal fuel but I didn't know how the airplane would actually handle at high altitude because no one had ever got an Allison-powered Mustang above 24,000 or 25,000 feet.

45

The first Merlin Mustang to fly was AL975/G, on 13 October 1942. It is seen here following roll-out at Hucknall. Powered initially by the Merlin 65, it was fitted with the 70 and 71 versions for further development testing. Total airframe time on Merlin test work was 195 hours 30 minutes before the aircraft was struck off charge on 5 April 1945. *(Frank Compton)*

''Ordinarily the two-stage blowers, the early ones, were manually operated on the Spitfires. I had just begun to think it was time to change blowers—I hadn't even inquired where the handle was for changing it—when all of a sudden I got this big ''chug'' and a thump around 16,000 feet and of course it was then in high blower. But I was about ready to make sure my chute harness was okay, and wishing I could change my drawers! There was an automatic supercharger gear change and it was a complete surprise.

''I got up to about 33,000 feet with it and it was so maneuverable; and I could tell without making any speed runs, assuming the airspeed indicator was calibrated reasonably carefully, that it was performing wonderfully. I just couldn't believe some of the things I saw after doing a couple of speed runs with it.''

It did not take long to set up comparative trials with the new Mustang. On 23 December 1942 AM203 was delivered to the AFDU at Duxford for trials with a Merlin 66-powered Spitfire IX. Interim Report No 64, released on 9 February 1943, revealed the following results: ''In level speed the Mustang is 12-22 mph faster than the Spitfire up to 30,000 feet. In rate of climb the Spitfire is better than the Mustang by about 800 ft/min up to 20,000 feet. In the dive the Mustang is able to out-pace the Spitfire without difficulty. In turning and rolling manoeuvres the Spitfire is the better, save that at 400 mph, IAS, with standard wings it was a little inferior to the Mustang in rate of roll. The Mustang suffers badly from lack of directional stability and adequate rudder control, both of which detract seriously from its fighting capabilities. Modifications are in hand to improve these qualities. The view for fighting and search generally from the Mustang is inferior to that from the Spitfire. The Mustang carries 150 gallons as compared with the Spitfire's 85 gallons.''

P-51B versus P-51A, P-47D, P-38J, P-39N, P-40N

One of the early P-51B-1s in RAF camouflage and carrying an RAF fin flash and serial number. Note the mid-1943 red-bordered national markings. *(Paul Coggan)*

Above: **The beautifully clean lines of the Merlin Mustang are evident in this mid-1943 shot of one of the production P-51B-1-NAs. Note the oil from the breather port covering the side of the fuselage.** *(NASM)*

Left: **This P-51B was flown in an all-matt-black finish devoid of national markings for testing as a night fighter; 21 February 1944, Wright Field.** *(USAF)*

Below: **One of the P-51C-10s built at the Dallas plant.** *(Paul Coggan)*

Once the final configuration of the P-51B had been settled at Inglewood, North American and the AAF wasted no time in getting the first production model out. Bob Chilton flew it on 5 May 1943. By the middle of that year the USAAF had set up tactical trials for the P-51B at Eglin Field, Florida, in which the new Mustang would be tested against each of the service's first-line fighters: the P-51A, P-47D-10, P-38J-1, P-39N-0 and P-40N. Excerpts from that report follow:

ARMY AIR FORCES BOARD PROJECT NO. (M-1) 50
TITLE: TACTICAL EMPLOYMENT TRIALS ON NORTH
AMERICAN P-51B-1 AIRPLANE

LEVEL SPEEDS

The P-51B-1 is capable of very high speeds at altitude. It is important in operations to keep the wing skin and the finish in good condition, free from rough spots, dents, and deep scratches. Airflow disturbances in the boundary layer region will materially affect speed performance. The average level flight maximum speed is about 435 mph at 30,000 feet, at 3,000 rpm and 61″ Hg manifold pressure . . .; two 1,000 pound bombs reduce maximum speed by about 45 mph. The bomb racks alone cost approximately 15 mph loss in speed. From sea level to 11,000 feet, the P-51B is from 7 to 10 mph slower than the P-51A, which is the fastest fighter below this altitude . . . Between 14,000 and 22,000 feet, the P-51B is about 15 to 20 mph faster; and from 22,000 feet up, the P-51B, in high blower, widens the speed advantage up to 75 mph true, at 30,000 feet. From sea level, the P-51B gradually gains on the P-38J and the P-47D until, at 16,000 feet, it has a speed of about 420 mph, which is about ten miles faster than the P-38J and about twenty miles faster than the P-47D . . . Above 27,000 feet the P-51B can no longer get war emergency power, but its speed of about 430 mph at 30,000 feet is equal to that of the P-47D and about 20 mph faster than that of the P-38J, both using war emergency . . . . The P-51B is capable of 400 mph at 40,000 feet.

CLIMB

The P-51B-1 is by far the best climbing airplane of all current American fighter types, [taking] about 4½ minutes to get to 15,000 feet, as against about 5 minutes for the P-38J-1, and about 7 minutes for the P-47D-10. The P-51B maintains a lead of about ½ minute over the P-38J to 30,000 feet, and reaches that altitude in about 11 minutes, which is about 6½ minutes faster than the P-47D.

ZOOM CLIMBS

In zooming the P-51B with the P-47D-10, from level flight at cruising and high speeds, and from high speeds out of dives, the P-51B gains speed rapidly and leaves the P-47D far behind. In zooming the P-51B with the P-38J, from level flight at cruising speed, the airplanes climb evenly at the start; however the P-51B falls off while the P-38J keeps climbing. In zooms from high speeds (425 IAS), the P-51B pulls away from the P-38J, and its zoom ends considerably higher.

DIVE

The diving characteristics of the P-51B are superior to those of any other fighter type airplane . . . . It is exceptionally easy to handle and requires very little trimming. The P-51B dives away from all other fighters except the P-47D, against [which] the P-51B jumps several hundred feet ahead in the initial pushover and then holds that position, apparently neither gaining nor losing distance.

AILERON ROLL

With the new seal balanced ailerons, the P-51B has a faster rate of roll at all speeds than any other fighter except the P-47D, [the two being] equal at cruising speeds.

SEARCH VIEW

The search view in the P-51B is better than in the P-51A, but is still obstructed above, to both sides, and to the rear, by the canopy construction. The view forward over the nose is considerably improved over the P-51A by the relocation of the carburetor air intake scoop, the elimination of the clear view panel on the left side of the windshield, and lowering of the nose of the engine one and one-half degrees.

FIGHTING QUALITIES
(Each aircraft carried normal combat load)

GENERAL

The fighting qualities of the P-51B were compared with those of the P-47D-10 and the P-38J-5, and, briefly, with the P-39N-0 and P-40N. The only maneuver the P-39 and P-40 have, that is superior to the P-51B, is a slight advantage in turning circle. In all other maneuvers, as well as performance, they are both far inferior. The P-51B has good performance at all altitudes, but above 20,000 feet the performance improves rapidly, and its best fighting altitude is between 25,000 and 35,000 feet . . .. The rate of climb is outstanding, with an average of about 3,000 feet per minute from sea level to 25,000 feet. Above 20,000 feet, the overall fighting qualities of this aircraft are superior to those of all the other types used in the trials.

P-51B-1 VERSUS P-47D-10

The P-51B has a much smaller turning circle than the P-47D-10, and is able to get in behind the P-47D in one and one-half to two turns, after a head on approach. The war emergency speed of the P-47D-10 is comparable to that of the P-51B up to 30,000 feet, but above this altitude the speed of the P-51B increases rapidly over that of the P-47D . . .. If the P-51B is jumped by the P-47D, it can turn into the P-47D and rapidly maneuver on to its tail. Dive, rate of climb and acceleration of the P-51B [are] superior to those of the P-47D. The P-51B also holds its high speed longer than the P-47D in level flight after a dive, because it decelerates much slower.

P-51B VERSUS P-38J-5

The turning circle of the P-51B is smaller than that of the P-38J-5 at all altitudes. It has a far faster rate of aileron roll through all speeds. The P-51B accelerates rapidly away from the P-38J in a dive, after reaching speeds of 325 IAS . . .. When full power is applied, the P-38J will pull several hundred feet out in front before the P-51B can reach maximum acceleration and overtake the P-38J . . .. If the P-38J has built up speed in a dive and is not seen in time, the P-51B can turn sharply into the P-38J and evade its fire. The P-38J cannot follow the P-51B at high diving speed at altitude, due to its lower limits of allowable diving speeds. At high speed, it is impossible for the P-38J to keep its sights on the P-51B due to the P-51B's rapid rate of aileron roll, allowing it to reverse its direction of turn faster than the P-38J can follow.

ESCORT

With its long range, high cruising speeds, and excellent fighting qualities, the P-51B airplane is very good for escort work. Pilot fatigue caused by poor cockpit ventilation and the not too comfortable seat are disadvantages for long range flights.

SERVICING

Complete servicing of the airplane with fuel, oil, oxygen, ammunition, radio check, and coolant for both systems requires approximately 18 minutes with a crew of nine men.

When the above report came out in late summer 1943, the 8th Air Force bombers were beginning to take their hardest beatings over occupied Europe. The concept of a strategic bomber that could defend itself was being proven woefully mistaken. But to begin with the Merlin Mustang modifications were rejected by 8th Air Force commander Maj Gen Ira C. Eaker in March 1943 because he believed that the British engine was too heavy for good performance at high altitudes. In fact, before and during the first part of America's involvement in World War II the Air War Plans Division of the USAAF, in formulating a strategic aerial offensive against Germany, did not even refer to the possible need for escort fighters. That the P-51B became available at all was a stroke of luck.

Escort Fighter

With the end of World War I, air power pioneers in the US and in Europe, notably Billy Mitchell and Lord Trenchard, placed a great deal of emphasis on the potential of strategic bombardment based on the central principle of Dòuhet: take long-range bombers and hit the enemy's war-making potential far behind his own lines. By the 1930s the bomber became the dominant air force weapon among Air Corps doctrinal thinkers. There were however notable exceptions among instructors at the Air Corps Tactical School, the foremost being Capt Claire Chennault. But he was brushed aside with the assertion that current bombers were faster than fighters and better armed. It was firmly believed that the only way to stop a large air armada was to destroy its aircraft on the ground. Rather than the various delays in getting the P-51 through testing and procurement, it was the struggle to overcome this doctrinal prejudice that kept the aircraft from entering combat on a larger scale any sooner. With the exception of a few "there will always be a fighter" advocates such as Ben Kelsey, most described the pursuit aircraft as strictly a defensive weapon.

It was not until early in 1942 that the subject of range extension for fighters came up in high places. On 20 February a small conference was held in Hap Arnold's office. According to Official Materiel Command documents, "During the conference several cablegrams from the various theaters of operation were presented for discussion and in almost all cases they expressed a demand for increased range in pursuit, dive bomber, and light bombardment types of airplanes. Following the discussion, verbal instructions were issued by telephone, to initiate immediate action on studies covering means of extending the range on the above-named types of aircraft. Later, on 21 March 1942, a conference was held at the Materiel Division, Wright Field. At this conference it was pointed out that the major problem in range extension was that of ferrying pursuit airplanes in order to avoid serious delay and relieve the 'bottleneck' of available ocean-going [transports] ... Thus, range extension was applied at first to pursuit airplanes."

Kelsey had already unofficially devised long-range tanks for the P-38, and he was more than ready for Arnold's conference. For his part, the latter did not conceal his surprise, then his delight, at what the Pursuit Projects Office had done. Air Materiel Command's *Case History of Fighter Airplane Range Extension Program* continues: "Study and flight test of fighter airplanes indicated that the P-51B consumed an average of sixty-four gallons of fuel an hour, the P-38J an average of 144 gallons an hour, and the P-47D an average of 140 gallons ... The P-51 carried enough fuel for four hours and forty-five minutes and, therefore, needed an additional 112 gallons in order to meet the required 'six hours plus thirty minutes for reserve.'

"By August 1943, there was already developed a leakproof, droppable fuel tank of 150-gallon capacity for the P-38

and a similar tank of 75-gallon capacity for the P-51 ... At the same time, the Materiel Command initiated action to construct a paper tank similar to the British 108-gallon paper tank ... Adequate production quantities of the various range extension tanks became available as a result of the decided increase in production after October 1943. The production schedule called for 22,000 tanks to be delivered during the month of November 1943. This monthly volume was not actually achieved until April 1944, when approximately 25,000 tanks were delivered. In June 1944, over 48,000 tanks were delivered by eleven prime contractors.

"Additional fuel, it was believed, could be carried in the thin outer portion of the wing of the P-51 by means of a wing change. However, this change was not advised. It would require such redesign that production would be "far in the future". Moreover, the rate of roll of the airplane would be decreased and the additional weight caused by leakproofing the thin tanks would be uneconomical for the small fuel increase.

"But the internal fuel capacity of the P-51B and C airplanes was increased by the installation of one 85-gallon self-sealing fuselage tank. This increased the built-in fuel capacity to a total of 269 gallons and, at the same time, increased the weight, including fuel, approximately 650 pounds. As was to be expected, this weight increase resulted in considerably reducing the performance of the airplane. The rate of climb was reduced by about 470 feet a minute and the flying characteristics at altitudes above 25,000 feet were seriously affected. Furthermore, the airplane was sluggish and the acceleration obtainable without stall was very low. When the additional fuel tank was placed in the rear of the fuselage, the longitudinal stability was marginal until the rear tank was partially emptied."

By fall 1943 the P-51B was clearly the answer to the 8th Air Force's long-range escort needs: an aircraft to stick close to the bombers and defend them from enemy fighter attack. On 3 September, while inspecting the 8th Air Force, Arnold cabled that P-51s be provided to escort the bombers as soon as possible. The result was that immediate action was taken to re-equip two P-47 groups in Britain with P-51s. It was believed that six groups of Mustangs could be ready for operations from England by December, but the first P-51B did not reach VIII Fighter Command until 17 September, and this was for a unit on detached service from the 9th Air Force, the 354th Fighter Group. In December the 363rd Fighter Group was assigned to the 9th Air Force. By February 1944 there would be but one additional Mustang group, the 357th, attached directly to VIII Fighter Command.

In November 1943 long-range escort finally became official AAF doctrine. By this time P-47s and P-38s were already crossing the borders of Germany using external tanks, but the fighters were still tied to the bombers, much to the frustration of General "Monk" Hunter and his fighter pilots.

An experienced World War I fighter pilot, Hunter knew that

Left and above: **Escort fighter supreme: with long-range 75-gallon drop tanks, the P-51B became the hope of the Army Air Force. This fighter, though suffering numerous teething problems, would make all the difference in keeping daylight bombing a major part of the war effort.** *(NAA via Norm Taylor)*

Right: **Late 1943, Lockheed Reassembly Plant, Speke Aerodrome, Liverpool. This new P-51B has just been made airworthy after shipment from the US. Theater markings have not yet been applied. Mustangs were being sent to England at a furious rate to meet the need for a deep-penetration escort fighter.** *(USAF)*

Right: **The 9th Air Force's 354th Fighter Group was the first Merlin Mustang outfit, entering combat on loan to the 8th Air Force on 1 December 1943 under the leadership of 4th Group CO Don Blakeslee. This 353rd Squadron Mustang is being looked over by men of the 401st Bomb Group on 27 December 1943.** *(USAF)*

Right: **Another 357th Group P-51B, which belonged to Jim Browning from the 363rd Squadron, visiting the 78th FG at Duxford. The Cessna Bobcat next to the P-51 was popularly known as the ''Bamboo Bomber,'' a reference to its wooden structure.** *(Russell Hunter, 78th FG Assn)*

Below: **This P-51B was flown by Capt Dave Perron with the 8th Air Force's first Merlin Mustang unit, the 357th Fighter Group.** *(Arval Roberson)*

Above: **On 23 March 1944 the white noses began to be supplanted by group nose colors. Here the 357th FG Mustang of Harry Ankeny sits at Leiston with new nose colors and 75-gallon drop tanks.** *(H. A. Ankeny via Merle Olmsted)*

Left: **Base Air Depot 2, early 1944. Few among many: Mustangs were far outnumbered by Thunderbolts until the middle of 1944. Early ETO markings consisted of white noses and white stripes on wings and tail to help gunners recognize Allied aircraft.** *(USAF)*

Top: **In early March 1944 another group, the 355th, gave up its P-47s to fly with VIII Fighter Command. Here 354th Squadron P-51Bs fly in echelon bearing early ETO markings. Note the non-standard camouflage gray sweeping up under the tail of WR-Y.** *(William P. Dumas)*

Above: **Lt-Gen James H. "Jimmy" Doolittle, commander of the 8th Air Force from 6 January 1944, flying a P-51D. Until Doolittle made the decision "to take our fighters off the bombers and put them against the German fighters," fighter pilots were not free to roam and hit the Luftwaffe. He considered it his most important decision of the war.** *(Benjamin S. Kelsey)*

as long as his fighters were used defensively there would be no opportunity to prove their true potential. He wanted flexibility to use his pilots as offensive, aggressive hunters of the enemy. The bomber commanders, including Eaker, demanded close escort. As Haywood S. Hansell put it in his book *The Air Plan That Defeated Hitler,* "Fighters were required literally to fly formation with the bombers and were permitted no latitude of judgment . . . The fighters had to fly at low speed and were at serious disadvantage when they were 'jumped' by German fighters. It had been the same in World War I."

The P-51B, a superbly offensive tool, was thrown into the middle of this problem along with a new commander for the 8th Air Force, Lt Gen James H. Doolittle, who arrived to take command on 6 January 1944. The defensive fighter tactics were an obvious failure and Doolittle wasted no time in reversing the trend. Doolittle recalls: "Adolf Galland, in his book, said that the day we took our fighters off the bombers and put them against the German fighters—that is, went from defensive to offensive—Germany lost the air war. He, however, erroneously credited my superior, General Spaatz, with the decision. I made the decision and it was my most important decision during World War II. As you can imagine, the bomber crews were upset. The fighter pilots were ecstatic."

Even though German fighter production continued to increase as 1944 wore on, American fighter pilots began a killing spree that did not end until there were virtually no German pilots left to face. To quote Haywood Hansell again, "One is compelled to conclude that the air offensive against the aircraft and engine factories was not a primary cause of defeat of the German Air Force . . . The Luftwaffe was defeated not so much by air attacks on production facilities as by elimination of vital aviation gasoline and by combat attrition. Gun crews aboard the B-17s and B-24s did their share, and so did the long-range P-51, P-47 and P-38 fighters." Combat rather than strategic bombing defeated the Luftwaffe, something that the AAF planners had not foreseen.

Mustang III versus Spitfire IX and XIV, Tempest V, FW190A, Me109G

Above: **FW190A-8s of IV./JG 3, one of the units that opposed the massive American formations in 1944 and 1945. The 190 gave the P-51 more problems than any other German piston-engined fighter, but when loaded with more weapons and armor plate its performance suffered severely.** *(Alfred Price)*

Below: **The Me109G-14, one of the later versions of the 109. This one was assigned to III./JG 3 to fly high cover for the Gruppe's heavily armed FW190s. As the 190s pressed in on the bombers, the lighter 109s were there to tackle the American fighter escort, which almost always consisted of Mustangs.** *(Oskar Romm via Alfred Price)*

On 26 December 1943 a new Mustang III (P-51B/C), FZ107, was delivered to RAF Wittering for tactical trials against the Spitfire IX and XIV, Tempest V, FW190A and Me109G. The following excerpts from the report on the trials give a good look at how these friends and enemies performed against what was then the new Merlin Mustang:

One of the last versions of the FW190 was the D-9. These two IV/JG 3 aircraft are at readiness (note parachutes on tails) in March 1945 at Prenzlau. The "Dora 9" was one of the few aircraft capable of meeting the Mustang on almost even terms during the latter part of the war. *(Oskar Romm via Alfred Price)*

FLYING CHARACTERISTICS

The Mustang III is very similar to fly and land to the Mustang I. It is therefore delightfully easy to handle. It is as easy to fly as a Spitfire IX with the exception that rudder is needed whenever changing bank (in order to prevent skid, and to prevent the sight from swinging off). This soon becomes automatic. The engine feels very smooth.

Flying Controls

These are well balanced and positive, especially at high speeds. In comparison with the Spitfire IX:

(a)   The rudder is heavier. It is far more effective as only a small amount of re-trimming is necessary at high speeds (over 400 I.A.S.) to keep the aircraft straight. There is no lateral wander.

(b)   The ailerons feel lighter, especially over small movements and in general flying. There appears, however, to be a cushioning effect when full aileron is applied. This is because considerably more stick force is necessary when a quick change of bank is desired.

(c)   The elevators are considerably heavier. They are not tiring, partly because the change of trim with speed is less.

Formation Flying

Because the aircraft is clean, one would expect station keeping to be difficult, but engine response is so steady that formation flying is very easy.

TACTICAL COMPARISON WITH SPITFIRE IX

A very close comparison can be made because the two engines are of very similar design and capacity. The tactical differences are caused chiefly by the fact that the Mustang III is a much cleaner aircraft, is slightly heavier, and has a higher wing loading than the Spitfire IX (43·8 lbs per sq ft of the Mustang III, against 31 lbs per sq ft).

Endurance

The Mustang III with maximum fuel load, has between 1½ and 1¾ the range of a Spitfire IX with maximum fuel load. The fuel and oil capacities are 154 [183 US] gallons and 11·2 [13·3 US] gallons respectively, as opposed to 85 [100 US] gallons and 7·5 [9 US] gallons of the Spitfire IX, both without long-range tanks. With long-range tanks, the Mustang can carry a total of 279 [330 US] gallons of petrol [two 75 US gallon long-range tanks] as opposed to the Spitfire IX's maximum of 177 [210 US] gallons (1 × 90 [107 US] gall "slipper tank").

The fuel consumption at similar boost and rev settings is approximately the same for the two aircraft, but the Mustang III is approximately 20 mph faster in level flight. Therefore, if the ranges are compared directly according to the fuel capacities of the two aircraft when the long-range tanks are fitted, the Mustang will still have something in hand.

Speeds

In general for the same engine settings the Mustang III is always 20-30 mph faster in level flight at all heights. This is also true for the maximum engine setting of 3,000 rpm 67″ (+18 lbs) or whatever is available, depending on the height. The best-performance heights are similar, being between 10,000 and 15,000 ft, and between 25,000 and 32,000 ft.

Climbs

The Mustang III has a considerably lower rate of climb at full power at all heights. (In a formation take-off, Spitfire IX maintains formation with 5 lbs less boost.) At other engine settings and 175 mph, the two aircraft have a similar climb. The Mustang has, however, a better zoom climb in that it can dive 5,000 feet or more and regain its original altitude at a greater speed. It needs less increase of power to regain its previous altitude and speed.

Dives

The Mustang III pulls away very rapidly in a dive. At the same revs the Spitfire IX requires from 4 to 6 lb more boost to remain in formation.

Turning Circle

The Mustang is always out-turned by the Spitfire IX. Use of flaps on the Mustang does not appear to improve the turning circle. There is adequate warning of the high speed stall in the form of elevator buffeting, followed by tail buffeting.

Rate of Roll

Although the ailerons feel light, the Mustang III cannot roll as quickly as the Spitfire IX at normal speeds. The ailerons stiffen up only slightly at high speeds and the rates of roll become the same at about 400 mph.

Search

The all-round view from the pilot's cockpit is the same as the Mustang I, therefore generally inferior to the Spitfire IX, but better forwards and downwards on either side of the fuselage. A sliding hood has been designed and is being fitted to Service Mustangs. This makes its rear view at least equal to, if not better than the Spitfire IX.

BRIEF TACTICAL COMPARISON WITH SPITFIRE XIV

Maximum Endurance

By comparison, the Spitfire XIV has no endurance.

Maximum Speed

There is practically nothing to choose in maximum speed.

Maximum Climb

The Spitfire XIV is very much better.

Dive

As for Spitfire IX. The Mustang pulls away, but less markedly.

Turning Circle

The Spitfire XIV is better.

Rate of Roll

Advantage tends to be with the Spitfire XIV.

Conclusion

With the exception of endurance, no conclusion should be drawn as these two aircraft should never be enemies. The choice is a matter of taste.

BRIEF TACTICAL COMPARISON WITH TEMPEST V

Maximum Endurance

By comparison, the Tempest V has no endurance.

Maximum Speed

The Tempest V is 15-20 mph faster up to 15,000 ft. There is then no choice until 24,000 feet when the Mustang rapidly pulls ahead, being about 30 mph faster at 30,000 feet.

Maximum Climb

These compare directly with the results of the speed tests. At similar performance height, the Tempest has the better zoom climb.

Dive

The Tempest tends to pull away.

Turning Circle

The Tempest is not quite as good.

Rate of Roll

The Tempest is not so good.

Conclusions

The Mustang has endurance and general performance above 24,000 feet. The Tempest has a better speed and climb below 10,000 feet.

BRIEF COMPARISON WITH FW 190 (BMW.801D)

Maximum Speed

The FW 190 is nearly 50 mph *slower* at all heights, increasing to 70 mph above 28,000 feet. It is anticipated that the new FW 190 (DB.603) might be slightly faster below 27,000 feet but slower above that height.

Climb

There appears to be little to choose in the maximum rate of climb. It is anticipated that the Mustang III will have a better maximum climb than the new FW 190 (DB.603). The Mustang is considerably faster at all heights in a zoom climb.

Dive

The Mustang can always out-dive the FW 190.

Turning Circle

Again there is not much to choose. The Mustang is slightly better. When evading an enemy aircraft with a steep turn, a pilot will always out-turn the attacking aircraft initially because of the difference in speeds. It is therefore still a worth-while manoeuvre with the Mustang III when attacked.

Rate of Roll

Not even a Mustang III approaches the FW190.

Conclusions

In the attack, a high speed should be maintained or regained in order to regain height initiative. A FW190 could not evade by diving alone. *In defence a steep turn followed by a full throttle dive should increase the range before regaining height and course.* Dog-fighting is not altogether recommended. Do not attempt to climb away without at least 250 mph showing initially.

BRIEF COMPARISON WITH Me 109G

Maximum Speed

The Mustang III is faster at all heights. [The Mustang's] best heights, by comparison, are below 16,000 ft (30 mph faster approx) and above 25,000 ft (30 mph increasing to 50 mph at 30,000 ft).

Maximum Climb

This is rather similar. The Mustang is very slightly better above 25,000 ft but inclined to be worse below 20,000 feet.

Zoom Climb

Unfortunately the Me 109G appears to have a very good high speed climb, making the two aircraft similar in a zoom climb.

Dive

On the other hand, in defence the Mustang can still increase the range in a prolonged dive.

Turning Circle

The Mustang is greatly superior.

Rate of Roll

Not much to choose. In defence (a tight spot) a rapid change of direction will throw the Me 109G's sight off. This is because the 109G's maximum roll is embarrassing (slots keep opening).

Conclusions

In attack, the Mustang can always catch the Me 109G, except in any sort of climb (unless there is a high overtaking speed). In defence, a steep turn should be the first manoeuvre, followed, if necessary, by a dive (below 20,000 feet). A high speed climb will unfortunately not increase the range. If above 25,000 ft keep above by climbing or all-out level.

CONCLUSIONS

The Mustang III is a delightful and easy aircraft to fly.

Its advantages over the Spitfire IX lie in a considerably greater range and greater all-round speed. It can outstrip the FW 190 in a dive, followed if desired by a shallow climb. Its only serious drawback is a slightly less rate of climb than the Spitfire IX, particularly at height.

A pilot needs to understand the effect of compressibility speeds. Practices should *not* be attempted.

AFDU/3/21/36
8th March, 1944

(signed)
Wing Commander,
Commanding, AFDU

Temperamental Thoroughbred

A 355th Squadron, 354th Fighter Group, P-51B on take-off at Boxted. The pilot has just pulled the gear handle to the UP position, as shown by the large fairing doors, which are just beginning to extend. The group spent only 20 days working up with its new fighters in November 1943 before entering combat. *(USAF)*

The P-51B was seen as a very fortunate answer to the USAAF's urgent need for a long-range escort fighter. The P-47 did not have enough range and the P-38, though only a little less "long legged" then the P-51B, was encountering numerous problems in Europe.

North American Aviation was pushed hard for both the P-51B and P-51C. The C model had flown for the first time from Dallas, Texas, on 5 August 1943. The XP-51D, a modified P-51B-1 with a bubble canopy, got into the air on 17 November 1943 in the hands of Bob Chilton. Everything was done in a rush and defects inevitably crept into the machines rolling off the lines. But the fact that the P-51B had never been designed for an 85-gallon fuselage tank ultimately did not matter in the face of the paramount need for more range.

On 7 November 1943 the pilots of the 354th Fighter Group, the first to get Merlin Mustangs, began checking out in P-51As from the 67th Photographic Reconnaissance Group at Membury, England. The first five P-51Bs were received on 11 November from 8th Ferry Service Command, and three days later the group moved from Greenham Common to Boxted, Essex.

On 1 December 1943, just 20 days after getting their new Mustangs, the group got 24 aircraft off under the leadership of 4th Group deputy commander Lt Col Don Blakeslee on their first mission, a sweep to Knokke—St Omer—Calais. Kenneth R. Martin, the group's first CO, recalls: "My maintaining command of the 354th rested on the answer to one question by General 'Pete' Quesada [9th AF commander]: how soon could I get our pilots checked out in these new aircraft and have both planes and pilots ready for combat missions? My answer of 3 weeks satisfied him."

Blakeslee flew the next six missions with the 354th, then flew one of the Mustangs back to Debden for his men to see. He was enthralled with the new "kite". It was reminiscent of the Spitfire, which the group had flown before getting P-47s. His group would be next on the list for the aircraft after the 8th's first P-51B group, the 357th, became operational after being transferred from the 9th Air Force. On 11 February 1944 the 357th flew its first combat mission and on the 28th, after a quick conversion course, the 4th took P-51Bs into combat. In the meantime, the 363rd Fighter Group, 9th Air Force, had flown its first P-51B mission in January.

The problems that arose from rushing the new Mustang into combat brought cries for help from the pilots. Cass Hough was given an unproven airplane, and told to make it work. "There were problems you wouldn't believe," recalls Hough, "but because the airplane had such great potential all the brass wanted to rush it into combat. They wanted to turn their backs on any problems there might be, for fear they would be denied the number of airplanes they wanted in the theater."

One of the first major disappointments centered on the very thing that made the P-51B what it was, the Merlin engine. When Packard had first undertaken license production of the engine, it was readily apparent that there were major differences between the UK and US Merlin engines. Most of the drawings from Rolls-Royce had to be changed and Packard found itself involved in building what was virtually a new engine. The Merlin 66 became the V-1650-3, and suffered serious teething problems in the European weather and under combat conditions.

Bernard R. Ginsberg, an engineering officer with the 356th Squadron of the 354th Fighter Group, recalls those early frustrating days: "The P-51 was entirely new to us and when we picked them up in England, all we got was the aircraft. The special tools and part packages had got separated from the aircraft, so we had planes, but no parts. And this went on for some time before the parts began to be available through regular channels. Thus we were forced to scrounge, steal, improvise and finally cannibalize grounded planes for parts. Of course, the crunch came when the word came down from Col Martin that we were to put the cannibalized airplanes back together as soon as possible; this really caused some night requisitioning.

"Some of the troubles that I remember were:

"Propeller seal leaks: This oil leak came from the seal between the dome and the propellor and put oil on the windshield. We had to replace the seal to correct the problem.

"Coolant radiator regulator trouble: This regulator was supposed to control the coolant temperature automatically. To begin with, when it malfunctioned, we had to replace the unit, which was difficult and the unit was in short supply. Finally, one of my mechanics studied the problem and came up with a way to adjust the unit in the aircraft. This solved the problem.

"Drop tank trouble: In many cases, the drop tanks would not draw at altitude. This caused a number of aborts. The solution to this was to pressurize the tanks.

"Rough engines: We had our share and the causes were numerous. However, the chronic cause was fouling of the spark plug in the front cylinder of the left bank. Beads of lead from the fuel would form on the electrodes of the plug and short it out. This problem seemed to be much worse at times and we thought that possibly there was excessive lead in the fuel. There was no way to check this, so we had to live with it and ended up changing this particular plug before each mission. We also advised the pilots to run the engine at 50" Hg just before take-off and check the mags at this setting. This cleared out engines that had loaded up taxiing."

All four Mustang groups suffered numerous aborts on every mission: the records list oxygen equipment, coolant leaks, engines cutting out or rough, magneto failure, high oil temperature, electrical system failure, prop leaks and high-blower failure. One-third early returns per mission was normal, and to get 20 aircraft per group up for a mission was a minor miracle. To watch a comrade bail out over enemy territory when his engine stopped was an agonizing experience, and several pilots ended up in captivity this way.

But there was one problem that was by far the most serious, and it resulted in pressure to have the type withdrawn from combat indefinitely. The first known casualty to result from this was Lt Mark O. "Mo" Tyner of the 354th. Over Boxted on a test flight, he entered a turn and the entire engine broke away. There was no way he could get out of the tumbling, engineless airframe and he was killed. All Mustangs in the theater were immediately grounded.

From 13 to 15 March 1944 all the wing bolts were replaced and the engine mounting bolts were checked. Some engine mounting bolts were found to be cracked; others had snapped completely, leaving broken pieces in the bottom of the

The Hun Hunter From Texas **was flown by Henry W. Brown, who became one of the 355th FG's leading aces. At this point in early 1944 he had four kills.** *(T. R. Bennett)*

cowling. Lt Knopka of 354th Headquarters drove to Burton-wood and scrounged enough engine mounting bolts to restore the group to flying status after only one day off operations, but the problem was far from solved.

On 17 March Burtonwood finished manufacturing new engine mounting bolts, but even these turned out unsatisfactory and in April North American had to rush 250 sets of new bolts to Britain. The problem was traced to faulty heat treatment.

Another problem was the continual jamming of the four 0·50-caliber guns, which plagued the groups from the very beginning. Any time a pilot pulled more than 1½-2 g the guns would jam; this effectively limited firing to straight and level flight, a grave limitation in air-to-air combat. Many of the stoppages were caused by the failure of rounds to extract from the belt. During maneuvers the pressure on ammunition in the belt increased to more than 17 pounds, at which point the guns jammed. The design of the gun installation, with the guns canted and the belts feeding over and down into the breeches, was poor. The ideal solution was to reposition the guns and feed belts, but this could not be done without a major modification (it came with the P-51D). The stopgap solution was a booster motor that was activated by a contact which closed under 17 pounds pressure and helped the belts to feed; but even then it was some time before all the P-51s were retrofitted.

The 85-gallon tank behind the cockpit, which shifted the center of gravity a long way rearwards, created another problem. If the tank was over half full, any abrupt stick movement aft could cause the aircraft to enter a high-speed stall and snap-roll out of control. Official AAF procedures worked out for the P-51B in the USA called for the internal tank to be burned off first, followed by the drop tanks. In the light of operational experience this was quickly reversed after many a frustrated pilot had ended up jettisoning full drop tanks when bounced by enemy fighters.

Before long it was found that the full 85 gallons in the tank caused such severe tail-heaviness that the P-51 could not even get off the ground safely with a full load. From that point on the tank was limited to 65 gallons. 354th Group ace Glenn T. Eagleston found that the Mustang would stall without much provocation when the rear tank was full and external tanks were carried. He learned to lead a turn with forward stick and then compensate by letting the tank give back

Charles Lenfest flew a series of fighters named *Lorie* (I to IV) with the 355th FG. Here he leaves his last Thunderbolt for a new Mustang in March 1944. All of his aircraft were coded WR-F. *(T. R. Bennett)*

BAD 2's *Spare Parts* in flight. This P-51B-5 was accidentally dropped into the sea while being unloaded in a crate at Liverpool. When it was recovered it was found that the fuselage was badly bent, and the aircraft was sent to Warton for spare parts. However, the men in the hangars volunteered to rebuild it as a two-seater in their spare time; note the passenger in what would normally be the radio compartment. It was lost in 1944 as a result of engine trouble, going down into the Irish Sea after pilot and passenger bailed out. *(George Gosney)*

pressure on the stick to make the turn. In spite of the problems of flying in this manner, Eagleston preferred to hang on to his fuselage fuel for extra range and burn that in the drop tanks first. If he got caught with too much fuel in the fuselage tank, he had the ultimate escape maneuver. He would whip into a right-hand turn and high-speed stall the fighter, snap inverted back to the left, and then look back to see if his opponent had been able to follow. The maneuver was so rapid that it usually succeeded.

In spite of these difficulties the pilots preferred to stick with their troublesome aircraft, for when the P-51 worked, it was better than its opponents. Indeed, Eagleston made some of his 18½ aerial kills with just one gun firing.

Recalling those months spent introducing the Merlin Mustang to combat, Eagleston gives much of the credit to Don Blakeslee's tactics. The line-abreast two-ship formation was used for mutual support. The group was taught to fight as a team, without lone-wolf attacks. Pilots were advised always to keep airspeed up, so that maneuvering energy would be available. The motto became "When in doubt, attack!" When the enemy had the advantage, the best tactic was to force him to reduce his airspeed or increase one's own speed; the same was true of altitude. A pilot's instinctive reaction is to make a left turn, so Eagleston forced himself to become a right-turn artist.

One serious tactical problem with the P-51B was its similarity to the Me109. Everything with squared wings and tail was treated as German, and friendly fighters often bounced the Mustangs. In fact on 10 February 1944 Eagleston himself was shot down by P-47s, though he managed to bail out safely.

One of the 354th's first squadron commanders was former "Flying Tiger" James H. Howard. Trained as a US Navy pilot, he was 30 years old when he arrived to fly Mustangs. On 11 January 1944 he was leading the group to Oschersleben and Halberstadt. Deep into enemy territory the bomber formation was intercepted by numerous German fighters and Jim Howard dispatched the three squadrons to intercept: "On that first pass I wasn't in a turning dogfight so all my guns

stayed in operation and I got an Me110. But on engaging the next several planes I found that my guns went from four down to three, two, then one, then none firing. By the time I got to none I,just made feinting passes at enemy planes and that apparently was enough to drive off the Germans.

"I found also after my second attack on the German planes that I was hovering around one particular B-17 group which turned out to be the 401st Bomb Group. I realized that I was alone and that the other planes had been dispersed to boxes of B-17s to the rear, so I thought to myself: 'Why not just stay here and do my job of trying to protect this particular group of bombers', about 20 of them, which I did.

"So I was in a constant climbing and diving operation in and around this particular group, driving off the enemy planes and shooting them down. In fact, when one of my guns operated I would make a pass at an airplane and that was enough to drive them off. But I didn't get too low as I realized if I dived down 10 or 15 or 20,000 feet a lot of German fighters would be coming along to shoot down my bombers. My main object was to protect the bombers rather than to shoot enemy aircraft.

"Well, after about 35 minutes there were no enemy planes around. The bombers had dropped their bombs and headed back for the North Sea so I turned for home, picked up a couple of my fighters and headed on back to England."

At interrogation the bomber crews were unanimous in their praise for the lone Mustang, wanting to find him regardless of where he might be. 401st Group commander Harold W. Bowman said: "For sheer determination and guts it was the greatest exhibition I've ever seen. They can't give that boy a big enough reward." "That boy" had claimed six destroyed and was awarded the only Medal of Honor given to a USAAF fighter pilot flying against the Luftwaffe.

The Mustang's problems were far from over, however. When the P-51D began to arrive in the combat zones, most assumed that the bugs had been ironed out, a misapprehension that cost the lives of some pilots until the hard-working technicians pinpointed the problems.

John T. Godfrey (left, in flying helmet) and Don S. Gentile are greeted warmly on 10 April 1944 after returning from a strafing mission in France. At that time Gentile was credited with 30 air and ground kills (later officially reduced to 27.8), and Godfrey ultimately became the 4th Fighter Group's leading ace with 30.6 air and ground kills. Gentile had scored his last three kills, FW190s, three days earlier. On 13 April 1944 he buzzed Debden for the newsreel cameras and flew his *Shangri-La* into the ground. Group commander Don Blakeslee was furious and sent the pilot home to Ohio. *(US Army)*

At the Base Air Depot at Warton, Lancashire, hundreds of Mustangs were modified, assembled, repaired and flight tested each month from the end of 1943 to mid-1945. On 12 June 1944 Lt Bill Clearwater took off from Warton in a new P-51D after combat modifications had been made to the aircraft. David G. Mayor later recalled: "Fifteen or twenty minutes later the usual sounds of assorted engines were blotted out by the ungodly scream of a Merlin gone mad. It was a never-to-be-forgotten sound that stopped every man in his tracks. Hundreds of eyes snapped skyward to the sight of a '51 in a nose-high attitude, twisting toward the earth from 1,500 feet. The engine was running wild and off to the west a few hundred yards the right wing fluttered down like a wrapper from a stick of chewing gum. In seconds the shriek of the mistreated Rolls stopped dead; the silence was deafening as the fighter buried itself in the tidal flats on the south side of the River Ribble." The pilot was killed.

Fourteen days later Orville Wrosch was watching Lt Burtie Orth take off from Warton on a P-51D test hop when he noticed the fighter slowly rocking left and right. Suddenly the right wing tore loose at the root and slammed against the canopy, and the aircraft went in with its pilot. Two men were now dead, and there were reports of P-51Ds losing wings in combat. The pieces of the P-51Ds were brought to Hangar 4 at Warton, where it was found that they had come off at identical points. Once again the AAF's leading fighter was threatened with grounding.

Fortunately, the cause was soon found: the landing gear had extended in flight and the abnormal aerodynamic load had twisted the wings off. As David Mayor recalls: "It is well to consider the design changes that had been made in the D Model as compared to the B and C. The landing gear structure itself had not been changed, but the up-locks for the main wheels and the fairing doors had been changed from a two-stage operation with latches to hold the landing gear and doors closed, to a sequenced hydraulic system with automatic latches at the front and rear corners of the fairing doors. The purpose was to simplify the lowering of the landing gear to a one-step operation by simply placing the gear selector in the down position without having to manually release the up-locks." But the hydraulic pressure was not enough to hold the gear up, particularly in a high-speed dive. The fairing doors were sucked open, allowing the slipstream to suck the gear out and tear it off.

Pilots were ordered to leave the gear selector in the UP position, rather than neutral, after retracting the gear. But the real answer came with modifications to the up-locks which were later incorporated on factory-built aircraft.

The wing failures did not all stop with these modifications, however. It was found that high g loads on P-51s with fuel in the fuselage tank caused the wings to break off at the inboard end of the gun bay. Following are excerpts from a report by Louis Wait, administrative test pilot at North American, Inglewood, explaining much of the mystery behind the Mustang's problems:

BRIEFING
FOR P-51 PILOT INSTRUCTORS
by
LOUIS S. WAIT
Administrative Test Pilot
NORTH AMERICAN AVIATION, Inc
Inglewood, California
AUGUST 8, 1945

Early P-51 types . . . were designed for a combat weight of 8,000 pounds, good for an ultimate pullout factor of 12g, with a pilot allowable applied factor of 8g. As a result of equipment and fuel tank location, the airplane was positively stable under all conditions of flight . . .; the pilot always had to pull more pounds on the stick to produce more g in a turn; when this force was released the airplane immediately stopped turning. The same was true of the aileron and rudder forces . . .. The changes in trim tab settings for climbing and diving were negligible.

The new, heavier, more powerful Packard-built Rolls-Royce engine made necessary a heavier radiator for proper cooling, and a heavier four-blade wide-chord propeller to utilize the increased engine power at altitude . . .. The P-51B and C Airplanes, the result of these modifications . . ., was an overloaded airplane since the combat weight was increased from 8,000 lbs to slightly over 9,000 lbs . . .. As later results demonstrated, the decrease in g factor alone was not a serious complication . . ..

However, other adverse characteristics did become apparent. The increased engine power and four-blade propeller caused a marked decrease in directional stability. Whereas the pilot previously had to use increasing rudder pressure for increasing sideslip or yaw angles, the rudder forces now tended to decrease at yaw angles greater than 10°, and if the pilot did not apply sufficient opposite rudder, the airplane tended to increase the skid or sideslip all by itself, eventually resulting in an unintentional snap roll or entry into a spin.

This condition became serious at high speeds, as the snap maneuver resulting from excessive skidding imposed a higher unbalanced load on the horizontal stabilizer than that for which it was designed. Horizontal stabilizer failures began to occur, and since the highest incidence was in slow roll maneuvers, slow rolls were immediately prohibited. Even though [the P-51B and C were cured by reworking the tail surfaces and] strong enough to take very high speed snap maneuvers, slow rolls were still prohibited because the inverted snap maneuver which often occurred . . . was catching the pilot unawares . . .. It became necessary to increase the directional stability of the airplane by adding a dorsal fin, and by rigging the rudder trim tab to give opposite boost.

As an interesting sidelight, many pilots using the P-51B and C airplanes in combat had discovered an excellent use for the directional instability just mentioned. The first well-described use came about when a P-51 combat pilot following an enemy airplane down in a steep dive glanced in his rear view mirror and mistook his wingman (who was following along as a good wingman should) for an Me109. Since evasive action was apparently mandatory, the pilot proceeded to push all the controls into the northeast corner of the cockpit, and the consequent series of inverted snap rolls, entered at over 450 indicated, seperated subject P-51B pilot from his target, his wingman, and almost from his airplane. The fact that the stabilizer fell off in the hands of the crew chief during inspection after the airplane had flown to its home base did not deter other pilots from using the same tactics, when necessary . . ..

Although several pilots who had used the above described maneuver complained that they could not any longer obtain their usual evasive action because of the addition of the dorsal fin and change in the rudder boost tab, it is believed that the increased directional stability overcame all of the difficulties previously encountered . . ..

The first objectionable feature [of the 85-gallon fuselage tank] was that the weight . . . without external tanks was increased to about 10,000 pounds, which decreased the ultimate pullout factor from an original 12g down to 9·5g, [but this] was not as serious as the fact that when the additional fuel was added, the airplane's center of gravity was placed so far aft that the airplane became longitudinally unstable. This instability was particularly dangerous in that a pullout at high speed was always accompanied by a stick force reversal which, unless opposed by the pilot, would quickly carry the airplane into an accelerated condition where the wings would fail . . . at the inboard end of the gun bay.

With full fuselage tanks and two 110-gallon external tanks, the gross weight of the [P-51D] is over 11,600 pounds, nearly 50% more than the design weight of the airplane. The pilot's allowable pullout factor is 5·0g and the ultimate wing failure load occurs at 7·5g . . .. Although additional weight has been added to the P-51 airplane, the ultimate and allowable load factors have not been decreased sufficiently to prevent the pilot from accomplishing any combat maneuver . . ..

The only way to obtain increased strength or any substantial amount of increased stability is to start from scratch and design a new airplane. This has been done in the P-51H. Actually the model designation of this airplane is somewhat confusing because the airplane is structurally no longer a P-51—it is a brand-new airplane. The P-51H is designed to develop over 11g ultimate pullout factor at a design gross combat weight of 9,600 lbs. Further, the arrangement of the airplane has been changed slightly so that it is always stable, regardless of the disposal of fuel or armament load . . .. The P-51H [is] a truly worthy successor to all previous P-51 Series airplanes.

The P-51's problems were serious enough for grounding to have been considered on at least two occasions. However, the genuine leap forward in all-round performance which it offered pulled the aircraft through. Ironically, when the aircraft was in the very midst of these troubles, during March and April 1944, such units as the 4th Fighter Group achieved more kills than at any time in their history.

Range was the central factor in keeping the Mustang alive—that and excellent maneuvering performance. On 25 November 1944 the Army Air Forces Proving Ground at Eglin Field released a report on tests designed to determine the maximum combat radius of the P-51D as an escort for heavy bombers. They revealed "that a single P-51D, taking off with two 75-gallon droppable tanks, can perform the following flights under either partial or total escort conditions:

(1) Radius of action 900 miles; reserve after landing 40 gallons.

(2) Radius of action 780 miles; reserve after landing 75 gallons.

With two 110-gallon droppable tanks, [the P-51D] can fly a radius of action of 1,000 miles under total escort conditions and land with a reserve of 55 gallons."

The following table from AAF documents shows how the P-51 compared with the P-38 and P-47 at various combat loads:

RADIUS OF ACTION: P-51, P-47 and P-38 COMPARED

	Take-off weight (lb)	Bomb weight (lb)	Fuel (US gal) Internal	Fuel (US gal) External	Radius (miles)
P-38L	19,500	1 × 1,000 underwing	410	1 × 165 underwing	400
	18,500	2 × 500 underwing	410	—	260
	19,500	2 × 1,000 underwing	410	—	250
	19,500	—	410	2 × 165 underwing	600
	17,500	—	410	—	290
P-47D	14,500	—	370	—	280
	15,150	—	370	1 × 108 centerline	400
	16,150	2 × 500 underwing	370	1 × 108 centerline	360
	15,500	2 × 500 underwing	370	—	260
	16,500	2 × 1,000 underwing	370	—	230
	16,400	—	370	2 × 150 underwing	575
P-51B, C, D	9,800	—	269	—	350
	10,800	2 × 500 underwing	269	—	325
	10,800	—	269	2 × 75 underwing	650
	11,200	—	269	2 × 108 underwing	750

Conditions: **1** Warm-up and take-off equivalent to 10 min at normal rated power. **2** Climb to 10,000 ft at normal rated power (distance covered in climb is included in radius). **3** Cruise out at 10,000 ft at 200 mph (P-47), 220 mph (P-38, P-51). **4** Drop external tanks on arrival in target area. **5** 5 min combat at war emergency power and 15 min at military power. **6** Cruise back at 10,000 ft and 210 mph (P-47), 230 mph (P-38, P-51). **7** No account is taken of decreased fuel consumption during descent. **8** Allowance is made for 30 min reserve at minimum cruising power. **9** No allowance is made for formation flight or evasive action other than 20 min combat.

For all the Mustang's growing success, there was one hazard that would never change: it was a very dangerous aircraft to ditch. The belly scoop, for all its advanced aerodynamic qualities, was a frightening liability when alighting on water. RAF Report No Aero 1896, December 1943, related the problem quite clearly: "The ditching performance of the Mustang is so bad that pilots should bail out on every occasion if sufficient height exists to do this. It is necessary to reduce ground speed below 70 mph to prevent catastrophic diving (deceleration up to 8g) which is caused by the radiator. This is only possible with considerable headwind, 20-30 mph, with dead engine...."

Mustang, Lightning, Thunderbolt:
A Combat Commander's Assessment

Col Hub Zemke with his P-51D in September 1944, when he was commander of the 479th Fighter Group, Wattisham.
(Hub Zemke)

In the history of air fighting only a few commanders have demonstrated a legendary ability to lead and employ fighter aircraft. One such is Hubert A. "Hub" Zemke, the only man to lead P-51, P-38 and P-47 units into combat as a group commander: first of the 56th Fighter Group with P-47s, then of the 479th Fighter Group with P-38s and later with P-51s. In the following account he describes the combat abilities of these aircraft from an air leader's perspective.

"**P-51** By far the best air-to-air fighter aircraft of the three below 25,000 feet. It had a very good radius of action for the type of work we did in Europe. The acceleration from slow cruise to maximum performance was excellent compared with that of the competition.

Its rate of roll was good and it maneuvered easily to a learned hand. Dive and acceleration were rapid. Visibility in all directions was ample. As an instrument flying aircraft it was a bit touchy, and it could easily be overcontrolled in turbulence.

On the question of armament, it carried sufficient machine guns. Why I say this is that after viewing numerous combat films where pilots fired at extreme range or over-deflected, I came firmly to a conclusion that one should fight for a combat position of 10° or less deflection. At close range—250 yards or less—there is no doubt what would happen when the trigger was depressed: it was a matter of ducking the flying pieces after that.

P-47 A rugged beast with a sound radial engine to pull you along. It was heavy in fire power, enough to chew up the opponent at close range. It was best suited to the ground support role, as everything in the armament arsenal was hung under its sturdy wings.

It accelerated poorly and climbed not too much better from a low airspeed. Once high cruising speed was attained, the P-47 could stand up to the competition.

Strangely, the rate of roll and maneuverability were good at high speeds. In fact, the aircraft had many a forgiving feature. With its high-altitude supercharger its performance at altitude—above 25,000 feet—appeared superior to that of the other two US fighters. At high altitude the higher level speed, better climb and more solid response to control were reflected in the tactics that the 56th Fighter Group developed early in combat.

The P-47, once it had gained altitude, could exceed any of the contenders in speed of entering a dive and the dive itself, and had a very good zoom recovery to altitude again. Naturally a fighter pilot endeavors to fight his aircraft from the strengths of his machine's performance rather than from its weaknesses. With this in mind I repeatedly impressed upon the 56th Fighter pilots that our tactics were to 'Hit and recover, hit and recover. If you can't get the opponent by an altitude of 15,000 feet, then break off and recover to altitude again.'

P-38 Though this aircraft had some virtues, for me it was the poorest of the three US Army Air Corps fighters in the European Theater. The fact that the extreme cold at altitude affected its performance hardly endeared it to me. The turbo-superchargers were controlled by an oil regulator and at altitude the oil had a tendency to congeal, which caused serious problems. On two occasions I recall entering combat with enemy single-seaters, and it became a matter of life and death to get away and survive, though I had started with the advantage. On both occasions the engines either cut out completely or over-revved when the throttles were cut or advanced.

The second factor that detracted from the combat capability of the P-38 was that it was limited to a maximum diving speed of 375 mph indicated. A common tactic of the Luftwaffe single-seaters was to split-S for the clouds or the deck. Often their head on-attacks on the bomber formations ended with a roll over and dive for the deck to confuse and outdistance the flexible machine guns. P-38s had little chance to pursue.

Now the above statements should not lead one to conclude that the P-38 had no good features. It did! As a gun platform it was as steady as a shooting stand. With two engines there was no torque. With a little trim for build-up of speed in a dive, a pilot could ride directly into a target. As to the armament installation, I have seen no better. Four machine guns and a cannon mounted close together directly in front of the pilot. This armament being so close to the gunsight, there was no need for the guns to converge their fire, as on the other two fighters."

Europe

As the Mustang bolted into combat its sterling qualities rapidly became evident in spite of the many problems, and before long several 8th and 9th Air Force groups were converting to the new type. The results of the switch to the Mustang are reflected in the 20th Fighter Group's unit history, *King's Cliffe*. The group completed conversion from Lightnings to Mustangs on 24 July 1944: "87 of our pilots were lost while flying P-38s over Germany and German-occupied Europe. 89 enemy planes were destroyed in the air and 31 on the ground.

"Lt Col Cy Wilson, who was Group Commander at the time, had strong feelings on the matter . . . . 'Well boys, pretty soon we will be flying fighter planes, instead of airborne ice wagons.'

"From 24 July '44 to the end of operations our intelligence reports commonly contained the words '15 FW190s were spotted by one of our squadrons. They were attacked and in combat from 28,000' to the deck, 6 were destroyed, without loss.' When enemy aircraft were encountered on P-38 missions the narrative of operations would commonly read: 'At 1115, 20 Me109s were spotted queuing up to attack the bombers. 79th Squadron prevented the attack but were unable to engage as the Hun split-essed and left the scene.'

D-Day for the 361st Fighter Group. *(USAF)*

"During the 1st month of operations with P-51s the Group destroyed 70 enemy aircraft. This was the same number the Group destroyed from February 22 to July 24, 1944. The destruction of these 70 aircraft in P-38s cost the 20th 51 pilots killed or missing in action. 70 victories in one month of operations with P-51s cost the Group 14 pilots. Even this low ratio of loss to victories improved as time went on."

Once VIII Fighter Command released its fighters to seek and destroy the enemy at will, kill tallies, both in the air and on the ground, began to rise dramatically. Even though losses in strafing attacks were four times greater than in air combat, the fighters sought ground targets continually. In a paper on ground attack, 4th Fighter Group commander Donald J. M. Blakeslee outlined his tactics:

AIRDROMES

Surprise, speed and a variation of the attack—these are the things to keep in mind when strafing a Hun airdrome.

I consider surprise as one of the chief factors in a successful strafe. When my group is assigned to strafe a particular target I ask for all the photographs available . . . . I want my intelligence officer to get the best information he can on the defense, the pin-point positions of flak posts, if possible. I want to know what kind and how many aircraft are reported to be on the field and just where on the field I can expect to find them parked . . . .

With this I can plan the approach best calaculated to achieve surprise. I use terrain—hills, gulleys and trees—for cover, and such airdrome installations as hangars, etc, to screen my approach. I never come right in on an airdrome if I can help it. If I have planned to attack an airdrome beforehand I pick an I.P. some 10 miles away . . . . I have my course from there to the drome worked out. Once in the air I take my boys right past the airdrome as if I had no intention of attacking it at all. At my I.P. I let down and swing back flat on the deck. I usually try and have another check-point on the course from my I.P., not far from the airdrome, and when I pass that I know I am definitely coming in on the right field . . . . Once I hit the drome, I really get down on the deck. I don't mean five feet up; I mean so low the grass is brushing the bottom of the scoop.

For a squadron attack on a Hun airfield I do not recommend sending sections in waves. This is a good way to get half the outfit shot down. In my own group, I want as many as eight in at one time, if possible. These should be well abreast and, knowing our target beforehand, we go right in full bore in a straight line. Once you start an attack of this kind, don't turn or swerve. If you do there is danger of collision or entering another man's pattern of fire.

I plan only one pass on an airdrome and after my first pass I climb to about three or four thousand feet well beyond the field and circle and look back to observe the damage in the form of smoke or fire. I see where the rest of the boys are and call up on the R/T and ask how the flak was. If there wasn't too much on the first pass and I figure we can afford to have a go a second time, we line up and repeat the performance. This time I usually leave eight aircraft up for top cover. These should be at four or five thousand feet—well beyond the range of small arms fire. On the first pass I never bother with top cover as we are all on the deck and any Hun that wants to bounce us is welcome to try.

After the attack on the field stay on the deck for a good mile beyond the drome before pulling up. The break should consist of rudder yawing. Never cock a wing up. If you must turn on the drome, do flat skidding turns. Don't give the Hun a better target to shoot at.

I prefer to get down low and shoot up at any aircraft on the ground rather than come in high and shoot down. Usually I fire a short burst from long range and correct for it as I come in . . . .

It's important to go in full bore. You want all the speed you can muster. The aircraft should be trimmed for high speed before you go in and not for cruising speed at which you go by the field . . . .

I have tried dropping belly tanks filled with gasoline and then strafing them to set targets afire, but to my mind it is not too successful. The trouble is the tanks fall different ways: some tumble backwards while others go straight down . . . .

In general, my pilots and I realize ground strafing involves a greater risk than shooting Huns down in the air. But it seems to be quite as important. Besides we get more fun out of strafing ground targets instead of airfields—no one really likes to attack these.

Concluding, I want to say a word about tactics. My feeling is that there is entirely too much emphasis placed on methods of strafing and on so-called tactics. Strafing is a simple process. You pick a target and shoot it up. As long as you are comfortable and get away with it, that's all there is to it. Every pilot probably has a different idea on how to do it. A general rule just can't be laid down, for one method is probably no better than another.

Elmer W. O'Dell was a member of the 382nd Squadron, 363rd Fighter Group, in the 9th Air Force from January 1944 to September 1945, flying for the most part a P-51B-10, *El's Belle, Ginny.* He vividly recalls his days with the Mustang: "I destroyed an aircraft on my first mission . . . unfortunately, it was a P-51. I was taking off on my leader's wing when I blew a tire and swerved toward him. Kicking opposite rudder, I avoided a collision, but by the time I got straightened out I didn't have enough speed or runway to get airborne. I cut the switches, held the stick in my gut, and closed my eyes. The plane ran off the field, across a sunken road which sheared off the gear, dropped on two full wing tanks, skidded across a field, tore off the left wing on a stump, and wound up with its nose in a chicken coop. I was told later that I killed a crow in a

Above: **A Kiwi in the AAF. After flying a tour with No 616 Squadron RAF, Flt Lt Jack Cleland, Royal New Zealand Air Force, flew another tour with the 363rd Squadron, 357th FG. While many Americans flew tours with Commonwealth nations, the reverse was rare and Cleland was the only RNZAF pilot to fly with the AAF. The two kill marks represent FW190s downed while with No 616 Squadron. Cleland also flew the Russia Shuttle mission with the 357th.** *(T. R. Bennett)*

Centre: **A flight from the 364th Squadron of the 357th Fighter Group: from left to right: C5-V (44-13678);** *Pappy's Answer,* **C5-E (43-6813), flown by Capt John Stern;** *The Shillelagh,* **C5-R (44-13546), Capt John Storch; and C5-T (44-13586), Capt Richard Peterson. The 357th made a habit of painting its natural-metal aircraft in the field, and RAF dark green was borrowed when normal Army olive drab stocks ran out, giving the Mustangs an appearance unique in the European Theater of Operations.** *(Merle Olmsted)*

Right: **Lt C. W. Ofsthun flew this P-51D with the 357th FG from Leiston.** *(C. W. Ofsthun via T. R. Bennett)*

Left: Jerome Jacobs was a 20-year-old replacement pilot with the 357th Group one month after D-Day. He flew Operation Market Garden over Arnhem on 17 September 1944, the next day shot down an FW190 and an Me109, and on 19 September (his 17th mission) shot down another Me109. 10 minutes later he was himself shot down by 190s and 109s, bailed out and was sent to hospital in Emmerich, Germany. That day he was to have started a 48-hour leave in London, and to save time he had dressed in his best uniform so that he would be ready to go out on returning to Leiston. *(Jerome Jacobs)*

Below: **Lt Charles G. "Toad" Todd in** *Faithful Fernie II* **leads a flight from the 355th FG.** *(William P. Dumas)*

Bottom: **One of Henry W. Brown's last** *Hun Hunter* **Mustangs from the 355th FG.** *(Mocerino via T. R. Bennett)*

Above: **Walter V. Gresham Jr's** Trigger III **of the 355th FG.**
(Crew chief F. Coraggio via T. R. Bennett)

hedge along the road and two chickens in the coop. The Mustang is rugged. I didn't even get a scratch.

"On the Berlin raid on 30 May 1944 my ship, El's Belle, Ginny, took three 20mm hits from a 109. After recovering from a violent spin, I found that on the left side there was only a hole about the size of a golf ball in the leading edge of the horizontal stabilizer. On the right side, the wing tip was missing, the next inboard top wing plate was curled up about 18 inches higher than the surface of the wing, the bottom wing plate was gone and the right aileron was extended about six inches past what was left of the end of the wing.

"With the extra drag from the damaged wing, plus normal torque from the prop, to maintain level flight I had to apply full left aileron trim and fly with the stick as far to the left as it would go. When I got back a little altitude and things settled

Below: Ginny Lynn **of the 355th Fighter Group.** (G. Hunsberger, 355th FG Assn)

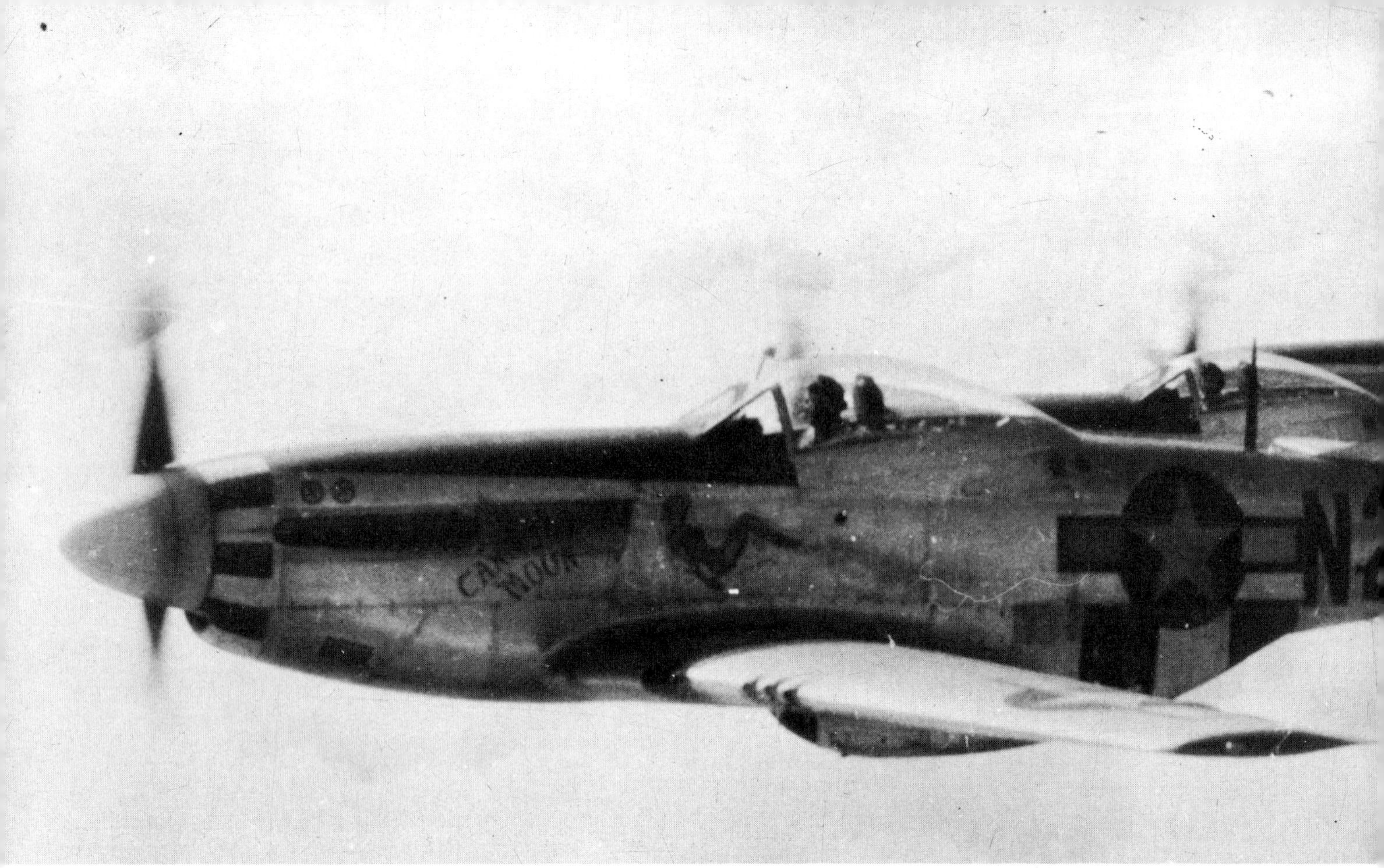

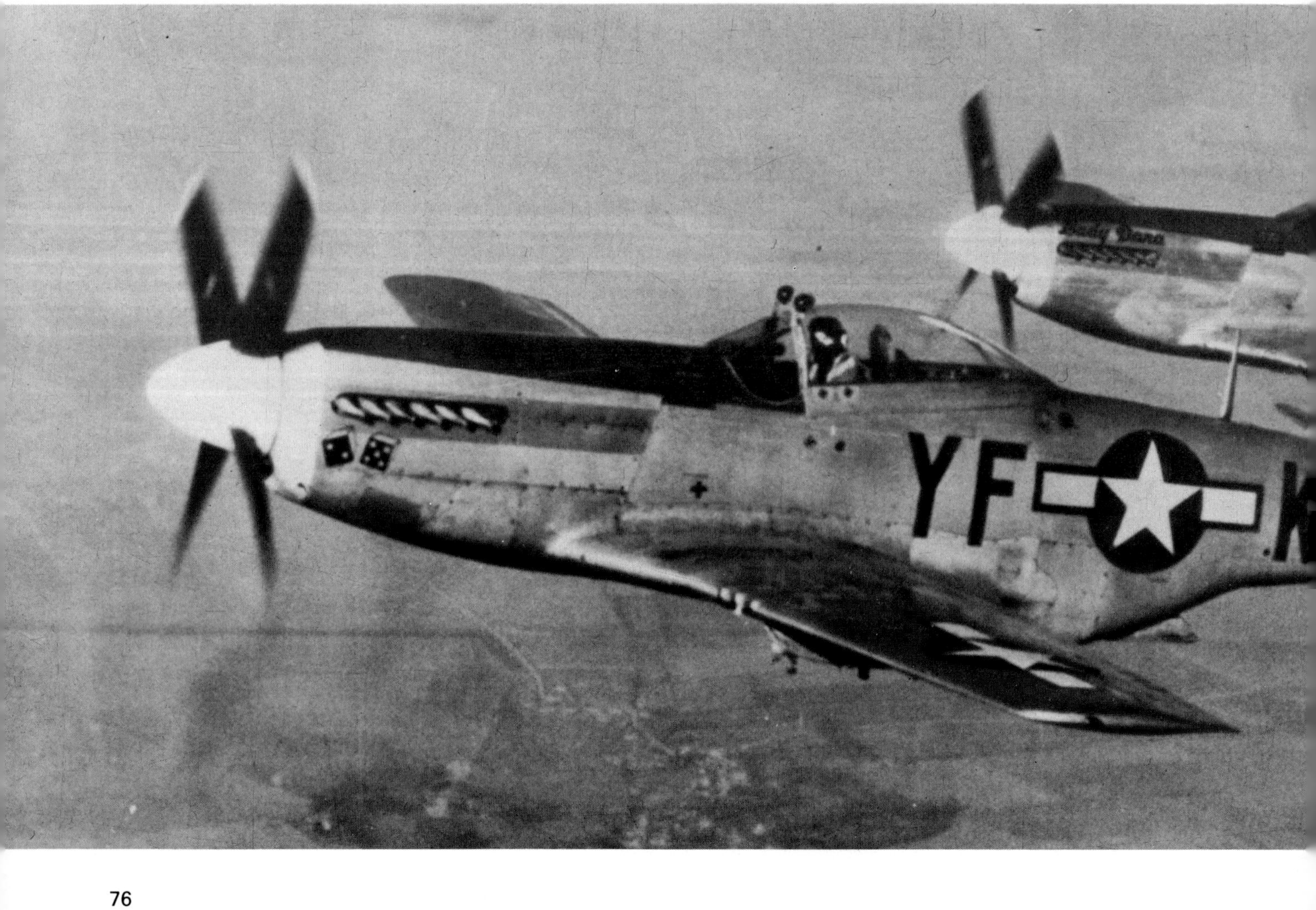
YF

Left: **A flight from the 364th Fighter Group in echelon in late 1944.**

Below: **A 20th Fighter Group Mustang over the English countryside early in 1945.** *(via Norm Taylor)*

Above: **355th Group commander Claiborne H. Kinnard taxis out for a mission in 1945.** *(T. R. Bennett)*

Left: **What used to be Ward H. Douglass'** *Baby Buggy* **leads Keo L. Snook's** *Lady Dana* **in a formation from the 358th FS, 355th FG. 44-13366 is one of the more famous P-51Ds, having been much photographed when it was flying out of the NAA factory and over Southern California. It went on to serve with the 355th; the dorsal fin was added by the group in England.** *(355th FG Assn, G. Hunsberger)*

James E. Duffy leads Norman J. Fortier in April 1945. Both men were aces in the 355th FG. *(Roy Vose via T. R. Bennett)*

Above: **Maj Carl W. Stapleton's** *Esie 4* **of the 364th FG, Honington, on 20 December 1944.** *(USAF)*

Right: **A flight from the 503rd Squadron, 339th FG, early in 1945.** *(J. Watson Noah)*

down, I let go of the stick to see what would happen. Before I could blink, the ship did the most vicious snap roll I ever experienced.

"I brought her in, wheels down, without incident. As I taxiied back everyone was looking at the ship, but surprisingly not at the wing but at the tail. When I stopped at my hardstand I found out why. All the movable surface of the left horizontal stabilizer was gone. The leading edge with the hole in it was practically all that was left.

"The third 20mm shell that hit the ship was the scariest. That 109 was swinging from left to right while he was firing. The first one took the stabilizer, the third hit the wing and made it spin. When he fired the second one he was dead astern—it left a two-foot crease along the fuselage directly below the right cockpit window and did not detonate! Incidentally, on that mission I was flying wingman to Jim Jabara, the first Korean War jet ace.

"I never found a problem with the CG after the fuselage tank was installed. Maybe it was because an incident in our

78th Fighter Group Mustangs at Duxford early in 1945.
(Walter Cannon, 78th FG Assn)

Top: **Robert L. Buttke's 55th FG Mustang in 1945. The 55th put the P-51's namesake on their aircraft, in this case on the rudder.** *(Dave Glover)*

Above: **By 1945 the 55th FG had taken to painting out the tail serial numbers on some aircraft.** *(T. R. Bennett)*

Below: The Impatient Virgin **of the 434th Squadron, 479th FG, in 1945.** *(T. R. Bennett)*

Left: **Lt Lahke of the 351st Squadron, 353rd FG, with his P-51D late in 1944.** *(USAF)*

Below: **339th FG pilot Lt George T. Rich had six kills as of 23 February 1945.** *(USAF)*

Bottom: **This 356th FG P-51D still has the black nose painted on at the assembly depot in late 1944 or early 1945.**

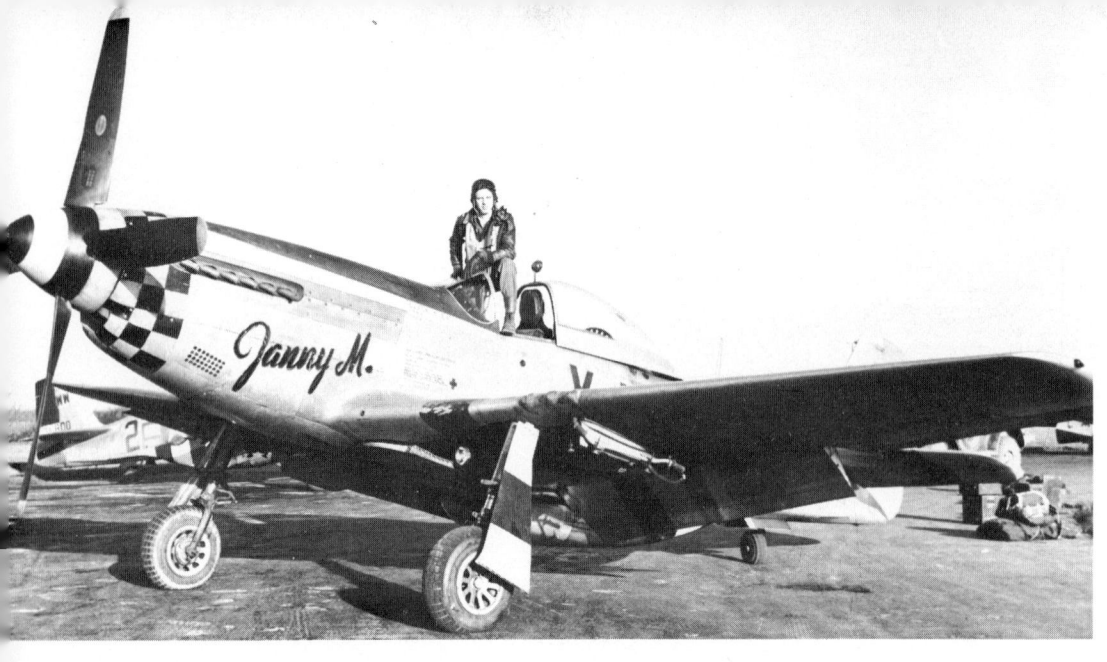

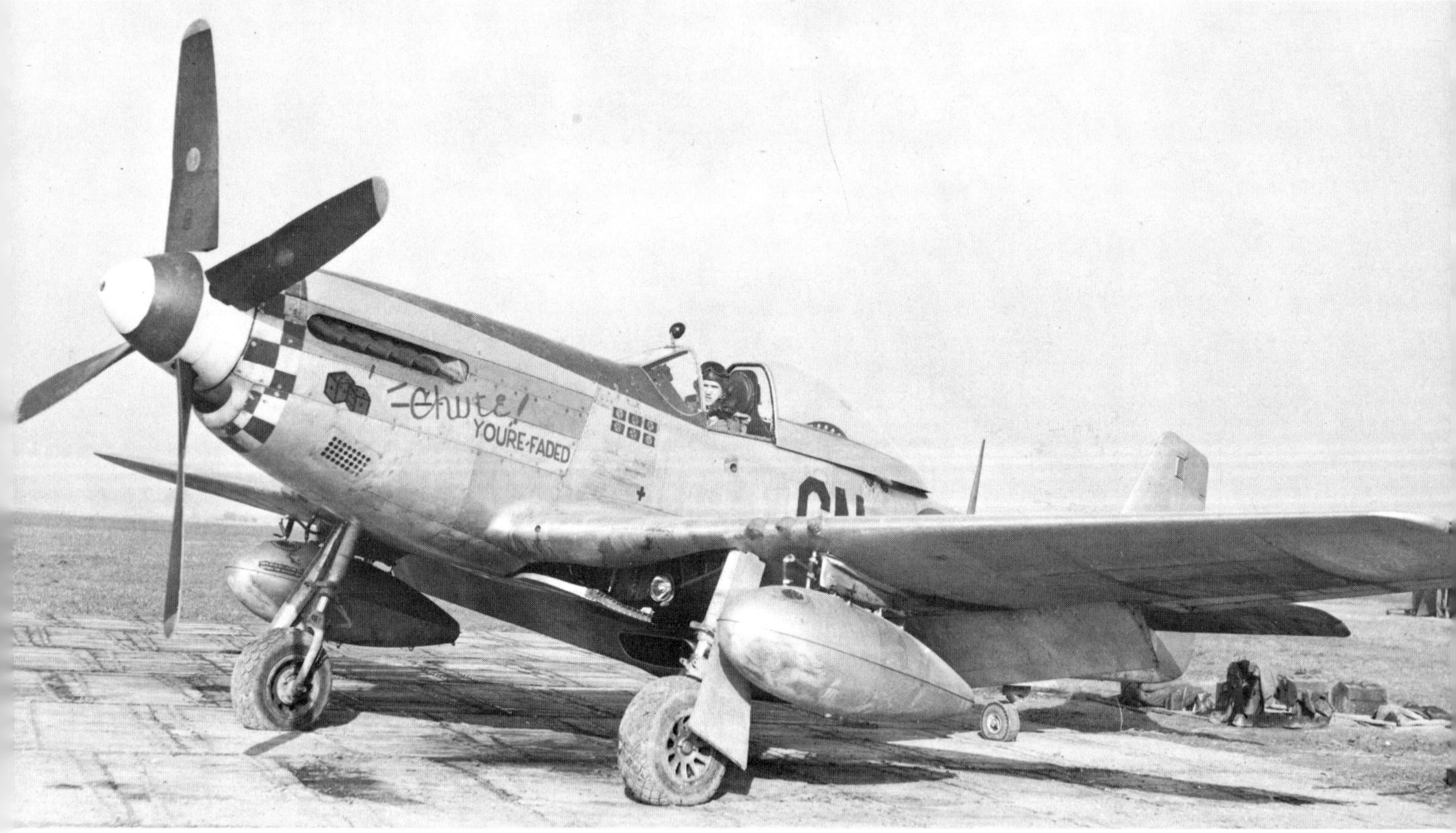

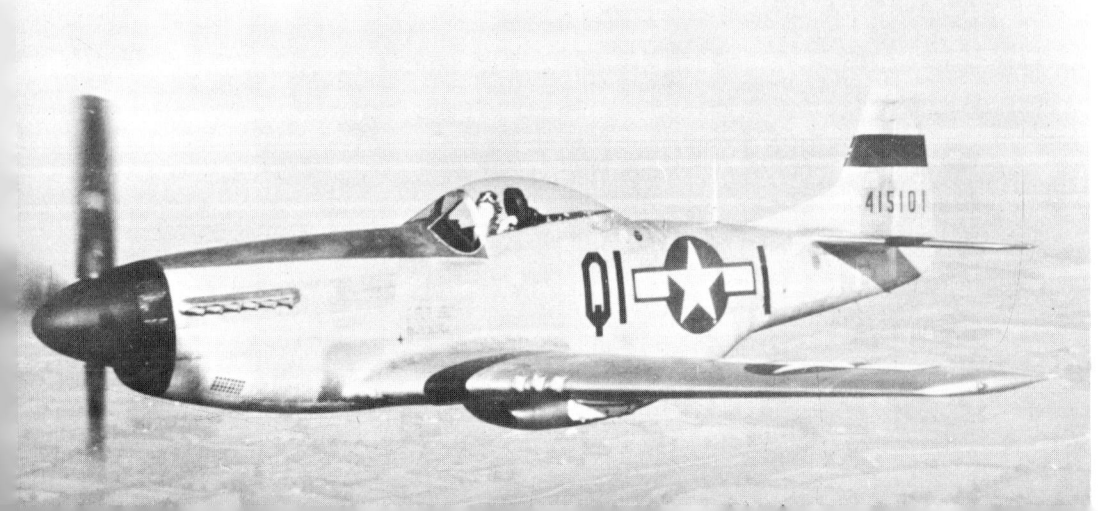

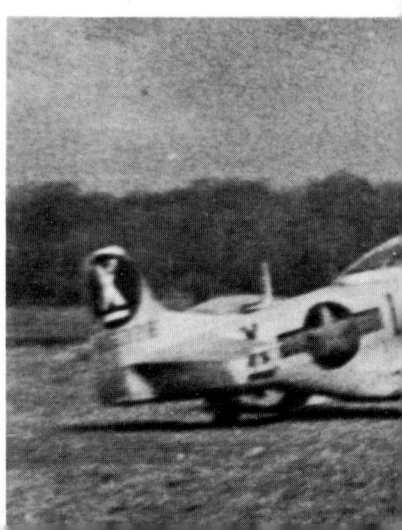

Above: This 4th FG aircraft was salvaged on 16 January 1945. (Edwin Rowe)

Right: Robert S. Voyles flew this Mustang with the 4th FG before being taken prisoner on 27 February 1945. (W. Johnson)

Below right: Paul Lucas' 4th FG Mustang early in 1945. The aircraft is parked near 335th Squadron HQ in the southwest flight line at Debden. (Romack)

Bottom: 77th Squadron, 20th FG, Mustangs at Glatton, home of the 457th BG, in early 1945. Note that the field-applied olive drab is peeling off the wings of LC-B. (J. Wilson via Jack Ilfrey)

A No 19 Squadron RAF Mustang IV (P-51K) in 1945. Flying from Peterhead, Scotland, this unit provided Coastal Strike Wing support, escorting Beaufighters and Mosquitoes on anti-shipping strikes into and around the Norwegian fjords.

364th Fighter Group P-51Ds over England in 1945. *(Hugo Lohr via Garry Fry)*

Above: **The 352nd Fighter Group Mustang believed to have been assigned to 18-victory ace John F. Thornell in 1945.** *(David Saffro via Garry Fry)*

Left: *Suzy-G* **belonged to Col Leonard H. Mottis, 357th Squadron, 361st Fighter Group, in mid-1944. Note the different sections of field-applied olive drab paint.** *(Col L. H. Mottis via Norm Taylor)*

squadron brought home to us the importance of running off the fuselage tank until it was down to 21 gallons. We had a practice dive bombing mission scheduled out over the Thames estuary one morning. The order went down to the line crew to drain the fuselage tanks to the prescribed level. For some reason it wasn't done to the plane of a good friend of mine. When he tried to pull out of his dive, the plane broke in half and he wasn't able to get out.

"13 August 1944 was my most satisfying mission, because it proved to me the value of operating by the book. As a countermeasure to Jerry's strafing the front lines at dusk to minimize interference by our fighters, we began patrolling the front every evening. On this date we had eight ships up and spotted 10-plus 109s heading east on the deck. I lined up behind one that seemed to be a leader . . . . As we came into range, my mind was suddenly filled with everything I had ever learned and practised for such a situation. Wait until his wings fill the ring sight. You're a little above him—pull the tit a bit out in front of his nose. Check the needle and ball—you don't want to be skidding. I squeezed the trigger and immediately everything from the four fifties converged on his engine, and he rolled over and went in.

"His wingman must have been surprised . . . I gave him a short burst. I guess the tracers passing over his wings was too much. He immediately jettisoned the canopy and bailed out. I circled as he floated down, and when he landed, he calmly pulled in his chute, tucked it under his arm, waved and walked away. The eight of us destroyed eight and damaged three . . . best day the squadron ever had.

"*El's Belle, Ginny* was a P-51B-10 and I flew all my missions with her. In June of 1944 I was offered a 51D, but I preferred to keep the B-10. I checked out the D and flew a number of mock combat missions in it, but to me it didn't have the delicate response of the B-10, which had four 0.50-caliber guns. When they built the D they added another gun to each wing. To do so, they had to alter the configuration of the wing. I maintain this caused a small reduction in maneuverability. I guess it was a personal thing, for obviously most pilots thought otherwise."

Lt Butler of the 317th Squadron, 325th Fighter Group.
(Arthur Fiedler via Bill Hess)

The Mediterranean

By the time the P-51A and the A-36 had reached their zenith with the 12th Air Force, the reputation of the aircraft had been established. News of the Merlin-engined Mustangs and their long range only sharpened the desire of commanders and planners in the 15th Air Force (created in November 1943) to employ the aircraft. Barrie Davis, a P-47 pilot with the 317th Squadron, 325th Fighter Group, recalls transitioning to the Mustang in May 1944 after 20 missions in the Thunderbolt: "Many were apprehensive about the liquid-cooled engine which powered the P-51. But we transitioned into the lighter, sprightly Mustang and quickly fell in love with it.

"One danger for the unwary pilot of the P-51 was the 85-gallon fuel tank located directly behind the pilot. When it held more than 15 gallons the center of gravity of the plane was dangerously rearward. In straight and level flight and normal maneuvers this posed no problem, but in a tight turn or pull-out from a dive ... the misplaced center of gravity tended to tighten the turn and could make the Mustang uncontrollable. Our squadron commander quite evidently made his first flight without a look at the manual. He picked up one of our first P-51s from Africa and flew it back to our base in Italy. To show his delight with the plane, he buzzed low over the tent area and pulled up into a steep climb, terminating with a roll. But he never completed the roll. The P-51, with its center of gravity out because of that full fuselage tank, went into an inverted flat spin. After exhausting his bag of tricks in recovery attempts, the squadron commander jettisoned the canopy and hit the silk. He watched as the hapless P-51 spun into the ground and exploded. This episode may have saved our lives later, because all of us never forgot what could happen when anything special was attempted with too much fuel in the fuselage tank.

"That same tank probably saved my life later. Our fighter group was the first to fly combat missions into and out of Russia [2-10 June 1944]. A Me109 got behind me without my knowing it and pretty near shot my P-51 to pieces. He hit all four propeller blades, shot over half my tail off, blasted off the canopy, and made scrap metal of the right wing tip. I was knocked out but the Mustang kept flying on its own until I regained my senses, then I flew back to our Russian base. Maintenance found an armor-piercing round lying in the bottom of the fuselage tank, where its energy had been spent as it hit the 15 gallons of gasoline which remained.

"As the war progressed, the fighter groups of the 15th Air Force took on interdiction missions along with their escort responsibilities, and we decided to try the P-51s as dive bombers. Even with the throttle back, the P-51 picked up speed rapidly. Since we found accuracy increased when the bomb was released at lower altitudes, we had to make an extremely tight pull-out.

"New pilots coming to our fighter group were invariably cocky to the point that they were dangerous to themselves. They thought the Luftwaffe was finished and that the P-51 could quickly and easily kill anything else that flew. To mod-

Capt John Nelson of the 307th Squadron, 31st Fighter Group, in late 1944. *(Norm Malayney)*

ify the attitude of newcomers, we used a war-weary P-40 which our squadron somehow acquired. I was in charge of putting new pilots through a quick, intensive training program, and the final flight included a mock dogfight with the new pilot in a P-51 pitted against one of us flying the P-40. I can tell you that until a pilot knows the strengths and weaknesses of both airplanes, the P-40 can make the P-51 look outclassed. Using all the P-40's strengths, an innovative pilot could outfly a P-51 at low altitudes until the P-51 jockey finally realized that there was something more to fighting in the air than simply having the best airplane. At that point the new pilot became ready to listen to everything we had to say."

On 1 April 1944 the 12th Air Force transferred its two Spitfire groups, the 31st and 52nd, to the 15th Air Force and both re-equipped with the P-51B and C. Daniel J. Zoerb, who had flown 70 missions in Spitfires with the 52nd Fighter Group, was one of a few in the group with Allison Mustang time. When word came that P-51s for the group were sitting in crates on Corsica, all of the pilots with Mustang time headed off to collect the new aircraft. There was no-one to check them out, so after the machines were assembled the pilots clustered around the new P-51s and pooled their memories. Zoerb recalls: "It was like a Chinese fire drill."

The 52nd Fighter Group's style changed a great deal: the Spitfire had been slower and with basically no range, but it was extremely maneuverable; the Mustang had superior speed and range, it could reach the heart of Germany, but it was less maneuverable. Dogfighting Macchi 202s had been no problem in the Spitfire VIII, whereas in the P-51 one had to outrun the very capable Italian fighter.

The Germans and Romanians had recognition problems with the new fighter, as indeed did the Americans. On a mission into Romania Zoerb entered the landing pattern of an Me109 base, put his gear and flaps down like everyone else downwind, and lined up on a 109 in front of him. He followed the fighter onto base leg and then shot it down. On final approach Zoerb cleaned up the P-51, pushed the nose down to get some speed and strafed the field before leaving.

Squadron leader's Mk IV of No 3 Squadron RAAF while flying with No 112 Squadron RAF. *(Frank F. Smith)*

April 1944: Dan Zoerb of the 52nd Fighter Group has just traded in his Spitfire VIII for a P-51B on Corsica. Check-out was informal to say the least: "Like a Chinese fire drill," recalls Zoerb. *(Dan Zoerb)*

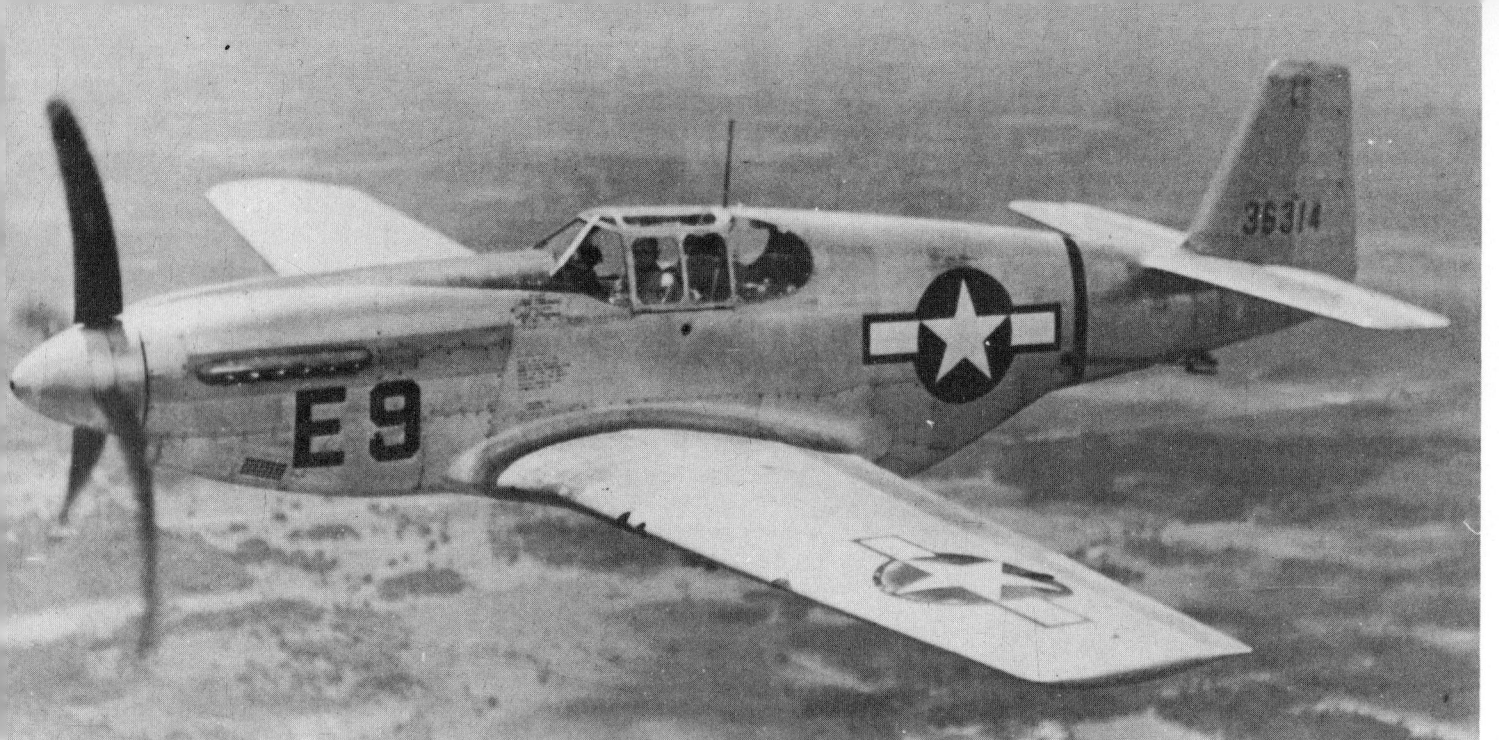

Above: **Mid-1944: the 332nd FG warming up for an escort mission from Rametelli, Italy.** *(USAF)*

Left: **After a brief stint in P-47s the all-black 332nd FG was equipped with Mustangs. Here Capt Ed Toppins, 99th FS, sits at the head of the line at Rametelli, Italy, in mid-1944.** *(AFM via Tom Ivie)*

Right: **On 2 June 1944 the first Russia Shuttle mission was flown by the 15th Air Force, covered by one fighter group, the 325th. As the cross-Channel invasion was being carried out on the other side of the theater on 6 June 1944, these 325th Mustangs were warming up for a mission to Galatz, Romania, from Eurk, Russia.** *(USAF)*

Left: **Dan Zoerb, 2nd Squadron of the 52nd Fighter Group, flies his P-51B-5 before group markings were standardized to red noses and yellow tails. Zoerb became an ace, flying Spitfires and Mustangs named** *Hey Rube I* **to** *IV. (Dan Zoerb)*

Right: **Lee A. Archer's** *Apache II* **at Rametelli. Archer achieved five air and six ground kills in 138 missions with the 332nd FG, the** *Red Tails.* **Behind the aircraft's red spinner the crews painted blue and white checks.** *(AFM via Tom Ivie)*

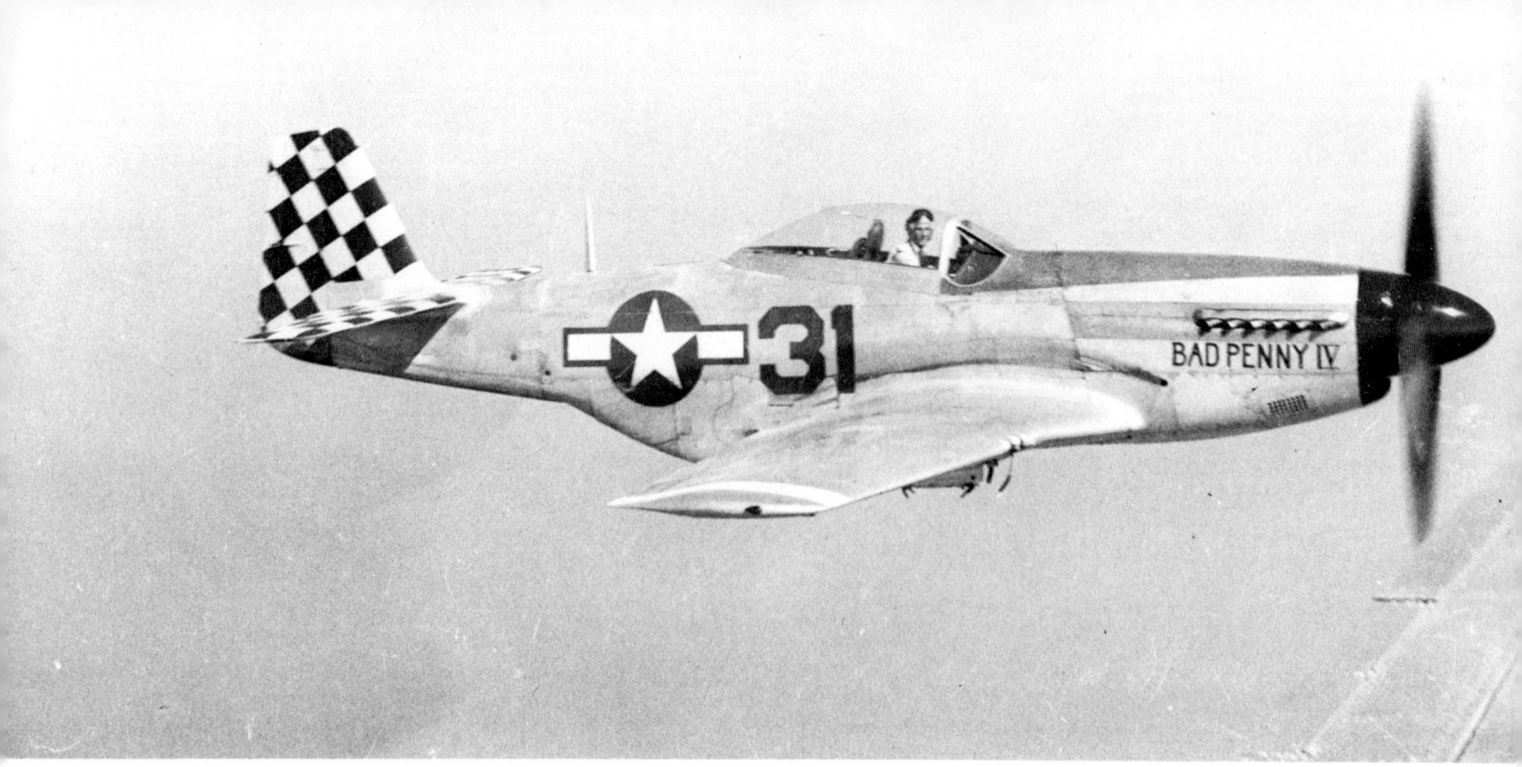
31
BAD PENNY IV

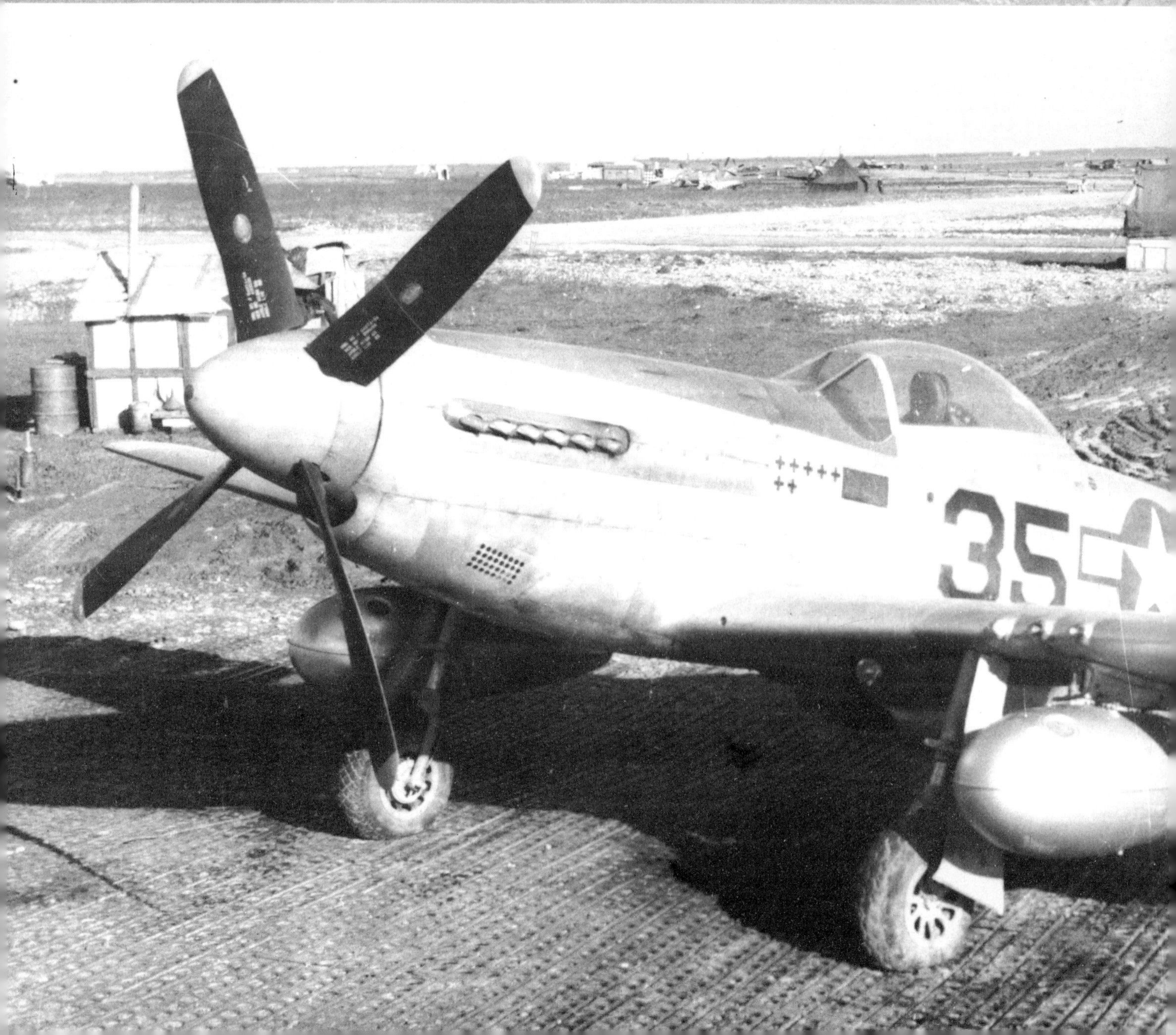
35

Left: **Lt Terry of the 317th Fighter Squadron, photographed 10 minutes before he was killed. During a dive-bombing demonstration either a wing or the horizontal stabilizer failed and he went straight in.** *(Arthur Fiedler via Bill Hess)*

Right: **Lt Fisher (15) and Lt Dowiatt (16) of the 325th FG. Both were later killed in a mid-air collision.** *(Arthur Fiedler via Bill Hess)*

Below: **Arthur Fiedler's** *Helen* **of the 317th Squadron, 325th FG, at Lesina, Italy, late in 1944 before the checkerboards were extended forward of the tail.** *(Arthur Fiedler via Bill Hess)*

Late in the day at the 325th Fighter Group, Lesina, Italy, in 1944. *(Arthur Fiedler via Bill Hess)*

A few days later the 52nd returned to the same field and the sky lit up with flak—the Romanians were not going to let the same mistake happen twice.

In May 1944 another fighter group transferred from the 12th Air Force to the 15th: the 332nd Fighter Group, flying P-47s before transitioning into Mustangs in June. It had the distinction of being the only all-negro group in the Army Air Force, with a core of combat veterans. Unfortunately there was no integration, since the AAF held to the policy of "separate but equal," and consequently there was a chronic shortage of replacement personnel. Little exchange of combat data took place before the pilots and ground crews shipped overseas, but once in combat *esprit de corps* developed rapidly and the 332nd became an accomplished outfit.

Lee A. Archer became the leading scorer of the group with five air and six ground victories. He and his comrades wanted to get into combat to prove a point as well as to fight

Early-model P-51Ds of the 4th Squadron, 52nd FG, without dorsal fins. *(T. R. Bennett)*

After getting rid of its Kittyhawks and moving to Italy, No 260 Squadron RAF worked up on Mustang IIIs. Here one of the unit's aircraft carries two 1,000lb bombs. *(Frank F. Smith)*

the Germans: "We felt that if we failed, society would say the black man had no ability." Official Army doctrine stated that blacks had less mental capacity than whites, that they had neither leadership potential nor the physical reflexes needed to become first-class fighter pilots. As wingman to Wendell O. Pruitt, the "character" of the 332nd, Archer learned the ins and outs of combat flying. On one occasion Archer and Pruitt tackled 13 Me 109s, claiming three and two respectively before the rest of the group arrived. Not one bomber was lost in the entire time the 332nd provided escort for the 15th's bomb wings. "It never occurred to me," remembers Archer, "to go leaping off after fighters and leave the bombers alone." Bomber crewmen came to respect the "Red Tails" and some came to prefer them as escorts.

Louis R. Purnell, who had served with the original all-black 99th Fighter Squadron, loved flying the Mustang after the P-40, P-39 and P-47. Evident prejudice never dominated Lou's AAF career: "When you fly nothing else matters. I could have been flying for the devil and it wouldn't have mattered".

One of the high points in the 332nd's history was the 24 March 1945 escort mission to Berlin. Col Benjamin O. Davis Jr, group CO, led them on a 1,600-mile demonstration of the kind of range the Mustang was achieving at that time. Encountering several Me262 jets, the 332nd claimed three of the eight downed by XV Fighter Command, with Lt Roscoe Brown making the first kill. On 26 April 1945 the 332nd claimed the last four enemy aircraft destroyed in the Mediterranean Theater of Operations.

A No 5 Squadron, No 7 SAAF Wing, Mustang III just about to touch down somewhere in Italy in late 1944. *(Frank F. Smith)*

In early 1945 Mustang IVs (P-51Ds and Ks) began to appear in the Mediterranean with the Commonwealth units. Here GL-N of No 5 Squadron SAAF lands in Italy. *(Frank F. Smith)*

In November 1944 No 3 Squadron RAAF gave up its P-40s for Mustangs. This is the Mk IV flown by Flt Lt A. F. Lane DFC out of Foggia in February 1945. Serial is KH676. *(A. F. Lane via Frank F. Smith)*

No 3 Squadron RAAF over Italy in 1945. CV-K is flown by Flt Lt Ken Richards. *(A. F. Lane via Frank F. Smith)*

Mustang versus Jet

When the Messerschmitt 163 and 262 and Arado 234 began to appear in combat, there was great consternation over what effect they might have on the Allied aerial offensive, for they had the performance to leave contemporary piston-engined fighters far behind. But the Mustang proved to be the very tool to deal with the German jets.

William C. Clark of the 339th Fighter Group recalls how 8th Air Force fighter units were getting ready to deal with the Me262: "In the late fall of 1944 the Me262 became fairly active in air defense. There was never any doubt that this fighter was the best that had ever been produced up to that time. The fact that it was late in being employed as an air-defense weapon, that the old fighter pilots had been killed or worn out, and that the Germans were having difficulties getting fuel, saved the air war for us. The USAAF had no real defense against this weapon if it was properly employed. It didn't do a bad job as it was, and would have cost us a lot more if several 8th AF fighter groups hadn't clobbered it with sheer numbers before it got started.

"In late December I decided that the Me262 should be our prime objective. In January we started planning how to get

The Messerschmitt 262 jet fighter. Throughout its career in action, which lasted less than a year, its technical superiority could not counter the far greater numbers of the Allied fighters, in particular the P-51 Mustang. *(via Ken Bokelman)*

them. We researched all we could (old intelligence reports, etc) into everything concerning the Me262. Where and how it was built, where they were based, when and how pilots were trained, where the fuel came from, and how it was stored, etc.

"Then we selected three known air bases where 262s were operational. We got photos and studied the terrain and defenses. We planned the best low-altitude approaches. Our idea was at first just to flush the 262s off the field and then shoot them down right after take-off. However, we found that they didn't flush out, so we shot them up on the ground and set as much of the air base on fire as we could. Always we left a whole squadron, 16 to 24 aircraft, up high to give the ground-attacking squadron cover and also to get anything that became airborne. There was another flight of at least eight aircraft which was ready to spread out and run down (force him to run out of fuel at low altitude) any 262 that got away from the high or attacking squadron. After about 20 minutes of beating up the air base we withdrew the attacking squadron (they were out of ammo anyway) and sent them home. Another flight of eight was left loitering in the area out of sight and its job was to knock down any 262 that had been missed somehow and was trying to land at home base.

"Of the three air bases we picked, we were able to attack only two. On the first (just northwest of Berlin) we claimed and were awarded five destroyed in the air. We didn't lose a single aircraft on this operation. I am more proud of this fact than anything else. On three planned missions similar to that I have described, we were credited with 14 destroyed in the

Here an instructor pilot of *Kommando Nowotny,* the first fighter unit to employ the Me262, teaches a student how to taxi the 262A in the autumn of 1944. Note the stone guards in place over the engine inlets and the bomb racks just below the shell ejection chutes. *(via Ken Bokelman)*

air and 26 destroyed on the ground, and probably caused the destruction of that many more without a single loss of our own. One must remember, though, that the German pilot flying the 262 was very much inexperienced, with little flying time. However, their ground flak was the best there was and the P-51's ability to work through this flak without loss was something very few people know about. We were successful because we pre-planned the mission, employed surprise, speed and natural screening to our maximum advantage.''

Probably the most famous pilot of the Me262 was the 258-victory ace Maj Walter Nowotny, commander of the first Me262 fighter unit to be declared fully operational. Until recently his death on 8 November 1944 had remained a mystery, but German and American records have now revealed what took place. On that day *Kommando Nowotny* scrambled several 262s to engage a large force of American bombers returning from an attack on the Mitteland Canal. Edward R. ''Buddy'' Haydon of the 357th Fighter Group recalls: ''I was flying wing for Capt Merle F. Allen. It was one of our last flights together. Our group had engaged the enemy and no longer maintained formation. Merle and I were flying at about 30,000 feet when we spotted a 262 approximately 10,000 feet below. We gave chase immediately. Because it was on my side, the port, and because my

aircraft was faster, I achieved the lead position with Merle on my right wing.

''The 262 was on a straight course, losing altitude, and we were closing steadily. When I was about 1,000 feet above the ground and almost in range to fire, I noticed two P-51s from the 20th Fighter Group at 5 o'clock off our starboard wing with a slight altitude advantage and closing slightly. The lead aircraft fired out of range. The tracers were dropping out half way to the 262 and there were no visible strikes. Almost immediately (I was about 500 feet off the ground) I saw that the 262 was headed for an airdrome. I called for Merle to break. He broke to the right and I broke left. The 262 was flat on the deck on a straight course . . . the pilot had never changed heading from the beginning of the encounter. The two P-51s from the 20th were instantly scattered and partially obscured by a heavy saturation of flak that came up from the airdrome. Noting that I was not being fired upon, I rolled level after about 45° of turn. Right in front of my nose I saw the 262, as if he were downwind, 180° from his prior position, perhaps one mile left. I rolled to the left and slid into a 90° position off his left wing tip moving nicely toward his stern. Each aircraft was 200 to 300 feet above the ground with, perhaps, 300 yards separation. I was closing acceptably. The pilot of the 262 saw me. He reacted violently, causing the 262 to snap left, directly into the ground. The pilot had no opportunity to leave the aircraft. There was an explosion and fire.

''Merle was there almost instantly. He was certain that I had fired on the 262 until I stated otherwise after we returned to home plate at Leiston, England. In debriefing I claimed the 262 and Merle confirmed it. Neither of us believed that the two 20th Fighter Group aircraft hit the 262 nor contributed in any way to its destruction.

''It is my opinion that the 262 had flamed out and that the

The Kommodore and his wingman: Maj Walter Nowotny (left) and Lt Rudolf "Quax" Schnorrer were two highly experienced pilots, and both gained kills with the Me262. Schnorrer was credited with 11 kills but Nowotny got only three before he lost his life in action on 8 November 1944. *(via Alfred Price)*

On 8 November 1944 Lt Edward "Buddy" Haydon of the 357th Fighter Group found himself behind an Me262 south of Dummer Lake. In an action during which neither Haydon nor 20th FG Mustang pilot Ernest Fiebelkorn scored a hit, Nowotny's 262 went out of control and crashed. Haydon and Fiebelkorn shared the victory over one of the Luftwaffe's most brilliant fighter leaders. *(Edward R. Haydon)*

pilot could not restart. The 262 showed no sign of damage. It simply did not have sufficient power to escape or fight."

Haydon's combat report stated that the airfield was south of Dummer Lake, which indicates that it was almost certainly Achmer, home of the *Kommando.* The lead 20th Group Mustang was flown by Capt Ernest Fiebelkorn. Nowotny's last understandable words over the radio before he crashed were: "Just made the third kill . . . . left jet has failed . . . been attacked again . . . I've been hit." The 262 crashed four miles north of Bramsche. Since neither Haydon nor Fiebelkorn hit the 262, it seems possible that Nowotny was downed in error by German flak.

The sheer number of Allied fighters placed the German jets at a continual disadvantage, with the P-51 doing most of the killing. Harrison B. Tordoff, who flew both P-47s and P-51s with the 353rd Fighter Group, made an Me262 kill on 31 March 1945 near Dessau after barely overtaking the jet: "My P-51 was bucking at the edge of compressibility." He recalls what it was like to engage jets that day: "I would not have had a chance against these jets, had it not been for the altitude advantage that let me get close enough. Had I reacted a second or two earlier, I'd probably had an easy chance at both of them since the 262's only advantage over us was speed. The German pilots knew this and avoided turning fights at all costs. Their very limited range made them vulnerable to our fighters, as we'd simply wait for them to come home out of fuel to the bases they were known to fly from.

"The Me262 was a great technological achievement. We were lucky it came so late in the war, when fuel was scarce and the sky over Germany was alive with P-51s that could afford to be patient."

Almost all the Me262s to go down during World War II suffered at the hands of Mustang pilots. One of the victorious pilots was Charles Yeager of the 357th FG, seen here with *Glamourus Glen,* named after his wife. Yeager went on to become the first man to fly faster than sound. *(W. Bruce Overstreet)*

Another 357th Group pilot who shot down at least two Me262s was Capt Donald H. Bochkay, seen here flying one of his ''Winged Ace of Clubs'' Mustangs. *(T. R. Bennett)*

China and the Pacific

In the late summer of 1943 the first Allison-powered Mustangs arrived in Assam, flying with the 311th Fighter Bomber Group of the 10th Air Force. Flying a mixed batch of A-36As and the first production P-51As, the unit was the first to get the aircraft into combat with the Japanese. Before long the Mustangs were providing escorts for B-25s and B-24s. By 24 November Allison Mustangs were also flying combat mission with the 23rd Fighter Group, 14th Air Force.

The 530th Squadron of the 311th sent a report in to the commanding general about their use of the new fighter between 1 November 1943 and 31 May 1944. The chief advantages cited were: "400 mph speed at the 15,000-17,000 foot level, extremely fine acceleration in a dive and unusually responsive aileron control at high speeds . . . proven ability to absorb punishment . . . has stood up extremely well under combat conditions. It is an effective dive bomber. If jumped

by enemy aircraft near the ground, it can easily outrun the enemy with superior speed. Its chief disadvantages are poor rear visibility, relatively poor rate of climb, and altitude limitations. The light armament is a drawback both in air-to-air and air-to-ground combat. From this it may be seen that the P-51A airplane has much the same disadvantages as the P-40 series and must be fought in the same manner. It is simply a better airplane for the same tactics."

In Burma the 5318th Provisional Unit took their P-51As into combat on 5 February 1944 in support of Orde Wingate's second expedition behind enemy lines. Flying with bombers, transports, liaison aircraft and fighters, the unit became the 1st Air Commando Group on 29 March under Col Phil Cochran. George Meacham, who flew with the 16th Fighter Squadron, recalls the excitement of getting the first P-51Bs in the 14th Air Force during February and March 1944: "I had by pure chance one flight in a P-51A in the summer of 1943 at Zephyr Hills, Florida, and was therefore ordered with seven other pilots from the 16th and 26th Squadrons to a special assignment. I was the only one of the group who had flown a P-51 so we gave ourselves a crash course in studying the tech orders and the same day we all made one flight in the P-51B.

"The next morning General Chennault called us into his office and outlined his strategy for us in detail. We were to be based at Liangshan, north of the Yangtze. We would refuel at

The first batch of production P-51As went to the 530th Squadron of the 311th Fighter Bomber Group, entering combat with the 10th Air Force over Burma in October 1943. This yellow-spinnered 530th Mustang is getting attention for battle damage at Kurmitola, where the unit staged when escorting B-25s.

Top: **Capt James J. England's P-51A** *Jackie* **(named after his wife), serial 43-6077, late in 1943. England was ops officer for the 530th FBS when the unit became the first to take the Mustang against the Japanese. He eventually claimed a total of 10 kills.** *(John Horne)*

Above: **The 1st Air Commando Group's Mustangs near Karachi, India, before transferring to a forward airstrip for operations over Burma.** *(USAF)*

The 1st ACG was originally the 5318th Provisional Unit until a designation change on 29 March 1944. The unit's P-51As first operated in support of Orde Wingate's raiders. This Mustang was the first to land at Broadway Strip, Burma, after an airborne invasion by the group, which also operated B-25s and C-47s. *(USAF)*

Col Philip Cochran flying his P-51A while commander of the 1st Air Commando Group in spring 1944. *(USAF)*

Fuel is hand-pumped into this 1st ACG Mustang at Hailakandi, India. *(USAF)*

Sian, very close to the Japanese lines at that time. Then we were to go in two-plane flights as deep as 500 miles into enemy-held territory, our primary mission being the disabling of the rail transport system that was supplying the building Japanese offensive from the north against the air bases south of Hankow. The General told us to alternate one plane as top cover and one at strafing level. Each of the four two-plane flights was assigned a different stretch of railroad.

"Our third flight in a P-51B was a long combat mission, and it proved Chennault's skill as a tactician. Our eight planes knocked out 27 locomotives plus some planes caught on the ground and some trucks. The General was so pleased that he gave us all the DFC and a letter of commendation. We lost one plane and a pilot, "Hose Nose" Dawson, who somehow landed on a Japanese-held field.

The 23rd Fighter Group, descended from Chennault's original Flying Tigers, began to receive its first P-51Bs in February 1944. This 75th Squadron aircraft has already been painted with the famous shark's mouth. *(Charlie Cook)*

Once the Mustang became available, it began to replace the older types in the theater, particularly the P-40. These P-51Bs and Cs, both camouflaged and natural metal, await combat assignments at a 14th Air Force field in China. *(USAF)*

Ed Bollen's P-51C, 75th Squadron, 23rd Fighter Group, in mid-1944. *(Ed Bollen)*

Rosalie was flown by "Chief" Joshua Sanford in the 75th FS. Sanford and his crew chief were both American Indians, giving rise to the team of "Big Chief" and "Little Chief". *(Ed Bollen)*

As the spring of 1944 progressed, the 311th was redesignated a fighter group as it received Merlin Mustangs in place of its P-51As and A-36s. Here a 529th Squadron P-51B sits on a 10th Air Force field next to a group of P-40Ns. *(Merle Olmsted)*

Col William M. Banks leads some of the Mustangs of his 348th Fighter Group, which was originally equipped with P-47s under the legendary Neel Kearby. Banks completed two tours before leaving *Sunshine* to return to the US. *(Norm Taylor)*

Early morning, Tingkawk Sakan, Burma, in June 1944: a P-51B-15 of the 528th Squadron, 311th Fighter Group. *(Kenneth M. Sumney)*

"As the Japanese advance overwhelmed the Chinese troops and moved south from Hengyang, our bases had to be evacuated. We moved to the next of the chain of airfields that extended down the center of China. When the enemy neared Liuchow we had several P-51s with damaged tail-wheel tires. In order to get them out ahead of the Japanese, since we had no spare tires, it was necessary to fly the sound planes to Nanning, take off the tailwheels, return them to Liuchow by C-47, and then fly out the remaining P-51s."

Don Lopez, who flew P-40s then Mustangs with the 75th Squadron, 23rd Fighter Group, remembers that the range of the P-51 allowed it to make some unusual "cargo" flights: often only one fuel tank was filled in India so that the other could be poured full of booze. Pilots had to make sure the lineman at home base did not put gas in the tank before the precious cargo could be offloaded.

Lopez learned about the danger of aerobatics with a full fuselage tank the hard way, after flying a new P-51C which had just been dropped off by a ferry pilot. As operations officer, he decided to show the new fighter off. In the P-40 the fuselage tank was always burned last, so Lopez emptied the

A Chinese-American repair crew works on a Mustang in a revetment at Liuchow on 6 October 1944. *(US Army)*

P-51s of the 16th and 26th squadrons, 51st FG, warming up for take-off at Nanning, China, on 16 November 1944. *(USAF)*

Often confused with the similarly shark-mouthed 23rd FG, the 51st FG painted all their Mustangs with the fierce decoration, while the 23rd normally carried the mouth on its 76th Squadron Mustangs only. Here Sgt Andrew Adamchik, an armorer, awaits the return of a combat mission. *(US Army)*

Above: **The P-51D of former Flying Tiger and 23rd Group commander Ed Rector. Note the three different-colored tail bands and the "football" antenna commonly fitted to 14th AF aircraft.** *(Don Lopez)*

Right: **F-6Ks of the 26th Squadron, 51st Fighter Group, at Nanning, China, on 27 July 1945.** *(US Army)*

wing tanks first, did a few rolls and then entered a loop. The P-51 did a half snap roll at the top as nice as could be. "Hey," thought Lopez, "that was neat, let's try it again." But this time the Mustang went completely out of control in a tumble. He chopped the power and finally brought the aircraft under control after having been taught a never-to-be-forgotten lesson. Lopez nicknamed the new maneuver the "Tootsie Roll."

Lopez did not particularly like the P-51B/C because the guns could not be fired if the aircraft was pulling excessive g; they jammed in China just as they did in Europe. He also wanted six 0·50s rather than four. The Mustang's lighter armament led him to regard the P-40 as a better airplane for the job in China, though the Rolls-Royce engine performed excellently at high power settings. The 23rd Fighter Group mounted bazooka tubes under the wings for ground attack, but they were inaccurate and created unacceptable drag.

The Mustang went on to re-equip other fighter units in China, including the Chinese-American Combat Wing made up of pilots from both countries. When the D model arrived, it roamed the skies at will. Donald W. Maggert entered combat in the P-51D with the 3rd Fighter Squadron, 3rd Air Commando Group, in January 1945, flying out of Leyte in the Philippines. Former Flying Tiger Arvid Olson commanded the group, while 56th Fighter Group veteran Walker M. Mahurin had the 3rd Squadron.

Since there were not many Japanese aircraft left to attack at this stage of the war, ground support became the 3rd ACG's speciality. By March 1945 the Mustangs were carrying five 100 lb fragmentation bombs over 600 miles into Formosa. On these 7-hour missions to China, flying for much of the distance over water, Maggert would take a thermos of coffee, sandwiches and cigars, trim the aircraft up nicely, and then prop himself up to relax until arrival over the target; then he would do the same thing on the way home.

Squirt, **a P-51D of the 47th Squadron, 15th Fighter Group, flyir**

The P-51D of Donald W. Maggert, 3rd Fighter Squadron (Commando), 3rd Air Commando Group, in early 1945. The Donald Duck emblem under the cockpit had the bird carrying a 0.50-caliber gun under one wing, smoking a cigar (a Maggert weakness) and wearing a top hat and bow tie. *(Don Maggert)*

Jima in 1945. *(Norm Taylor)*

Left: **The entire 3rd Air Commando Group just after arriving at Atsugi, Japan, from Ie Shima on 20 September 1945. The next aircraft after Maggert's** *Oh well!* **is Thomas J. Williams'** *Texas Longhorn* **(Williams on left). The 3rd Squadron's color was blue, the 4th's red.** *(Don Maggert)*

Centre left: **What was left of 44-15090 when Maggert ditched it after take-off when the engine cut out. Maggert got away with a cut above the right eye and a broken nose after the aircraft literally disintegrated.** *(Don Maggert)*

Below: **3rd Air Commando Mustangs over Japan after the surrender.** *(Don Maggert)*

Right: **The 3rd ACG was established as a part of the occupation forces, flying out of Chitose. Here 3rd ACG P-51s fly past Mount Fuji.** *(Don Maggert)*

P-51D versus Zero

The ninth P-51B built, 43-12102, served as the airframe for the XP-51D and tested the new bubble canopy. Bob Chilton flew the aircraft for the first time on 17 November 1943. The poor visibility from the P-51B and C resulted in North American being asked to fit a P-47 bubble canopy to their aircraft, but the company preferred to develop their own. The D model carried six 0.50-caliber guns in place of the four mounted in previous models. *(NASM)*

On 6 March 1945 the first Mustangs landed at Motoyana Airstrip Number One on Iwo Jima to serve with the 7th Air Force. Coming to grief here is a 47th Squadron, 15th FG, P-51, the third to land. *(USAF)*

Every unit has its "hangar queen", and in the 3rd Commando Squadron it was No 090, a Mustang that was never quite right. Maggert was scheduled to test-fly No 090, and its bad reputation inspired him to double-check everything. But at 50 feet off the ground the engine lost power, white smoke poured out of the exhausts and the oil pressure fell to zero. Maggert cut the switches and tightened his harness as the aircraft drifted down through a line of coconut trees and into high bamboo. There was a blinding flash and he was surrounded by water, managing to take a breath before he went under. The Mustang had hit a fishpond, run up on a dam and then slid back down under the water. With only a couple of feet of water over his head, Maggert calmly unfastened his harness and parachute, stood up out of the water and walked across what was left of the aircraft to the dam. The engine and cockpit were the only sections to reach the dam, and the wings, wheels and tail were strewn on the other side. Maggert came out with a cut over his eye and a broken nose.

Mahurin thought that the Formosan anti-aircraft fire was even fiercer than that encountered over Europe. Maggert had a 20 mm shell enter the fuselage and explode between the seat and the armor plate while he was strafing an electricity plant. It cut his parachute harness and knocked out the P-51's electrical system, but did not harm him.

At the end of the war the 1st Air Commando Group was still going strong. This is Leonard Kelly's P-51K. *Sigh!* was painted on the other side under the exhausts. *(Buck Holloway)*

The Mustang was assigned to provide very-long-range escort for B-29s of the 20th Air Force. This 7th Air Force P-51 is tucked in tight off the Superfortress's wing; July 1945, flying out of Iwo Jima. (USAF)

Mustangs of the 46th Squadron, 21st Fighter Group, parked at Iwo Jima for long-range escort missions to Japan. (USAF)

In April 1945 the AAF Proving Ground Command, Eglin Field, Florida, released a report entitled *Comparative Performance Between Zeke 52 and the P-38, P-51 and P-47*. A captured Mitsubishi A6M5 Type O Model 52 was flown against the P-38J-25, P-47D-30 and P-51D-5, the results to be disseminated throughout the Pacific combat commands. The same pilot flew the Zero throughout the tests, while combat-experienced pilots were rotated through the AAF fighters. The results were as follows:

Performance

AIRPLANE	ALTITUDE	MP	RPM	RESULTS
P-51D-5	10,000 feet	62·5"Hg	3,000	Approximately 80 mph true airspeed faster than Zeke 52.
Zeke 52	10,000 feet	38"Hg	2,750	
P-51D-5	25,000 feet	62"Hg	3,000	Approximately 95 mph true airspeed faster than Zeke 52.
Zeke 52	25,000 feet	33·5"Hg	2,750	

Combat Comparison–Zeke 52 vs P-51D-5

Level Turning Circle

10,000 feet. In both right and left turns, the Zeke gained an advantage in less than one 360° turn.
25,000 feet. Results were the same as those at 10,000 feet.

Level Flight Acceleration

10,000 feet. The run was begun from a line abreast formation at 200 IAS. At the end of one minute at full power, the P-51D had an estimated lead of 400 yards. After two minutes, the lead had increased to 1,500 yards.
25,000 feet. The run was begun from 190 IAS. Estimated lead for the P-51D was 300 yards after one minute and 1,000 yards after two minutes at full power.

Dive Acceleration

10,000 feet. Dives were begun from level flight line abreast formation at 200 IAS, with full power applied as the dive was entered. The P-51D began to pull ahead immediately. The selected red line airspeed (325 IAS) of the Zeke was reached after 27 seconds. At this time, the P-51D had a lead of approximately 200 yards.
25,000 feet. Results were much the same as at 10,000 feet. The Zeke reached 325 IAS after 20 seconds, and the P-51D was rapidly widening a lead begun shortly after the dive was entered.

Aileron Roll

At both altitudes, the rolling ability of the Zeke was slightly better than the P-51D below 220 IAS. At speeds above 220 IAS, the P-51D was superior, due to increasing control forces in the Zeke.

Zoom from Level Flight

10,000 feet. In a full power zoom, begun from level flight, line abreast formation at 210 IAS, the P-51D was approximately 300 feet above and ahead of the Zeke when airspeed had decreased to 130 IAS.
25,000 feet. Results of a full power zoom begun from 185 IAS (Zeke cruising speed) were the same as at 10,000 feet.

Zoom from Dive

10,000 feet. The P-51 gained an advantage of approximately 500 feet above and ahead of the Zeke after a zoom from a shallow dive, applying full power when the nose passed through the horizon.
25,000 feet. Results were the same as at 10,000 feet.

Spirals

Climbing and diving spirals were executed at 10,000 and 25,000 feet, with either airplane alternately leading in a line astern formation. Results were the same at both altitudes. The Zeke could stay in range within the P-51D's turn during either a climbing or diving spiral. With the Zeke in the lead position at the start of a spiral, the P-51D could hold the initial advantage for only a short time.

Combat

Results were essentially the same for the two individual combat comparisons at 10,000 and at 25,000 feet. The following three initial conditions were checked:

Head-On Approach. The two airplanes approached each other on the same level approximately 500 feet apart. As they came abreast each other, the Zeke immediately turned onto the P-51D's tail, but was unable to close range as the P-51D dove away. The P-51D was able to gain altitude after the dive and make repeated passes from above, for which the Zeke's only defense was turning to face the attack and firing a snap shot.

Zeke 2,000 Feet Above and Directly Behind. When the Zeke started a pass from above, the P-51D could dive away out of range and use excess speed to climb to a favorable attack position. The P-51D's higher climbing airspeed and superior climbing ability aided in keeping out of range until in position for a pass. The Zeke was able to turn into each attack for a short burst, but never gained the initiative.

P-51D 2,000 Feet Above and Directly Behind. The P-51D was able to climb for continued attacks after the first pass, and the only firing opportunity for the Zeke when attacked was to run into the P-51D for brief bursts.

CONCLUSIONS:

The P-51D, P-38J-25 and P-47D-30 are greatly superior to the Zeke in maximum level flight speed at both 10,000 and 25,000 feet.

Due to advantages in speed, acceleration and high speed climb, all three AAF fighters were able to maintain the offensive in individual combat with the Zeke 52, and to break off combat at will.

The Zeke 52 is greatly superior to all three AAF fighters in radius of turn and general maneuverability at low speeds.

RECOMMENDATIONS:

The pilots of AAF fighter aircraft (P-38, P-51 and P-47 types) should take advantage of high speed performance superiority when engaging the Zeke 52 in combat; speed should be kept well above 200 IAS during all combat; "hit and run" tactics should be used whenever possible, and following the Zeke through any continued turning maneuvers must be strictly avoided.

Warrant Officer Takeo Tanimizu with his Zero in 1945. On 3 November 1944 he was shot down by Lt Bolyard of the 74th Fighter Squadron as he and his wingman were taking off from Amoy airfield in the Foochow area. Although he went on to make 32 kills, this Japanese ace never forgot what the Mustang could do. *(Henry Sakaida)*

The performance superiority of the P-51 over the Zero and most other Japanese fighters allowed it to engage or disengage in combat at will, an extremely important capability. Warrant Officer Takeo Tanimizu, Japanese Imperial Navy, claimed 32 kills in World War II but he himself was a victim of the P-51's superiority. On 3 November 1944 Lt Bolyard and Capt Ries of the 74th Fighter Squadron took off from Kanchow to cover the Foochow area, looking for enemy shipping and ground activity. Nearing Amoy airfield, Bolyard spotted two Zeros on the approach. Tanimizu and his wingman were landing after providing escort cover for convoys, and Tanimizu had his wheels down. Without warning, his wingtips were hit by gunfire; he didn't see any enemy aircraft so at first he thought it was friendly fire. When Tanimizu looked back, his wingman was going down in flames under the guns of Ries. Bolyard closed in on Tanimizu, who was trying to retract his landing gear and increase power while making a sharp left turn. Bolyard fired a short burst from 500 yards and registered direct hits on Tanimizu's Zero, which caught fire immediately. Flying at 300 mph IAS, the Mustang pilot effortlessly zoom-climbed up onto the Zero's tail and fired a one-second burst. Tanimizu managed to get the canopy open and bail out as his fighter fell into the water, his parachute opening just before he went in. A veteran of the long Rabaul campaign, Tanimizu survived the war with a healthy respect for the Mustang.

Rustled Mustangs

On 25 November 1943 the 530th Squadron of the 311th Fighter Bomber Group began a series of air assaults from Bengal into the Rangoon area. The unit's P-51As, with long-range tanks, staged through Cox's Bazaar to escort B-25s of the 49th Bomb Squadron to hit Mingaladon airfield.

Shortly before noon, word reached the 64th Sentai, flying Nakajima Ki.43-II Hayabusa (Peregrine Falcon, or Oscar to the Allies) fighters, that American warplanes were on the way in. Lt Yohei Hinoki, 3rd Chutai leader, took off from Mingaladon with three other pilots and patrolled for an hour before Hinoki's radio equipment failed. Looking back to signal his flight, he spotted seven aircraft with unfamiliar pointed noses. "I could not tell if they were Japanese or American," recalls Hinoki, "so I tried to get closer. I was afraid that if they were Americans we would be in poor position because they were much higher than we were. We were slowly closing on them by taking advantage of the sun . . . about 200 meters below them I was sure they were Americans. Suddenly Lt Sumino, who was an instructor for our inexperienced pilots, tried to attack. I was extremely worried about him due to the risk in attacking from such a disadvantageous position. In addition to that, I could tell these were very advanced aircraft. 'Watch out, Sumino!' I said to myself; I had to rescue him as soon as possible. My first impression of the new airplane was its size, and that it moved so fast."

Sumino was bounced by one of the Mustangs and Hinoki attacked the American leader, getting a few pieces to fly from the Mustang, which dove for the ground. Warrant Officer T. Kinoshita attacked the enemy leader's wingman, who was about to get Hinoki. He pursued the Mustang until he caught up with it over Bassein, about 100 miles west of Rangoon, where he shot it up from 150 feet; the P-51 fell into a river. Sumino got away; then turned to attack a Mustang at tree-top height, shooting it down into the ocean.

After landing Hinoki and his men discussed the unfamiliar fighter, which they recognized as the P-51. They knew that the aircraft was an improvement over other US fighters, with a reputation for being sturdy and effective. The Mustang pilots claimed one Oscar shot down plus four probables, but Hinoki recalls: "We did all right this first time, escaping without any damage, which made me feel a little calmer after the intense dogfight. But at the same time I started to worry about the future." The 530th Squadron recorded the loss of two P-51As with two more damaged. Hinoki got a call the next day from the 64th's main control center, congratulating him on the unit's first experience with the Mustang and confirming that he had shot down Col Harry Melton, the commander of the 311th FB Group, who was taken prisoner.

On the 27th the 530th was back with its Mustangs, around 15 of them, as well as 20 B-24s and four P-38s. Capt Yasuhiko Kuroe led the Chutai up with seven Ki.43s and one Ki.44 Shoki (Demon, or Tojo to the Allies). A tremendous fight developed, with both American and Japanese aircraft going

down in flames. Hinoki recalls: "I was flying over the ocean and found four P-51s. Fortunately they had not noticed me yet, so I easily shot down one of them." Making a close pass on a B-24 after leaving the Mustangs, "I had an enormous shock from below—just like being pushed up from below. 'P-51, that's it!' I said to myself and saw one fly by so quick it

Lt Yohei Hinoki, leader of the 3rd Chutai, 64th Sentai, at Mingaladon in late 1943. Hinoki and his men were among the first to encounter the Mustang in combat and Hinoki managed to shoot one down on 27 November 1943. He was himself shot down the same day by a P-51A, losing one of his legs. After being fitted with an artificial leg he became an instructor and then made the last of his at least 12 kills, a Mustang, on 16 July 1945. He test-flew a captured P-51C at Akeno, Japan. *(Yokei Hinoki)*

Mid-1943: Lt Yohei Hinoki and pilots of the 64th Sentai warm up their Nakajima Ki.43-II Hayabusa fighters at Mingaladon. *(Yokei Hinoki)*

was like a flash-back. 'You made a mistake,' I told myself and felt my whole body go numb, especially below the waist. My plane was shaking badly as I clutched the control stick. I tried to get myself together but could not see clearly at all. Slowly I began to realize that there was blood on the floor all around my boots. I reached out and touched something warm—my foot was gone.'' After tying his thigh with his scarf to stop the flow of blood, Hinoki was attacked again, causing his Ki.43 to spin. Barely conscious, he just managed to land the aircraft.

The Japanese were now fully aware of the Mustang and its capabilities. But as 1944 began, newer P-51Bs and Cs began to arrive in China, and the Japanese were faced with an even better version of the Mustang. High on their list of priorities was the capture of a P-51 so that it could be taken back to Japan for evaluation. Finally a P-51C of the 51st Fighter Group, flown by a pilot named Strawbridge and nicknamed *Evalina,* came down intact in Japanese territory in China. Japanese insignia were painted over the US stars, but the bars and personal markings remained, including the kill flags below the cockpit and the shark mouth. Yasuhiko Kuroe of the 64th Sentai flew the Mustang back to the Japanese Army Air Inspection Center at Fussa (now Yokota Air Base).

No time was wasted in flying the P-51 against such types as the Ki.43, Ki.61 and Ki.84. Kuroe, an ace with 30 victories, knew he had a real fighter on his hands: ''I was astonished with its performance. Turn characteristics were splendid, almost the same as the Ki.84 in a horizontal turn. The radio transmitter was excellent, the armament and other miscellaneous equipment was very good, particularly when compared with their Japanese equivalents, and moreover it had a radio direction-finder.

''Its dash speed was inferior to that of our imported FW190A, but diving speed and stability during the dive were excellent. After fuel consumption tests we estimated it would be able to fly over the Japanese homeland from Iwo Jima. Some time later this came true.

''I flew the P-51 to various bases to let them get first-hand knowledge of the fighter's performance. I had such confidence with this P-51 that I feared no Japanese fighters.'' The consensus of opinion at the Air Inspection Center was that the Mustang lacked any major faults: it was easy to fly and had good speed, climb and maneuverability.

The captured Mustang was moved to the Akeno Flying Division for trials against current Japanese types. Among those asked to come and fly the Mustang at Akeno was Yohei Hinoki, now wearing an artificial leg: ''Maj Gen Imagawa asked me to master the P-51 and then demonstrate it to other fellow pilots. I did not have a great deal of confidence in my ability to fly such an advanced, high-speed aircraft with my disabled right leg, but I made up my mind to do my best.

''I flew to Omasa Airfield and finally got a look at the P-51. I could see the superiority of its equipment, and its shiny fuselage with the open red mouth of a dragon. I saw several red dots on the side of the cockpit, probably recording Japanese aircraft the pilot had shot down. With the radiator under the fuselage, it looked very sleek and deadly.

''It reminded me of the day I had first seen the P-51 in the sky above Burma on 25 November 1943. Maj Kuroe, who brought the P-51 back from China, told me how easy the P-51 was to fly. Getting in, I was very impressed by the roomy seat and I did not have any trouble with my artificial leg on the rudder pedal. For me there were several new things about the aircraft. First of all there was the bulletproof glass, with a better degree of transparency than the thin Japanese glass; secondly, the seat was surrounded by a thick steel plate which I had never seen in a fighter before; there was an automatic shutter for the radiator, and an oxygen system which was new to me. Overall, it was better equipped than any Japanese airplane I had ever seen.''

Hinoki's flights in the Mustang paid off on 16 July 1945. Back in combat in the Ki.100, he had had his artificial leg cut and shaped to fit on the right rudder pedal. On this day he spotted 12 Mustangs, then another 40 aircraft overhead. In one firing pass he downed one of the Mustangs and got away after a large air battle over Isewon. Hinoki finished the war with at least 12 victories.

A burned-out generator finally grounded the captured P-51 *Evalina* at Akeno. Two P-51Ds were later captured during 1945 after appearing over the homeland but there is no information on whether they were evaluated.

In Germany the Luftwaffe evaluated several P-51s, the opportunities to obtain examples of the aircraft being certainly greater than for the Japanese. On 10 May 1944 the Versuchsverband des Oberkommando der Luftwaffe had two P-51s flying, as well as a Mosquito IV, P-38, P-47, Griffon Spitfire and Spitfire IX. By 10 August 1944 a total of four P-51Ds had been added to the Versuchsverband's fleet. The "Zirkus Rosarius", as the unit was known, flew the Allied machines around to the various Luftwaffe units to give pilots a chance to see them.

Several experienced Luftwaffe fighter pilots had the opportunity to fly the Mustang, including 275-victory ace Günther Rall: "For a short period of time I was commander of the German Fighter Leader School. During this time I had the opportunity to fly the P-51 in two or three mock dogfights with Me109 and FW190 fighters. This was not extensive experience, and I certainly cannot claim any profound knowledge of the P-51, but what impressed me was the comfort in the cockpit, the ease of the electrical starting system, the long endurance of the aircraft and its maneuverability in a dogfight. However, the Me109 was superior in all steep climbing turns, in which the P-51 had a tendency, when low on speed, to snap over the outer wing." Overall, Luftwaffe pilots were impressed with the Mustang and, like the Japanese, considered it the best all-round fighter of the war.

A captured P-51C of the 51st Fighter Group, named *Evalina* **and originally flown by an American pilot named Strawbridge, in Japan. Maj Yasuhiko Kuroe of the 64th Sentai flew it back from China, visiting fighter bases and flying against pilots in Japanese fighters before taking it to the training school at Akeno. Japanese markings were painted over the US markings without removing the bars. The American markings were otherwise left intact, including the kill flags. Yohei Hinoki flew the aircraft against Kuroe, who was flying a Ki.100. Hinoki was amazed at the lack of oil leaks, since Japanese aircraft always leaked: "If there were no oil leaks, then there was no engine!"** *(Hiroshi Yamamoto via Yasuho Izawa)*

This captured P-51B flew from Hannover/Wunstorf, coded T9+CK, during June and July 1944. *(Paul Hermsen)*

Above: **This captured Mustang flew from Oranienburg in October 1944, coded T9+HK.** *(George Punka)*

Below: **A 354th FG Mustang soon after capture in 1945.** *Li'l Mike 4* **force-landed in Hungary.** *(F. Kovacs)*

WASP

A total of 78,000 engineering man-hours were required to get the NA-73X into the air, and another 3,193,000 hours were expended on developing the Mustang through to its last version. Altogether 15,682 Mustangs were built and at peak production in Inglewood the assembly lines produced one P-51 every 22 minutes, 570 a month. In 1942 the price of a Mustang was $58,698 compared with $58,824 in 1943, $51,572 in 1944 and $50,985 in 1945. In combat Mustangs claimed just under six enemy aircraft for every one that was lost.

In order to get such large numbers of aircraft into combat, they had to be tested and ferried on almost a production-line basis. This required large numbers of pilots who could handle expensive, high-performance aircraft. But most of the men who could meet this specification were already in the front line. Where then were the ferry pilots to come from?

Before America's entry into the war, Jacqueline Cochran and Nancy Love, both accomplished pilots, had tried to raise interest in a women's organization that could perform almost any flying job but combat. After Pearl Harbor, working independently of each other, they renewed their campaign for approval of such a program. The efforts paid off on 10 September 1942, when Love's Women's Auxiliary Ferrying Squadron (WAFS) was announced. For the first time in American history, women were a part of military aviation. The WAFS, only 28 in number, had an average of 1,100 hours flying time each when attached to the Air Transport Command, Army Air Forces.

In July 1943 the growing numbers of women pilots being trained for AAF service were consolidated into the Women's Airforce Service Pilots, the WASPs. By the end of the program 1,074 women had flown for the AAF, piloting every type of military aircraft from the B-29 to America's first jet, the P-59. Fighter aircraft, particularly the P-47 and P-51, were ferried in great numbers by the WASPs. These women loved the single-seaters and considered flying fighters the essence of what it meant to fly. One WASP fortunate enough to be assigned fighters for most of her wartime career was Jean Landis. Jean was sent to Brownsville, Texas, for fighter transition training, and when the time came for her first flight in a fighter, she drew a P-51.

Her instructor told her to take off, climb to pattern height, and then make a series of practice approaches, overshooting each time until she was confident that she could land the aircraft. As she came back to the pattern, the gear-down lights indicated red, a possible indication of unlocked landing gear. Flying low over the tower, she was told that everything looked down and locked; but there was no way to be certain. The 'hash wagon'' (crash rescue vehicle) was sent out to wait on the airfield as Jean turned final. Her first landing in a Mustang, and the gear might retract on touch-

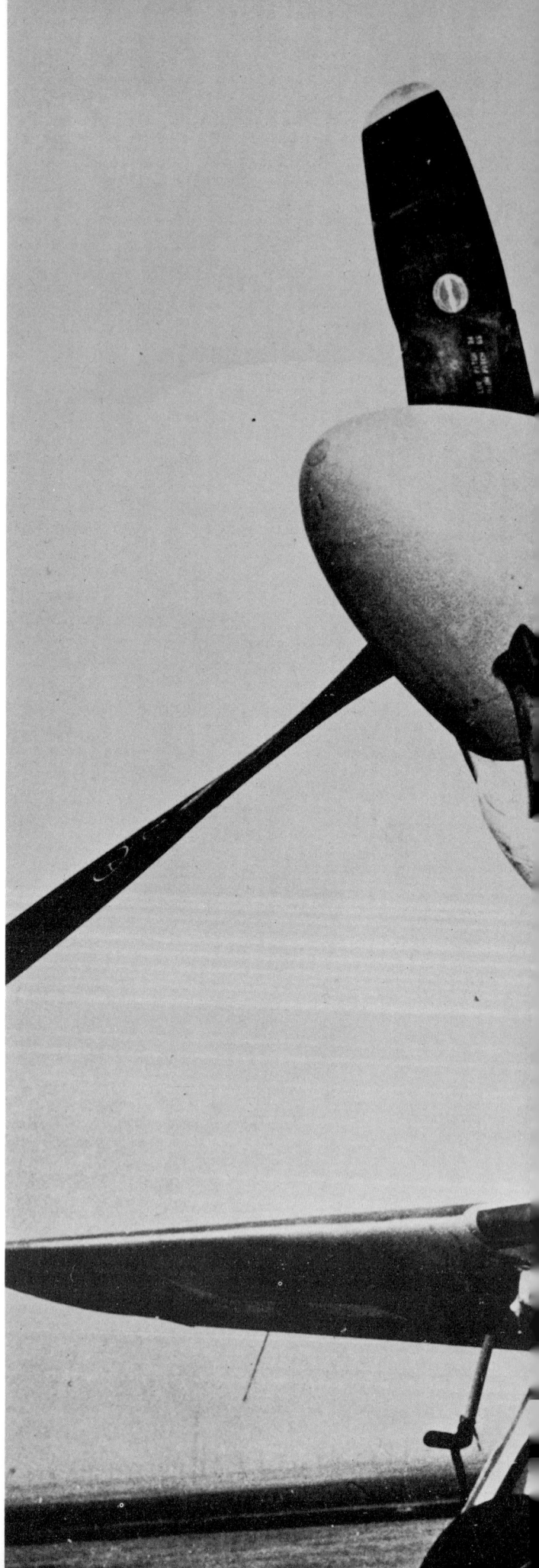

With the formation of first the WAFS (Women's Auxiliary Ferrying Squadron) and then the WASPs (Women's Airforce Service Pilots), women found themselves in the cockpits of every type of military aircraft in service with the USAF. This is Barbara Erickson with an early P-51B which she flew with the 6th Ferry Group, Air Transport Command (she was the WAFS/WASP commander in the unit), out of Long Beach, California. In 1943 she was awarded an Air Medal for making four transcontinental ferry flights in a little under five days, piloting a P-47, a P-51, a C-47 and a P-38. *(Barbara Erickson London)*

Some of the Mustangs on this ramp at Oakland, California, being processed for overseas shipment on 14 November 1944 were ferried by WASPs of the 6th Ferry Group at Long Beach. *(USAF)*

As more and more Mustangs rolled out of the Inglewood and Dallas plants they were ferried primarily to Oakland, California, and Newark, New Jersey, to be shipped overseas to the combat theaters. WASPs did a major portion of the ferry work until they were disbanded on 20 December 1944. An overnight bag and kit are strapped behind the armor plate above the radios. *(USAF)*

down! Much to the relief of all, however, the gear held; the malfunction had been in the warning-light circuits.

Jean also flew a number of other types, including the P-47: "The P-47 was a bucket of bolts compared to the Mustang; it was too heavy and sluggish. But when you got in a Mustang, it felt like you had just strapped the wings on. You didn't feel you had any fuselage around your body, you were a part of the airplane."

Jean had the good fortune to be stationed at the Ferrying Division at Long Beach, California, flying nothing but P-51s from then on. The new fighters were picked up at Inglewood and flown all over the country, particularly to Newark, New Jersey, where they were prepared for shipping overseas. Reactions to a woman climbing out of a P-51 were: "Varied, mostly startled. Once I flew into a field that was off-limits but

The cockpit of a P-51D. Note the early-style ball throttle, which was superseded by the rubber pistol-grip type. *(Paul Coggan)*

the weather was bad and I had a slight mechanical problem so I called in and asked for permission to land. I kept radioing 'P-51 ready to land; awaiting final landing instructions.' It was sort of garbled and they kept asking me to call in again and again. Finally they said: 'Waggle your wings if you receive!' So there I was waggling away and pretty soon they came back: 'Lady, the only thing we see up there is a P-51! Where are you?' I replied: 'That's me! I *am* the P-51!' They couldn't believe it—they were looking for a Piper Cub or something. Finally, when I landed, what a welcome I got. Word got around that a gal was flying that thing. They were darlings. By the time I had taxied up to the line, following the little Follow Me truck, there were lots of guys around to see what kind of woman was flying this P-51. They'd never heard of us, the WASPs.''

''We had to pay for all our clothing, had no medical or insurance benefits or many other military benefits,'' Jean recalls. The WASPs were subject to military discipline and lived in the Officers' Quarters, but they were not allowed most military privileges and received less money than men doing the same job. ''But we were there to fly and loved every minute of it.''

Then Congress decided that the WASPS should be deactivated, and no more women would fly after 20 December 1944. ''We wrote telegrams to Roosevelt, Arnold and others offering to fly, throughout the winter at least, for $1.00 a year. We received a very nice commendation, but deactivation came anyway. Here we were in a war; they needed us desperately, and we were deactivated at the wrong moment. I delivered the last P-51 to Newark just before we were deactivated. As I came into the New York area I felt the emotion welling up in me and I headed for the Statue of Liberty. Flying around her, I waggled my wings in salute and wept.''

Jean Landis about to climb into one of the many Mustangs she ferried. The WASPs were the first American pilots to wear blue uniforms. *(Jean Landis)*

Lightweight Mustangs

In 1943 North American Aviation, at the request of the British, had begun studies of ways of improving the Mustang while retaining the aircraft's proven qualities. The result was the XP-51F, which was actually a new aircraft, lighter than the previous Mustangs as a result of reduced stress criteria and some other improvements. It was followed by the XP-51G and J, which were essentially Fs with engine and propeller modifications.

Bob Chilton flew the XP-51F for the first time on 14 February 1944, and subsequently took it to a maximum speed of 493 mph in flight tests. The F, with its lightness, controllability and high power-to-weight ratio, was Chilton's favorite Mustang variant.

The XP-51G was first flown on 10 August 1944, with Ed Virgin at the controls. When Chilton flew the G on 14 August he reported: "At cruise I found the airplane to be directionally unstable and unfit for further testing." The XP-51J flew for the first time on 23 April 1945 with Joe Barton aboard. This marked the return of the Allison V-1710 engine to the Mustang, but supercharger problems ultimately made the machine a failure. Without telling Allison, North American adapted the Merlin's supercharger system to the Allison and came up with some fine performance figures. But then the war ended and with it went the requirement for the aircraft.

When the AAF asked for a fighter to be produced as a lightweight Mustang, modifications to the F airframe resulted in the P-51H-1. On 3 February 1945 Chilton made the first flight and found that he was aboard what was to be the fastest production Mustang of them all. It had a somewhat shorter range and lower service ceiling than earlier versions, but this was offset by having the best supercharger ratios at the altitudes at which combat was likely to take place. The cockpit was redesigned with long-range Pacific missions in mind, and the control stick and seat were moved closer together to reduce fatigue.

The H and the other lightweight versions of the P-51 were supreme dogfighters with low wing loadings, but they also had the power to disengage from a fight if necessary. The P-51H was never to see combat, however. Some 370 had been produced by VJ-Day but the type never saw action in the Pacific.

One of the first lightweight Mustangs, either the XP-51F or G, being run up at North American in 1944. *(NAA via Dave McLaren)*

Above: **The tall tails on the P-51Hs were supposedly standardized on the -5s, but this one, at Fort Dix, New Jersey, in December 1945, still has the short tail. It was used at Wright Field for vibration tests.** *(AAHS)*

Below: **Three P-51Hs of the 56th FG in formation as escort for Governor Kim Sigler on his visit to Selfridge Field, Michigan, in January 1947.** *(MXF Simpson via Dave McLaren)*

Above: **An 82nd Fighter Group P-51H. Note the T-6 in the background, used for transitioning into the aircraft, and the "PF" designator, which was later changed to "FF".** *(W. J. Balogh Sr via Dave Menard)*

Above right: **26 April 1948: 66th Squadron, 57th FG, Mustangs serving as part of Alaskan Air Command. The old World War II-style codes were dropped by the Air Force shortly after.** *(USAF)*

Right: **In the early 1950s both the D and H were used to train pilots to use the Mustang in Korea, although lack of spares prevented the H from entering action.** *(AAHS)*

Below: **Col Gerald Johnson's H when he was CO of the 62nd FS, 56th FG. Here the aircraft is a part of the 82nd FG, belonging to Capt J. B. Selkregg.** *(Robert O'Dell via Dave McLaren)*

K
O
E
464203
464705
464244
AC
AC
L
464698
AC

U.S. AIR FORCE
475021
FF-021
FF-191

Above: **220 and the next two Hs in line are all ex-64th FS, 57th FG, aircraft (note 64th insignia) transferred to the Ohio Air National Guard's 164th FS in Mansfield on 17 July 1949.** *(Dave Menard)*

Left: **Pulling up close to a SAC B-29 is one of the Air Defense Command F-51Hs that flew with the 85th Fighter Interceptor Squadron in late 1952 and early 1953 before F-51Ds replaced the Hs.** *(via Dave McLaren)*

In October 1946 the Air Proving Ground Command at Eglin Field, Florida, released its *Final Report on Service Test of the P-51H Airplane.* The following excerpts reveal why the aircraft never went into service in any great numbers:

Combat Comparison Completed between a P-51H-1 and a P-51D-25, comparison consisted of turning circle, rate of aileron roll, level flight and dive accelerations, and full power zoom from level flight and from a dive; these maneuvers were conducted at both 10,000 and 25,000 feet, and pilots repeated aileron roll and turning circle tests after exchanging airplanes. Throughout the comparison, the P-51D was limited to its war emergency rating of 67″ Hg manifold pressure and the P-51H-1 used the tentative rating of 80″ Hg manifold pressure with water injection.

At both altitudes, no real difference in minimum turning radius could be noted between airplanes. Maneuver flaps were used on the P-51H-1, but no advantage was gained.

For corroboration, rate-of-roll comparison was done at both altitudes, with the airplanes alternating in leading a shallow line-astern dive. Up to an indicated airspeed of 400 mph, the airplanes were about equal; then the P-51D had the higher rate of roll. P-51Hs and later series airplanes have been modified to increase aileron effectiveness, but no opportunity to investigate the modified system was presented.

In level flight acceleration and dive acceleration, the P-51H was superior to the P-51D due to the greater power available and the resultant speed advantage. At both altitudes, the P-51H gained approximately 400 yards advantage after three minutes of a level flight acceleration run begun from cruising power. At both altitudes, the P-51H pulled slowly away from the P-51D in shallow, full power dives begun from cruising power level flight.

In zooms from full power level flight, and from a full power dive, the P-51H had gained an average altitude advantage of approximately 500 feet when indicated airspeeds had decreased to 130 mph. It was noted that the P-51H was extremely sensitive to ram effect on power, manifold pressure decreasing materially in a zoom or turn begun from full power level flight.

Range The P-51D has a slightly longer radius of action than the P-51H due primarily to the larger internal fuel supply (269 gallons for the P-51D as compared to 255 gallons for the P-51H), but this advantage is considerably reduced by the fact that the P-51D is not sufficiently stable with a full fuselage tank to permit violent maneuvering.

Stability and Handling Characteristics During the course of tests on the P-51H-1 airplane, an undesirable elevator sensitivity and a tendency to porpoise during dives at high Mach number were encountered. Insufficient trim for high power climb was also noted. These discrepancies were later corrected by manufacturer's modification. No stick-force reversal was reported during high-acceleration turns with a full fuselage tank (this condition was most objectionable with the P-51D). The P-51H-5 was much more stable than the P-51D with a full external load (bombs, tanks or rockets) and was easily trimmed for various flight conditions. Stall characteristics, stability during final approach and landing, and visibility during landing and taxiing were better than the P-51D, and in general, the P-51H is easier to fly.

It was the opinion of pilots that the airplane is preferable to the P-51D as a gunnery platform, and as a dive-bomber. View over the nose for deflection shooting is better (approximately 10 degrees for the P-51H as compared to 5 degrees for the P-51D) and the airplane is more stable during a dive bombing run.

Cockpit Arrangement The cockpit arrangement of the modified P-51H [-5] is satisfactory. Moving the seat forward and the stick to the rear has aided pilot comfort. Functioning of the heater during test was satisfactory and the cockpit is better ventilated than is that of the P-51D.

Maintenance It is the opinion of maintenance personnel who have worked on both types of aircraft, the P-51H is more easily maintained than the P-51D. The accessibility of the engine accessories and other equipment is very good, making it much easier to accomplish necessary maintenance on the P-51H than on the P-51D.

Tail Wheel Down-Lock Throughout the entire time that the P-51H airplane was flown at this station, periodic difficulties were encountered with tail wheel collapse during taxiing and landing, resulting in considerable damage.

Wheel Brakes During the test, it was found that the Goodyear Three-Spot brakes are more easily burned out by extensive use than are the multiple disc brakes of the P-51D [although] the braking effect obtained from this type brake is considered superior to that of the multiple disc type brake.

CONCLUSIONS

a. The P-51H type airplane, without the use of water injection, is operationally suitable, but does not have sufficient advantage over the P-51D type airplane to warrant standardization.

b. The P-51H type airplane released for power ratings greater than 67″ Hg manifold pressure is a desirable replacement for the P-51D airplane.

c. The following conditions and characteristics found in the test aircraft are objectionable.

(1) The engine surge encountered near full throttle in the low cruising power range.

(2) The functioning of the tail wheel down-lock system is unsatisfactory.

The first AAF assignment of the P-51H was to Air Training Command fields in Florida and to the 412th Fighter Group at March Field, California. Most P-51Hs were shipped from Inglewood to either Hobbs Field, New Mexico, or to Kelly Field, Texas. The Hobbs aircraft were then made ready to equip the 57th FG at Shemya, Aleutian Islands, and the 56th Fighter Group. The 56th sent its 62nd Squadron to Ladd Field, Alaska, while the other two squadrons served as a long-range escort unit for Strategic Air Command, operating out of Selfridge Field, Michigan. When the 56th finally got P-80s in March 1947, its P-51Hs went to the 82nd FG under Lt Col Gerald Johnson. In the same year, when the USAAF became the US Air Force, all "P" (pursuit) designations were changed to "F" (fighter); thus the P-51 became the F-51.

By 1948 the F-51Hs were being turned over to Air National Guard units, most going to Ohio, Indiana and Texas. With the beginning of the Korean War, F-51Ds were transferred from ANG units into the regular Air Force, the vacuum being filled by the F-51Hs that had been stored at Kelly Field. Even though most of the restrictions on the early H-model's engine had been lifted to get all 2,218 hp, there were no longer enough spare parts to sustain combat operations. Thus the F-51H missed its opportunity to fight, while its older brother went overseas. Eventually 61 Air National Guard units received one or more F-51Hs, but by the end of 1955 all were out of the regular Air Force and ANG inventories.

Horace Q. Waggoner, a 353rd Fighter Group veteran of World War II, flew the Mustang through the Korean War, getting to know the F-51H at Tyndall AFB, Florida. He recalls Tyndall as the first place that he wore a hard helmet. This was due to the F-51H's tendency to lose its canopy; as it came adrift it would hit the pilot on the head, and this had resulted in some fatalities.

Waggoner recalls that the F-51H had engine runaway problems attributable to the Simmonds automatic manifold control. If the throttle was advanced at all on engine shutdown it would go to full power when restarted, causing the aircraft to nose over. The checklist was amended to warn of this failing, and ground crew always stood to the right of the nose during starting—if the propeller hit the ground, the broken tips flew to the left.

The F-51H also had a bad landing-gear problem: if the raising or lowering cycle was interrupted, the system was thrown out completely. One gear leg would come up as the other went down, with the fairing doors doing whatever they wanted. Once this happened there was no way to get the system back in line and several F-51Hs had to be brought in on one wheel as a result.

To clear up some confusion with P-51 designations, "E" was never used for the P-51 series. There was a single P-51M-1NT, serial number 45-11743, which was basically a P-51D-30NT rather than a development of the H. It had a V-1650-9A engine (as the -9 in the H but without water injection). The P-51L was to have been similar to the H but built in Dallas with the -11 engine; it was never built.

The H-equipped units flying in the early 1950s all had an air-defense role, although only the 113th FIS (an ANG unit) and the 85th FIS served as active ADC units during the Korean War. The fast H was well suited for the role. (Dick Phillips)

134

Above: **This 63rd Squadron, 56th FG, Mustang was used as a target tug, sporting a bright yellow tail.** *(W. J. Balogh Sr via Dave Menard)*

Below: **The H of Pennsylvania ANG commander Ed Bollen was named after his wife.** *(Ed Bollen)*

In the fall of 1954 the F-51H began to give way to newer types. The Pennsylvania ANG operated three different types during that time: CO Ed Bollen is flying the Mustang, Jack Love the F-86A, and AF advisor Earl Lupton the F-84F. *(Ed Bollen)*

Double-Breasted Mustang

In late 1943, with the need for long-range escort fighters becoming evident, the AAF asked the aircraft industry for a new aircraft that could perform the mission. North American began work on the XP-82 Twin Mustang in early 1944, just as the first of the lightweight Mustangs, the XP-51F, was being readied for flight testing. The F served as the basis for the new aircraft, the 82's fuselage essentially being a modified and lengthened version of the lightweight fighter's. As the aircraft took shape, P-51H outer wing panels and engines were fitted to the larger twin-engined aircraft. It was however the development of the P-82 that led to the refinement of the H, rather than vice versa.

Joe Barton and Ed Virgin took the XP-82 into the air for the first time on 16 June 1945. In November North American announced, rather optimistically, that production of the P-82 would supplant the P-51H line. With a combat range of 2,500 miles, the aircraft seemed ideal to support Strategic Air Command's very-long-range bombers. Pilots could take turns on long-range flights. The stick in the right-hand, co-pilot's, cockpit was removable, and the rudder pedals in either cockpit could be disconnected in flight and moved out of the way. The starboard cockpit had only enough instruments for relief and emergency operation. Firepower was

The second XP-82 built is escorted by a P-51D during tests in 1945. The aircraft was not two P-51Hs joined, but rather two P-51Fs. The advances made with the Twin Mustang were then incorporated into the H. *(NASM)*

The prototype P-82C night fighter, 44-65169 (actually a converted P-82B). *(NASM)*

formidable: six 0·50-caliber guns in the outer wings, which could be supplemented by eight more in a pod under the center wing. Bombs or rockets could also be carried, and photographic and radar pods were being considered for the centerline station.

Of the 500 P-82Bs ordered only 20 were built, and two of those were converted into prototype night fighters, the P-82C and P-82D. Merlin engines gave way to Allisons with the XP-82A and then the P-82E, which was basically a converted B with radar and an automatic pilot. The P-82Es were converted into night fighters as the F and G. Then came a change of designation to F-82, following the institution of the US Air Force. The F-82H was built as a winterized night fighter.

The justification for the continued procurement of the F-82 was the need for an all-weather fighter as well as an escort for the long-range B-50. In fact the P-82E was ordered as the P-82Z in November 1945. These "Z" aircraft, "in quantities of 20, were procured as an interim measure to keep some of the major aircraft companies in business during the period after termination of war contracts and prior to establishment of firm requirements for further production," according to the official Air Materiel Command history of the aircraft. The document goes on to say: "The airplane was to have the Allison V-1710-143 and V-1710-145 engines in lieu of the Rolls Royce V-1650 engines because one of the most urgent problems facing the Army Air Forces was the development and utilization of an American liquid-cooled engine." Delivery of 250 aircraft was to have begun in November 1946 and been completed by April 1948, but difficulties with the government-furnished engines resulted in the airframes being built and then stored without engines at Consolidated Vultee. All of the airframes had been completed by 30 April 1948, but final delivery of the completed aircraft was not carried out until a year later.

Such was the importance of the F-82E to the Air Force's support of Strategic Air Command, and the urgency of the need for a replacement for the P-61 night fighter, that in January 1948 priority was given to getting 100 of the fighters into SAC, with another 100 Fs and 50 Gs into other commands. Then a spare-parts shortage hit the aircraft, forcing cannibalization of existing airframes.

Don Maggert, after leaving the 49th Fighter Group in Japan, returned to fighter flying with the P-51-equipped 522nd Squadron of the 27th Fighter Group at Kearny AFB, Nebraska. In August 1948 the Mustangs were replaced by the "Double-Breasted Mustang", as the F-82 had become known. As a SAC outfit the 27th, under Col Cy Wilson, was flying 11 and 12-hour missions.

When the engines weren't backfiring or leaking oil the Twin Mustang was nice to fly, particularly with two pilots on long flights, and it handled well on one engine. The electronics were a nightmare, however: there were so many new gadgets. Nor did Maggert like riding as a passenger, particularly when the other pilot "was hurtling my pink body at the earth during gunnery or bombing." But the F-82 was excellent for giving hard-working crew chiefs an idea of how their charges performed in the air.

In December 1949 the F-82 was re-classified as a second-line aircraft, and in May 1950 Strategic Air Command declared a large number of F-82s to be surplus to its needs. As the decision was being made on whether to hold them in temporary storage or send them to the Air National Guard, the North Koreans invaded South Korea on 25 June 1950 and created a new lease on life for the F-82.

This Allison-engined F-82E served with Col Cy Wilson's 27th Fighter Escort Wing, Strategic Air Command. *(AFM)*

The 4th, 68th and 339th all-weather fighter squadrons, flying Twin Mustang night fighters, were a part of the Far East Air Force. When Korea was invaded they were assigned to fly combat air patrols over Inchon and the Seoul area. On 26 June a Yak piston-engined fighter approached two F-82s, but the American pilots were not sure whether to fire or not. The next day all that would change.

Right: Lt Henry Varnell with the last active Twin Mustang after flying from Ladd Field to Elmendorf in Alaska. The aircraft had been assigned to the 449th FIS. *(AFM)*

Below: On 27 June 1950 this F-82G, flown by Lt William Hudson and Lt Carl Fraser, made the first kill of the Korean war by downing a Yak-7U. *Bucket of Bolts* was attached to the 68th Fighter (All Weather) Squadron. *(James Gasser)*

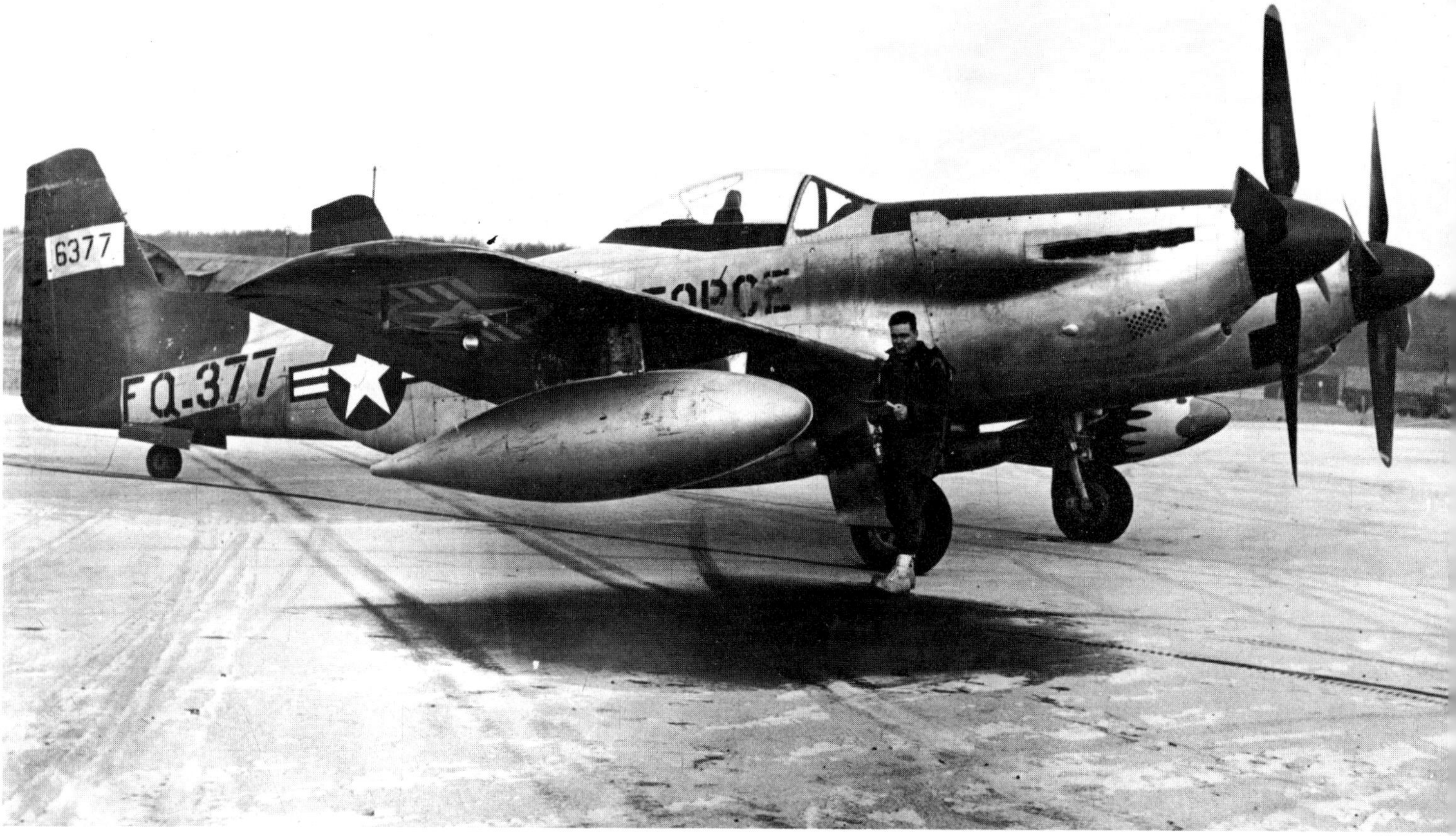
6377
FORCE
FQ-377

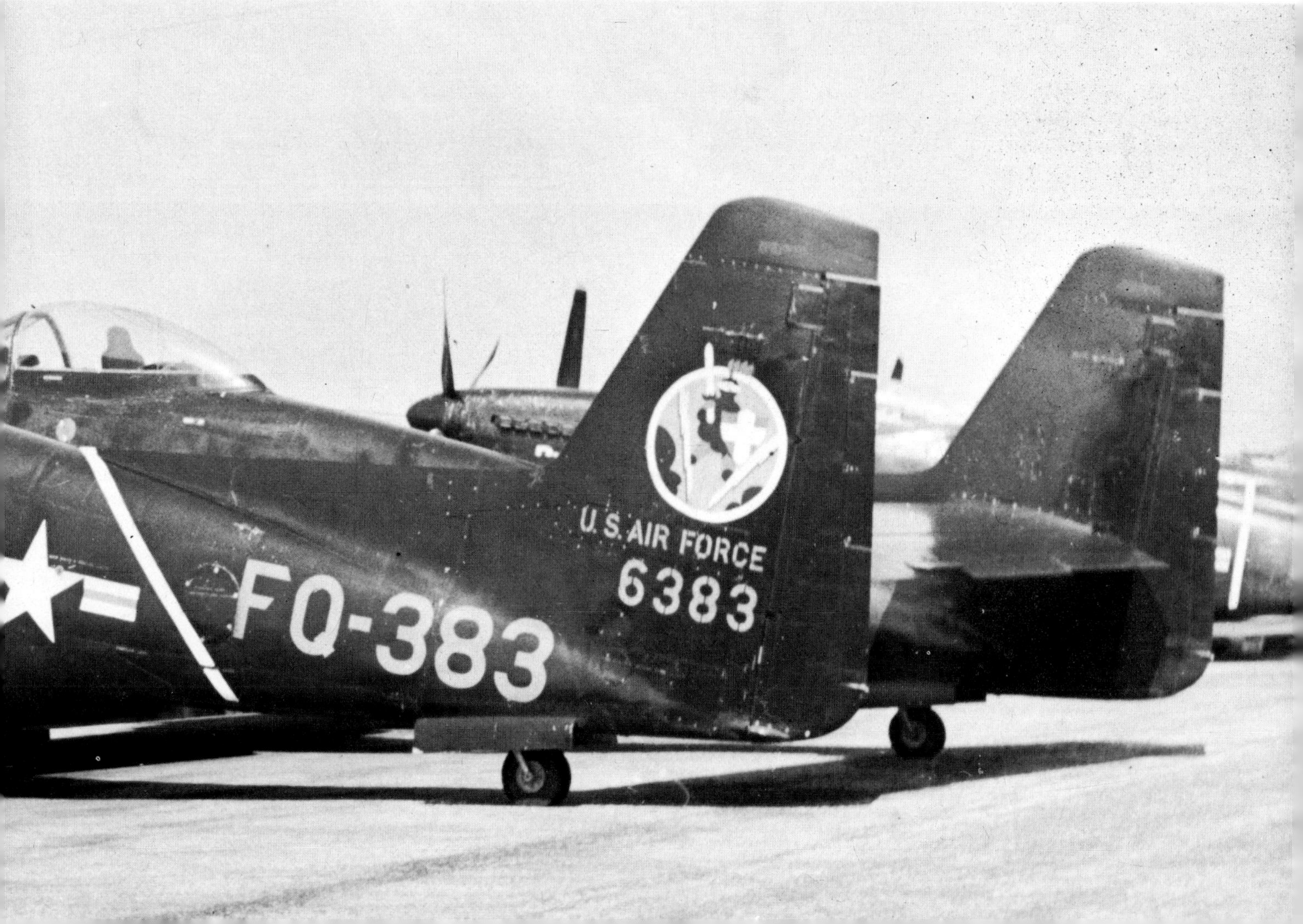
U.S. AIR FORCE
6383
FQ-383

Korea

On 27 June 1950 five North Korean Yak fighters were sent to strafe Kimpo Airfield. Covered by F-80s, Twin Mustangs shot down three Yaks, the first falling to Lt William Hudson of the 68th F(AW)S. He and his radar observer were flying an F-82G night fighter, No 46-383. These were the first three US kills over Korea.

Mustangs, both F-51s and F-82s, had been coming back into the Far East Air Force (FEAF), and in all there were three groups of F-51Ds in Japan by 1950, the 49th, 8th and 35th. Morale was not very high and most of the pilots were looking forward to returning home. Maj Ervin C. Ethell found his command of the 39th Fighter Squadron a challenge. In February 1950 the 39th converted to F-80s, as did other Mustang units. When the war began in June the 39th began to fly support missions with their jets, but combat damage and the shortage of replacement F-80s took their toll and the 39th was ordered to convert back to F-51Ds. Since several of the unit's pilots had just finished flying the Mustang, the 39th was a prime candidate for this apparent backward step. In the meantime Maj Jerry Brown took command of the 39th

Squadron, with Ethell remaining on for a short while to serve as his operations officer before moving to command the transition unit for F-51s at Johnson Air Base.

As the F-80s left the squadron Jerry Brown, a World War II P-38 ace and P-51 pilot, got the unit ready for combat in the Mustang: "All the pilots felt that they were going from a Cadillac (F-80) to a Model T Ford (F-51). However the F-80 could stay in the target area only about 15 minutes, while the F-51 could stay an hour longer, operating from the same airbase, Ashiya on the Japanese island of Kyushu. The F-51 could also land and operate out of bases in Korea when required.

"We had no air-to-air mission. We operated in flights of four or in two-ship elements. We would go to the area ordered and then contact a forward air controller, who was usually in a T-6 or a jeep. The enemy didn't move about when aircraft were in the area, so the F-51 was the more effective because it could stay longer and it carried quite a load of armament.

"It was practically impossible to stop the Russian T-34 tank with 0·50-caliber guns or 5-inch rockets: you needed napalm.

39th Squadron commander Jerry Brown in September 1950. Note the igniters sticking out of the top of the napalm tanks. Brown was downed by ground fire on 30 November and spent almost three years in Chinese prison camps. *(Jerry Brown)*

Right: **Maj Dean Hess USAF was assigned the job of rebuilding the Republic of Korea's Air Force during the first months of the war. After 80 hours in P-51s the Korean pilots were ready for combat.** *(USAF)*

Below: **31 July 1950, Taegu airstrip: the USAF F-51, from the 12th Fighter Bomber Squadron, 18th FBG (before the addition of shark mouths), is operating with the ROKAF.** *(US Army)*

143

As soon as we got it the F-51s could use it immediately; the F-80s had to be modified to carry it, and when they did their range was reduced.

"On 30 November 1950 we were operating out of Yonpo in Korea, a former Japanese base 60 miles north of Wonsan. I led a four-ship flight over the mountains to an area where the Chinese had broken through the South Korean lines. The forward air controller wanted us to burn up about 20 vehicles that had been caught and left in a roadblock, and then work over a small motor pool in the little town of Tokchon. We had all the vehicles in the roadblock burning and were working on the motor pool when I was hit.

"We had established a gunnery pattern when bullets started coming through the bottom of my aircraft. My throttle and gas selector were shot off and coolant hit. I pulled off the target and zoomed to about 400 feet but was too low to bail out. This was mountainous terrain, but alongside the railroad serving the town there was a small cornfield about 75 yards long and fairly level. I didn't have the power to climb so I set it down in the cornfield. This was a bivouac area for a whole Chinese division, so I was picked up immediately."

The Republic of Korea's Air Force was in a shambles after the first few days of the war. The US sent South Korea 10 Mustangs and pilots under the command of Maj Dean Hess to train Korean pilots and ground crews in F-51D operations.

Before long, combat became intense for all pilots flying in Korea. James A. Gasser, who had flown with the 357th Fighter Group in World War II, was happy to get back into the Mustang. He recalls: "Pilots and aircraft kept up a hectic pace from dawn till dusk. From two to five missions were flown daily, with an average of two hours per mission. 23 August 1950 was typical: 2 hr 5 min to Waegwan; 2 hr 15 min to Taegu; 2 hr to Seoul; 2 hr to Seoul; 1 hr to Taegu. Days like this were not rare and certainly could not have been accomplished without good ground crews and very dependable aircraft. After 100 missions I was grounded from combat

As the war heated up, the Australians sent No 77 Squadron to join the other F-51s at Taegu, where this shot was taken on 3 August 1950. *(US Army)*

Above: **By September 1950 the 12th FBS had added shark mouths to their aircraft, seen here at Pusan.** *(USAF)*

Right: **Attached to the 18th FBG, No 2 Squadron South African Air Force, the** *Flying Cheetahs,* **flew their first mission on 16 November 1950, when this shot was taken. The unit received 96 Mustangs from the USAF.** *(USAF)*

Below: **A No 2 Squadron F-51 just returned from a mission on 17 December 1950.** *(US Army)*

activities. The ground troops expressed much praise for the F-51 and the air support rendered by the 5th Air Force. No particular mission stands out from the rest, but it was always a surprise to see a haystack or hut blow up in your face when hit with six 0·50-caliber wing guns; we quickly realized the enemy was everywhere. To fly the F-51 in peace or war was an extreme delight; it seldom let you down and only when the pilot exceeded his capabilities did a problem develop.''

Even though the Mustang was not assigned to air-to-air combat, it got at least four Yak kills (three to Maj Arnold ''Moon'' Mullins of the 67th FBS) and tangled with the MiG-15. On 7 November 1950 a flight of Mustangs from the 36th FBS managed to get several hits against MiGs while not receiving one bullet hole in any of the F-51s.

Nevertheless, the Mustang was an antique in the jet age. From 1 January 1950 to 1 January 1952 there were 462 major accidents with the F-51, over half due to pilot error. The Mustang was a handful to a pilot used to bombers or larger aircraft, or to a pilot not used to the torque of a propeller-driven fighter with ''its nose wheel on the tail''.

Right: **The South Africans eventually transferred to Chinhae, where Capt G. B. Lipawsky taxis out for a mission on 17 December 1950.** *(US Army)*

Below: **This SAAF Mustang is carrying rockets and napalm, and has dropped flap to stay with the camera aircraft. Before converting to Sabres in December 1952 No 2 Squadron lost 74 aircraft and 34 pilots—two of the F-51s were downed by MiG-15s—in the course of 10,373 combat sorties.** *(John Lord via Dick Phillips)*

Arval J. Roberson, a World War II ace in the 357th FG, was not happy when he returned to Mustangs with the 67th Squadron of the 18th Wing, which also had to give up its F-80s for F-51s. The check-out was quick and confusing, though no trouble, but flying off pierced steel planking at night could be hair-raising. At Pyongyang the unit operated from a 2,500ft dirt strip. To get out to the runway, pilots had to taxi between the officers' quarters and the mess hall, with only 10-15 ft clearance, and then turn left at the security police post. Some of their deep interdiction missions ran over five hours, and at times the Mustangs would escort RB-29s. Roberson chalked up 100 missions before going home to fly F-51s with the Kentucky Air National Guard.

Erv Ethell, after a tour of duty as the Senior Air Advisor to the Korean Military Assistance Group and flying combat in T-6s, C-45s and forward air control aircraft, came home to

Centre right: **James A. Gasser's 8th FBG F-51 loaded with rockets and napalm.** *(Jim Gasser)*

Right: **20 April 1951: 35th FBG Mustangs are worked on at Seoul Air Base before a mission in support of the 3rd Infantry Division.** *(US Army)*

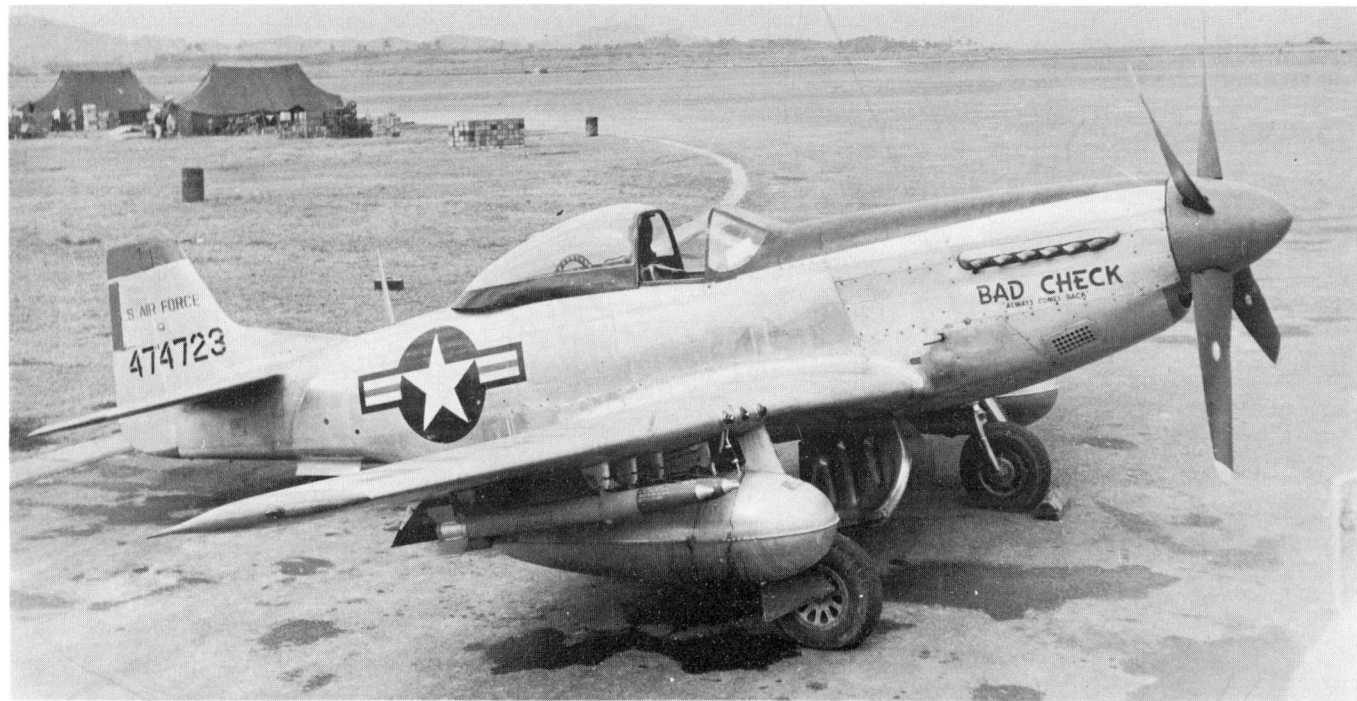

Above: Lt Col Ralph D. Saltsman Jr's gun-camera film of his victory over an Il-2 on 20 June 1951 while flying an F-51 with the 18th Fighter Bomber Group. *(USAF)*

Above: A 67th Squadron, 18th FBG, Mustang taking off fully loaded from a waterlogged steel-matted runway in August 1951. *(USAF)*

Above: **35th and 18th FBG F-51s being prepared for a close-support mission in October 1951.** *(US Army)*

...ow: **September 1951: a 35th Group F-51 with bombs and ...kets taxis through one of the many "water hazards" ...countered in Korea.** *(USAF)*

U.S. AIR FORC
44-64004

George Air Force Base, California. While serving as 192nd Squadron commander Ethell was approached by 131st Fighter Bomber Wing commander Woody Ramsey in the summer of 1952 about what was to be the last overwater military movement of Mustangs in the USAF. The government of Iceland, having been promised US aircraft for their air defense, made it clear that if the fighters did not arrive by 1 September 1952 the American presence in Iceland would no longer be welcome. The only fighters immediately available were the F-51s at George, and so they would have to go.

Some 35 aircraft were taken from eight separate units, along with pilots and support personnel. The F-51s were painted in arctic markings and made combat-ready. On 26 August 1952 Erv Ethell led the new squadron into the air from George. Three C-124s hauled the maintenance personnel and the spare parts. The aim was to have 30 aircraft reach the east coast, since there would be no time for major repairs en route.

The first leg to Tinker AFB, Oklahoma, and the second to Wright-Patterson, Ohio, went as planned, but 25 new batteries were needed before the third leg, to Presque Isle, Maine, could be flown. Ethell, a major, was flatly denied the batteries by an irate colonel during a 15-minute debate on the flight line. Only after he invoked the authority of Gen Virgil Zoller, who was following in a B-26, was Ethell reluctantly given the batteries.

From Wright-Patterson the Mustangs were split into flights of four and sent to Maine. But then the aircraft began to land all over the place between Otis AFB, Massachusetts, and Presque Isle. The new engines had not been run in, resulting in glycol leaks, magneto and other problems, but in the end everyone arrived at Maine. The North Atlantic weather briefing revealed a 50 per cent possibility of snow at Goose Bay, Labrador, the next stop, but Ethell decided to press on. As the last flight of four arrived there the snow began to come down hard. It lasted for two days!

Below: **Lt David L. Gray, 67th Squadron, 18th FBG, making a wheels-up landing after being damaged by ground fire in September 1952.** *(USAF)*

Top: **Some 25 F-51s were delivered to Iceland by 1 September 1952 under Ethell's command, but they served only seven months before being replaced by F-94s. This was the Mustang's last assignment in the USAF as a first-line fighter.** *(USAF via Dave Menard)*

Above: **18 May 1953: the Republic of Korea continued to operate Mustangs through to the end of the Korean War, flying most often from fields surfaced with pierced steel planking.** *(USAF)*

Left: **''O dark thirty,'' 26 August 1952, George AFB, California: Maj Erv Ethell is wished well by Lt Col Woody Ramsey (left) and Brig Gen James Furgeson, 9th Air Force vice-commander, as the last overwater deployment of Mustangs on active service begins. The aircraft were to be delivered to Iceland for air-defense duty.** *(Erv Ethell)*

The only way into the next field, Bluie West One in Greenland, was up a fjord between snow and ice-covered mountains. A total of 25 aircraft were selected for the flight from Goose to Bluie West One. At Greenland one went out with a coolant leak. On 1 September Ethell led his 24 Mustangs to Iceland, passing over Reykjavik in show formation before breaking up into flights to land at Keflavik. The F-51s taxied in and lined up for inspection as Ethell told those gathered that ammunition was on board the aircraft and that only the guns had to be charged. The USAF was in place as promised, with eight aircraft on alert and another 16 ready.

In fact the US presence was only a token one, as there was no air-defense radar or control system in Iceland. Maintenance crews went over the aircraft, but did not get all of them to alert status until 15 September. After three months Ethell, his pilots and airmen left and replacement personnel took over. Seven months later F-94s were flown in to replace the old F-51s and an era had passed. The North American Mustang, even though it would serve for a few more years in the Air National Guard, had finally been withdrawn from the nation's first line of defense.

Guard the Sky

At the end of World War II the USAF picked the P-51 as the primary equipment for the Air Reserve. Here Maj Larry Horras and Capt George Van Noy Jr of the 473rd AAF Base Unit in Miami, Florida, get some practice on 13 September 1946. As CO, Horras had to get former pilots checked out on the AT-6 before allowing them back to the Mustang. *(Larry Horras, USAF)*

Above: **In June 1948 all "pursuit" designations were changed to "fighter". These F-51s, from the 82nd FG at Eglin AFB, Florida, were photographed on 8 September 1948.** *(USAF)*

Right: **Late 1947 or early 1948: these Mustangs are serving out their time by keeping reserve pilots active.** *(Dick Phillips)*

Below: **F-6Ds of the 363rd Tactical Reconnaissance Group in late 1945 or early 1946.** *(Gen Bryce Poe III via Dave Menard)*

Below right: **In 1950 Mustangs still equipped several fighter-bomber wings and some, like the F-51, served as target tugs. Note the hard helmet.** *(Robert Stuckey via Dick Phillips)*

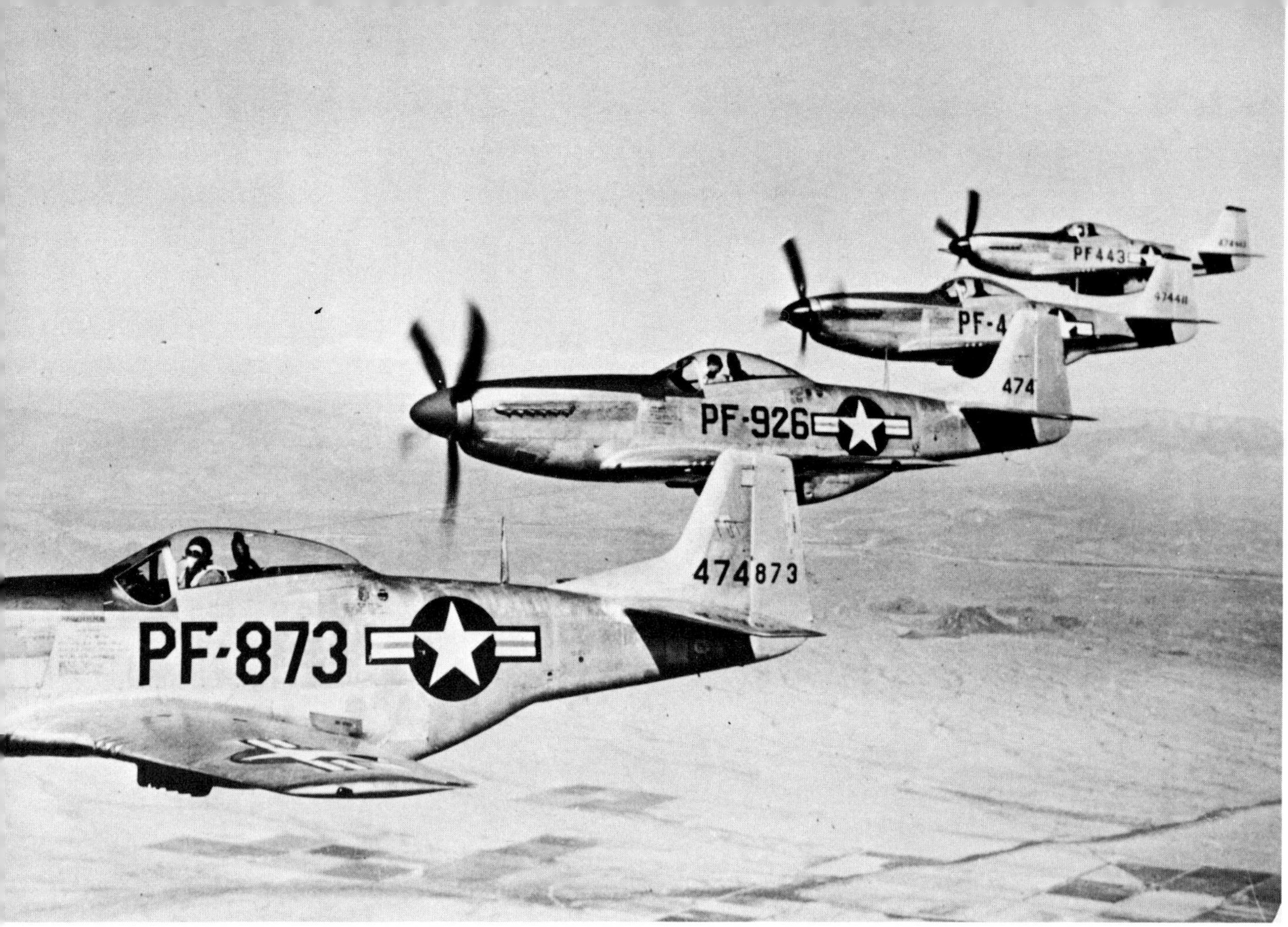
PF-873
474873
PF-926
474
PF-4
PF443

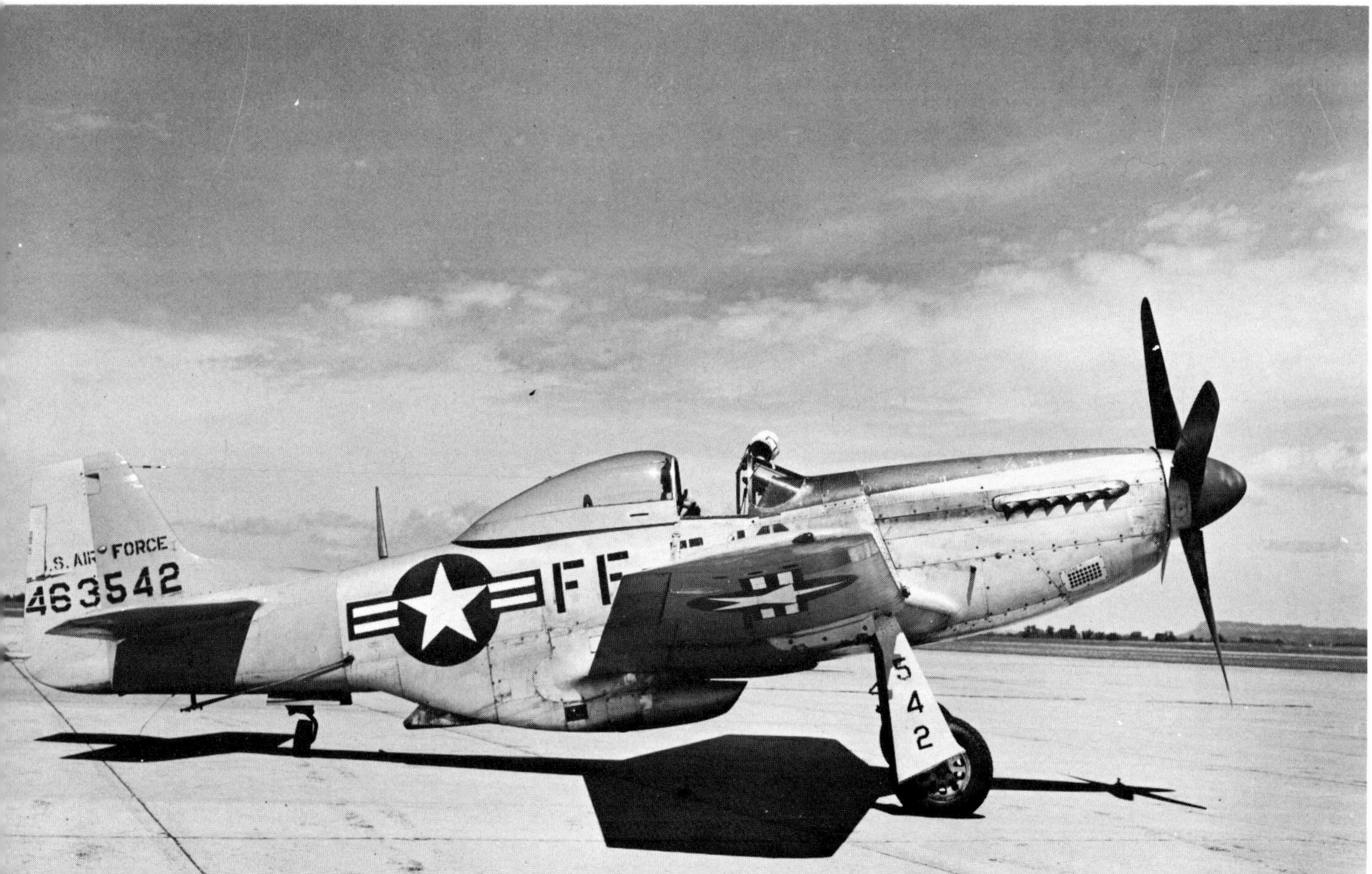
.S. AIR FORCE
463542
FF
5
4
2

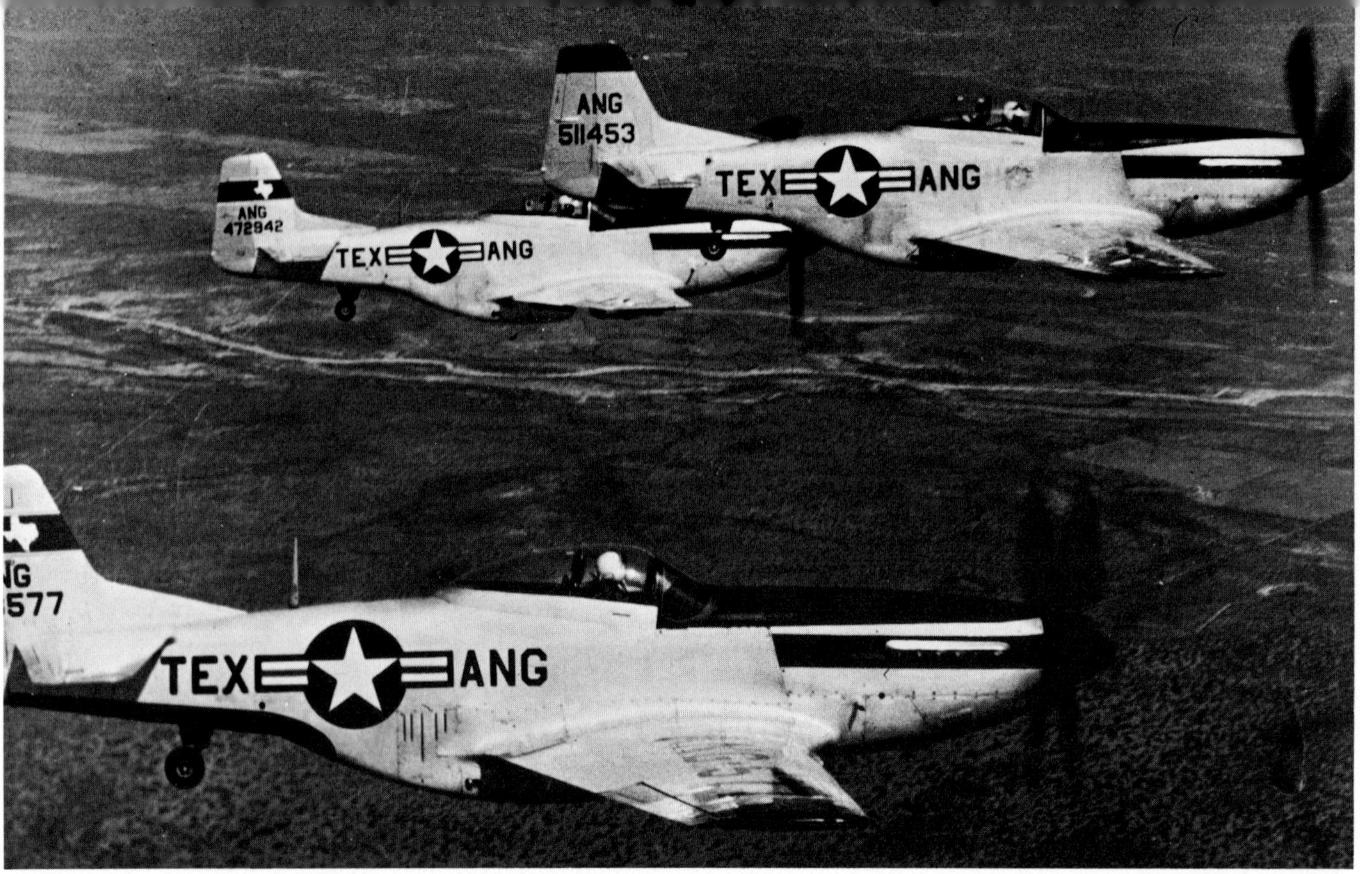
ANG
511453
TEX ANG
ANG
472842
TEX ANG
TEX ANG

ANG
0463536
NJ ANG
536

ANG
463803
KY ANG
03

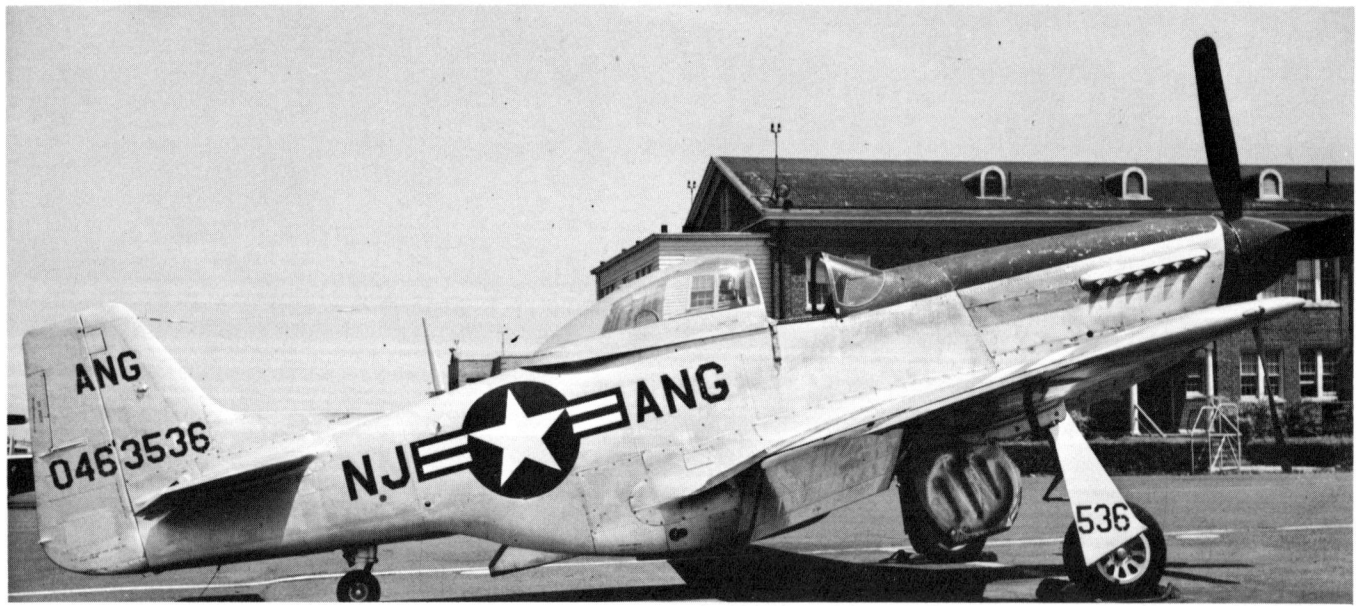

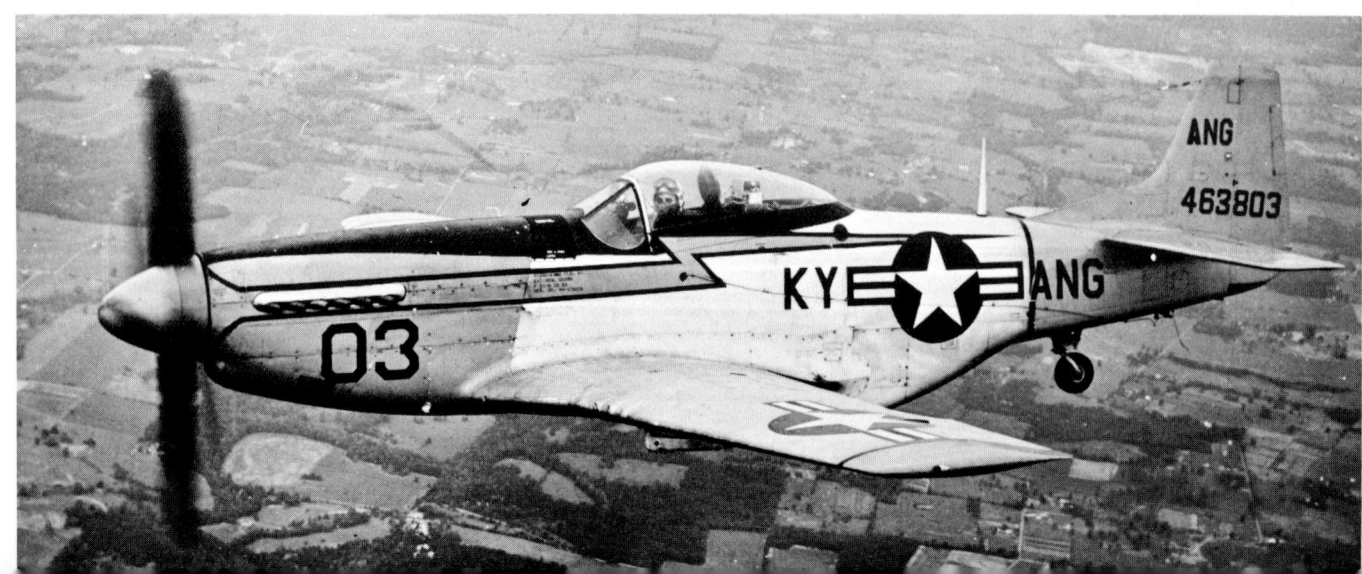

Pages 156-9: **In the 1950s the last active F-51s in the US went to the numerous state-based Air National Guard units. They were to guard the sky as a reserve force of citizen soldiers that could be called to active duty when needed. Some were recalled and went to Korea. As can be seen in some of these shots, on 19 January 1953 all of the F-51 units were ordered to disconnect the tailwheel retraction mechanism and lock the wheel in the down position.** *(Texas ANG via John Dienst; Roger Besecker; Norm Taylor; W. J. Balogh Sr via Dave Menard; North Dakota ANG; Logan Coombs; Robert Stuckey via Dick Phillips; Dick Phillips)*

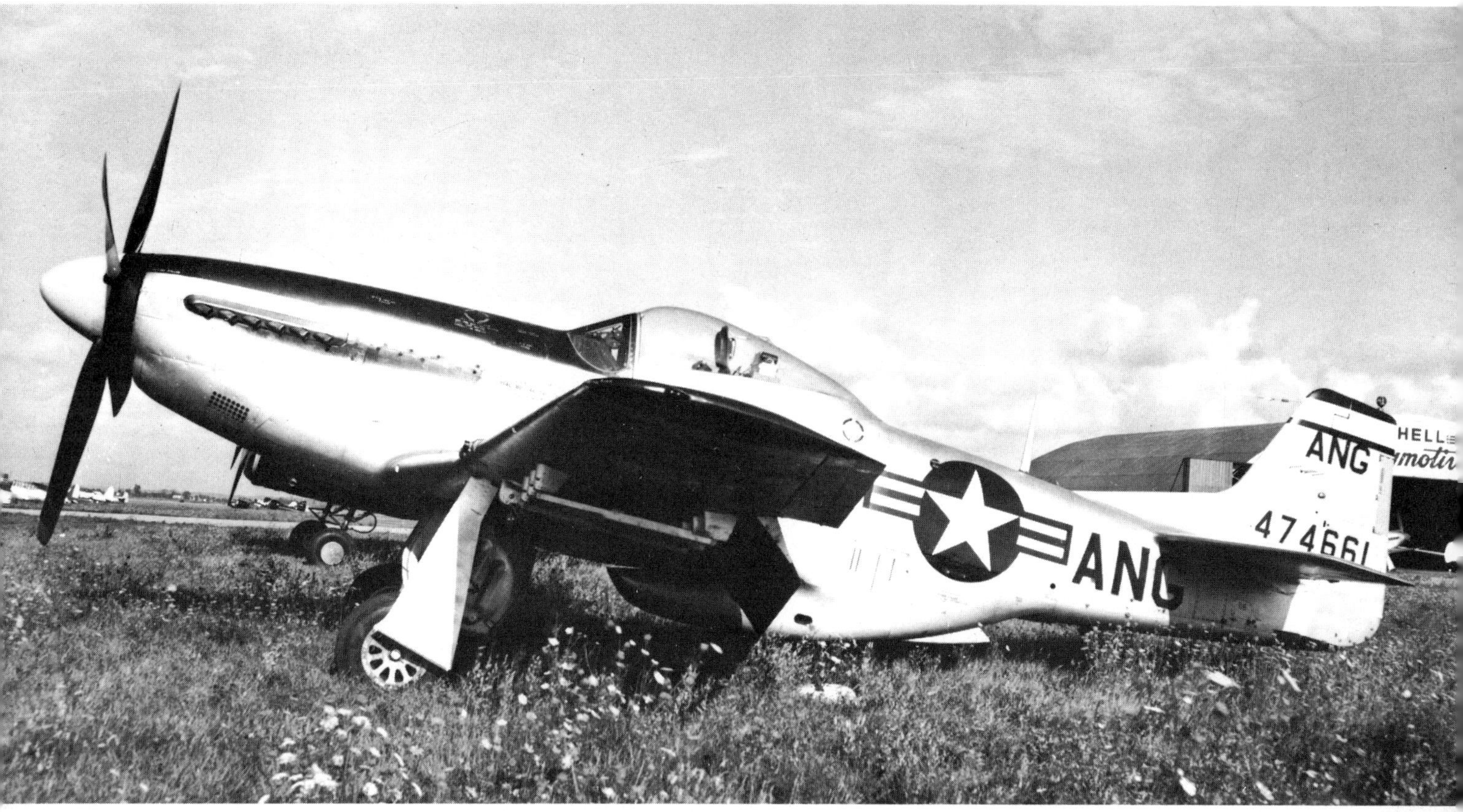
ANG
474661
ANG

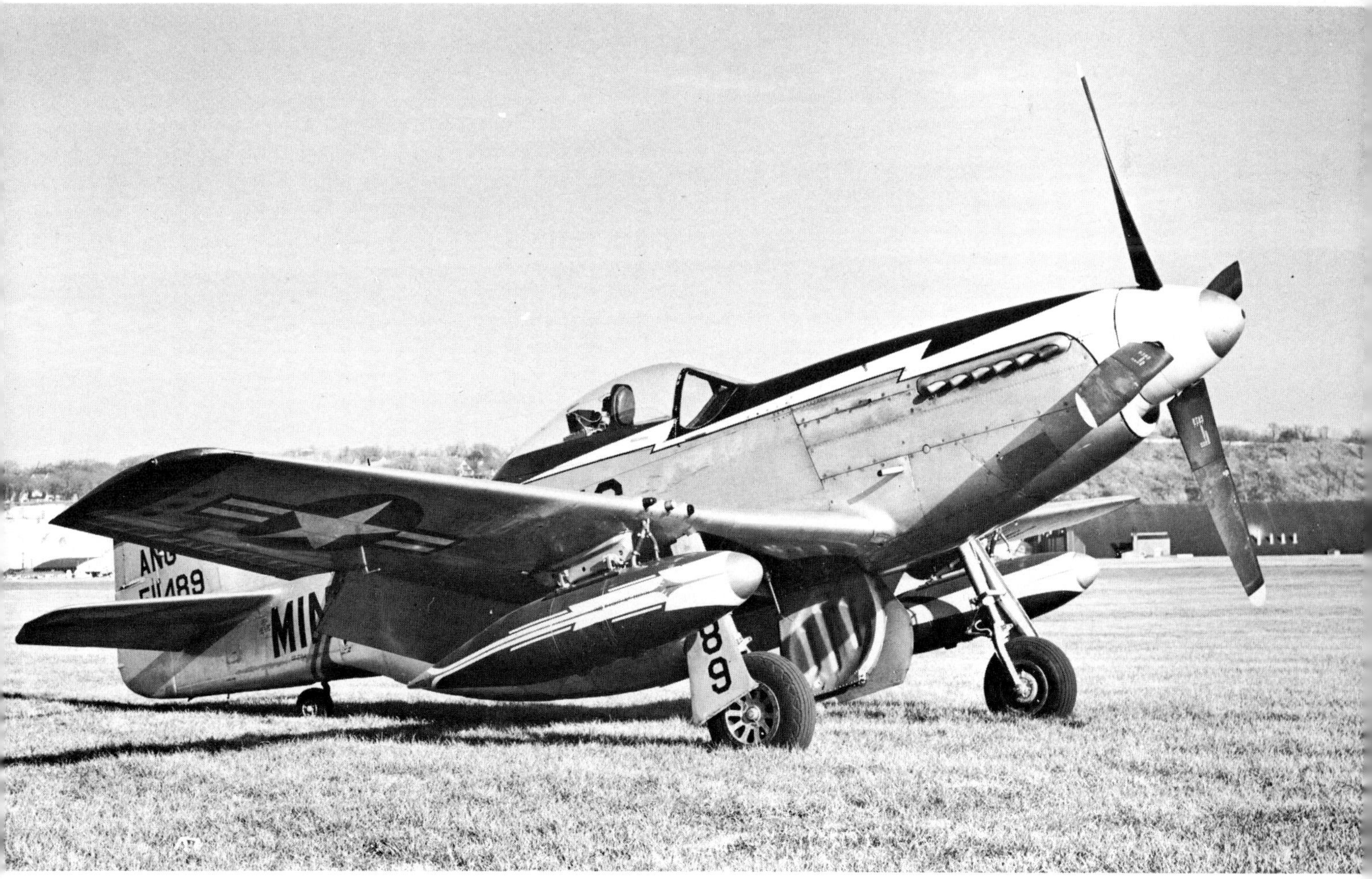
ANG

Below: **The Maryland ANG (104th Fighter Bomber Squadron) had an aerial demonstration team known as the Guardian Angels. The pilots were John F. R. Scott, Jesse D. Mitchell Jr, Malcolm E. Henry and William Marriott III.** *(Dave McLaren)*

Right and far right: **As the F-51 served out its last years in the late 1940s and early 1950s it remained a favorite with its pilots in spite of the advent of the jet age. The USAF's last propeller-driven fighter, it is one of the most famous of American combat aircraft.** *(Norm Taylor)*

Left: **Kelly AFB, Texas: Huge numbers of Mustangs were taken from storage and disposed of to the National Guard and civilian buyers in the 1950s. In those days the average price of a Mustang on the auction block was less than $1,500.** *(USAF via Norm Taylor)*

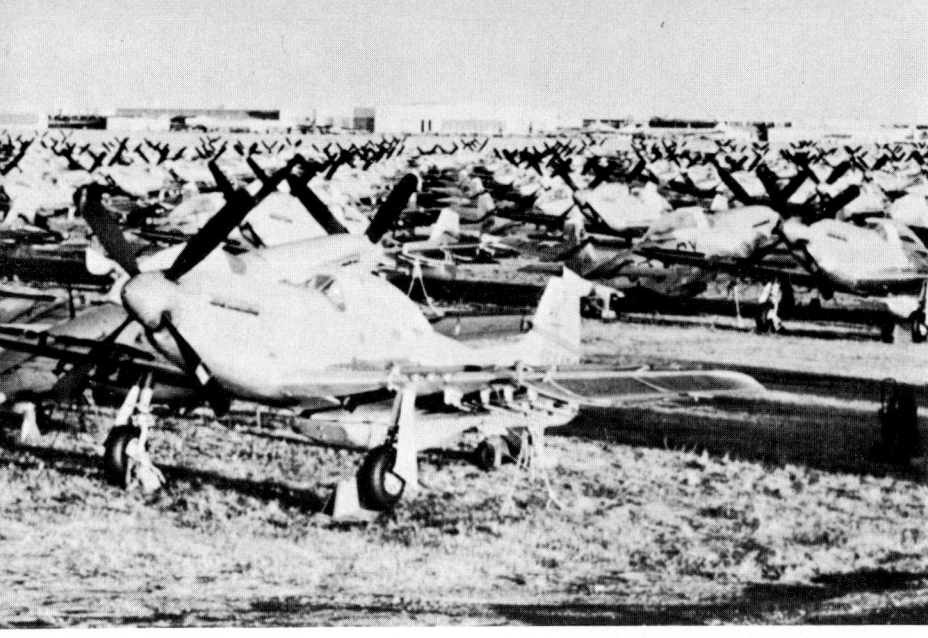

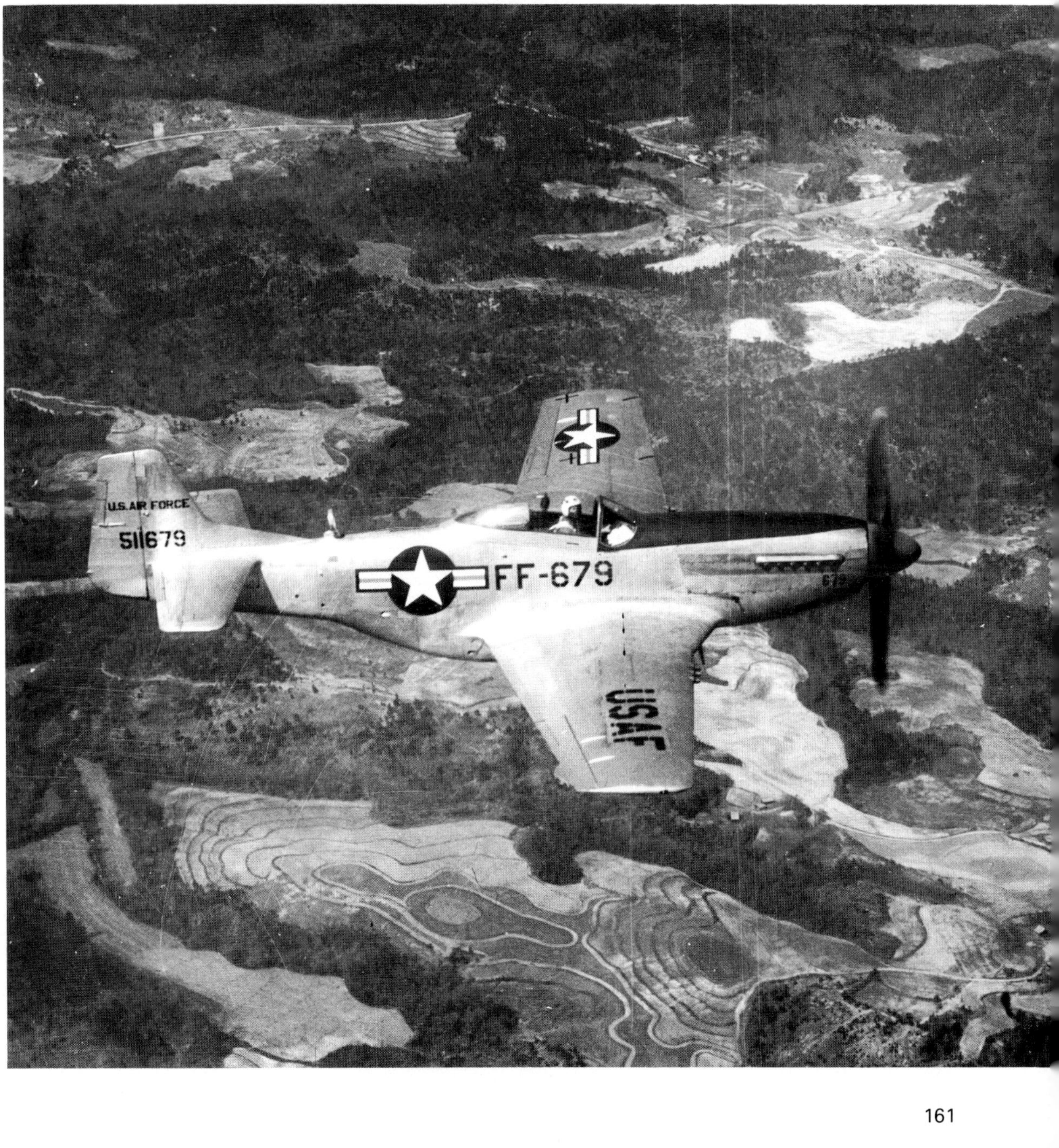

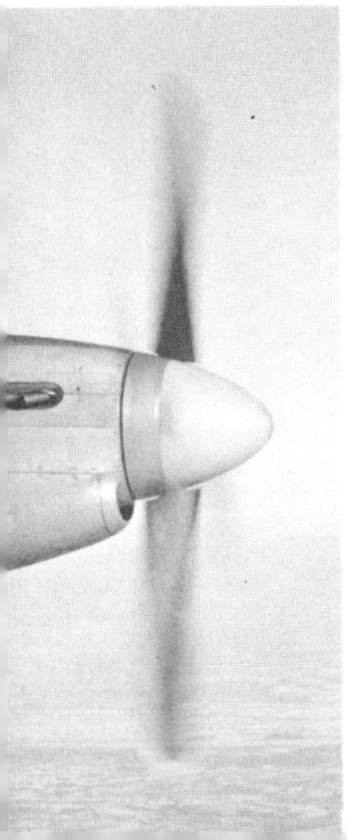

RF-51D-25-NT of the US Air Force. Tactical reconnaissance Mustangs were popular in Korea and served in this role without a replacement until jets phased the mission out.

Below: **27 January 1957: Maj James L. Miller taxis the last F-51 in the US military inventory (West Virginia ANG) at Wright Patterson AFB, Ohio, where it was handed over to the Air Force Museum. The aircraft flew for the last time on 14 February 1957 over Marietta, Ohio, for the première of the movie** *Battle Hymn,* **an account of Dean Hess' experiences with the ROK Air Force in Korea.** *(USAF)*

Under Other Flags

Above: **A P-51K fresh out of the factory for delivery to the Royal Air Force as a Mustang Mk IV. 594 Ks and 281 Ds were delivered to the RAF, which designated them all Mk IVs. (AAHS)**

Below: **2 May 1945: this Mk IV (P-51K-15-NT) is at Newark, New Jersey, the primary staging point for Mustangs destined to be shipped to Europe.** *(via Kenn Rust)*

Left: **Sqn Ldr A. Cox (LB-V) leads a No 84 Squadron flight out of Townsville, Queensland, Australia, on 4 July 1945.** *(Frank F. Smith)*

Right: **No 77 Squadron RAAF with their Australian-built Mustangs in the late 1940s or early 1950s. This unit saw extensive action in Korea before converting to Vampires.** *(via Bruce Hoy)*

Below: **Flt Lt Dave Hudson in 155 leads a No 22 (City of Sydney) Squadron scramble to intercept RAAF Lincolns inbound to ''attack'' the city in 1955 during Exercise Flying Link.** *(Dave Hudson)*

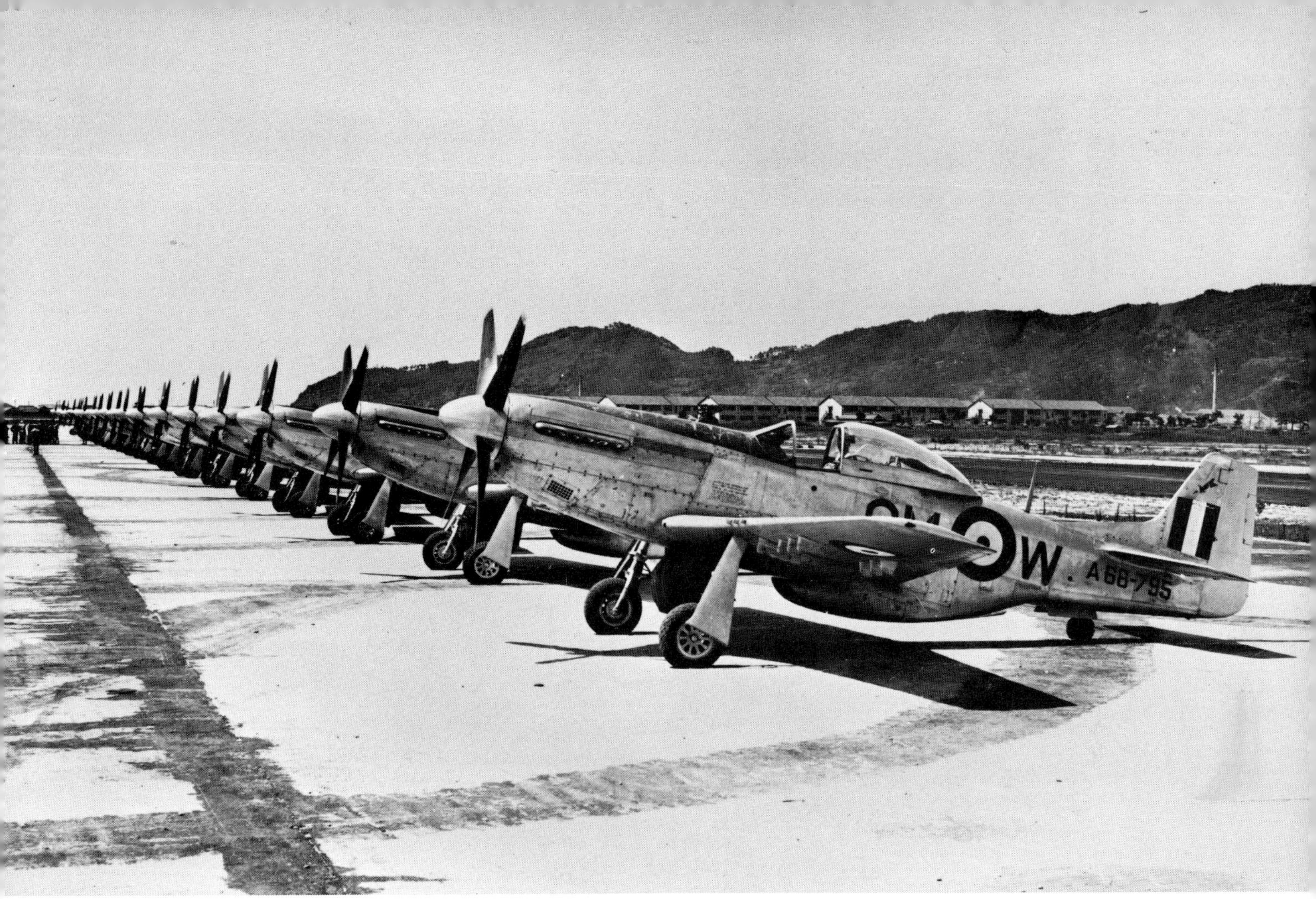

W
A68-795

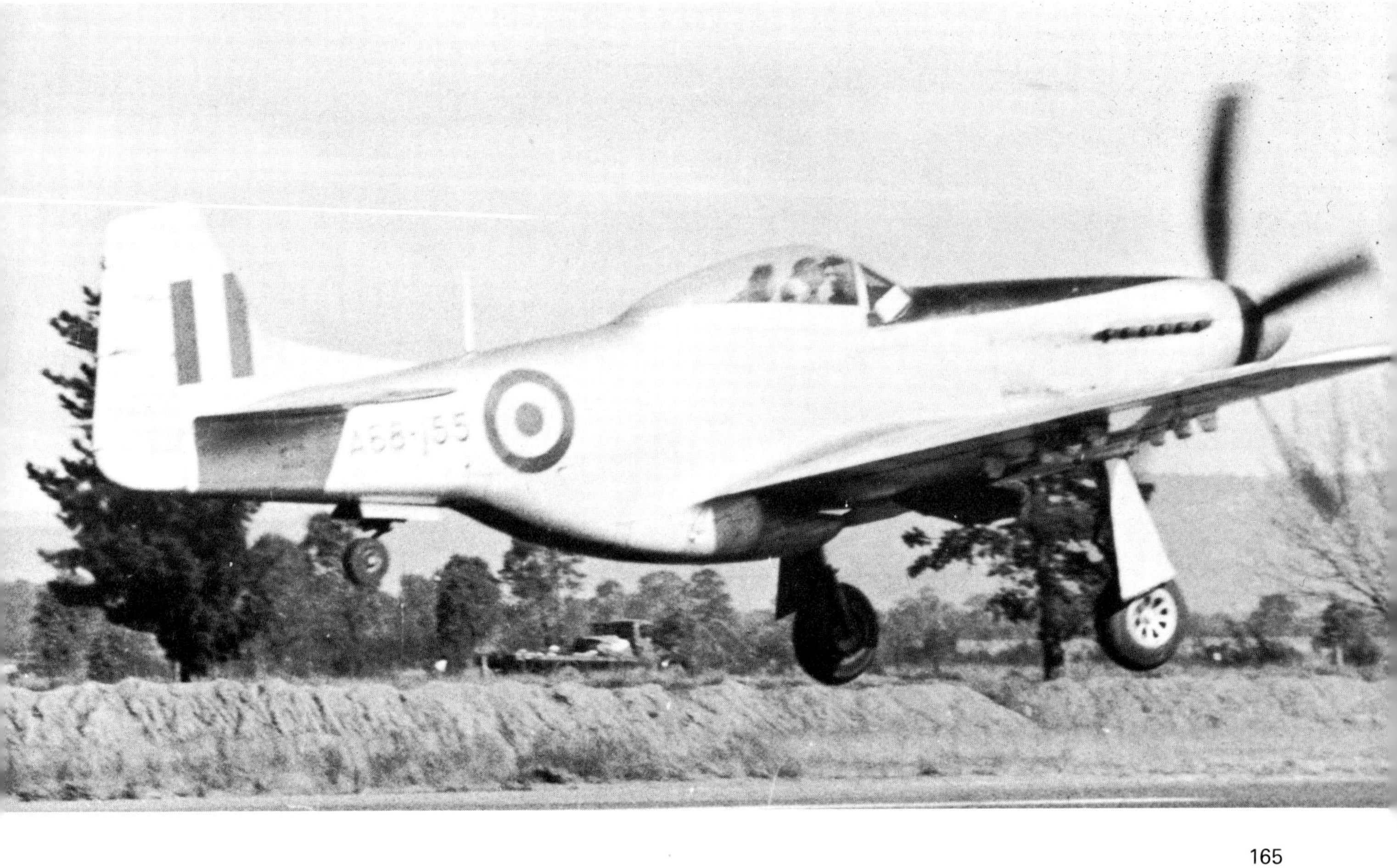

A68-155

Left: **Between April and August 1944 nine USAAF Mustangs force-landed in Sweden. Four entered the inventory of the Swedish Air Force as J 26 fighters. This P-51B, 43-3635, was impressed into service with the SwAF as a J26. At the time the picture was taken, July 1950, the aircraft was still in service with F 16 at Uppsala** *(Lars Olausson)*

Left: **Dave Hudson (left, with engine running) with another No 22 Squadron pilot in 1955 during Exercise Flying Link. The City squadrons were made up by the Citizens Air Force, composed mostly of part-time pilots. At the time Hudson was the only medical doctor who was also a fully qualified pilot in the RAAF; he was thus able to double as flight surgeon for the unit.** *(Dave Hudson)*

Below: **Sweden bought large batches of former USAAF Mustangs, which were delivered between March and November 1948. They equipped F 4 and F 16 as well as F 21, a reconnaissance wing which flew the Mustang as the S 26 (USAF F-6). F 20, the Air Force College wing, also flew the aircraft. National markings had been painted out on these aircraft, which are taxiing in on delivery on 1 February 1947, but the former 8th Air Force group and squadron markings are clearly evident. Nose markings indicate the 353rd, 339th, 352nd, 479th, 78th and 355th groups.** *(Lars Olausson)*

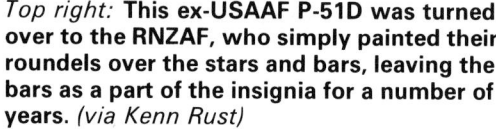

Above: **August 1950: Engineer Cadet Harald Werner flies a J 26 belonging to F 21 at Lulea.** *(Lars Olausson)*

Top right: **This ex-USAAF P-51D was turned over to the RNZAF, who simply painted their roundels over the stars and bars, leaving the bars as a part of the insignia for a number of years.** *(via Kenn Rust)*

Centre right: **The Armée de l'Air received several USAAF P-51s and F-6s. This one was photographed at Munich, Germany, in 1949.** *(Merle Olmsted)*

Right: **A P-51D of Groupe Reconnaissance II/33 "Savoie," 2nd Escadre, at Dijon-Longvic. Most of the aircraft in this unit were F-6s.** *(P. Gandillet via Roger Freeman)*

Left: **September 1954: as the SwAF began to acquire jets, most of the Mustangs were sold to Israel.**

Right: **This Mustang flew with the RCAF's Central Experiment and Proving Establishment, based at Arnprior, Ontario.** *(NASM)*

Below: **A Mustang belonging to the Uruguayan Air Force in 1953.** *(via Kenn Rust)*

Bottom: **During September and October 1948 the Israel Defense Force/Air Force received its first Mustangs. They flew with Nos 101 and 105 squadrons, which also had Spitfires and Avia-built Me109s. As long as the aircraft were in first-line service they were left natural metal; camouflage was applied once they were consigned to secondary roles.** *(IDF)*

Right: **No 402 City of Winnipeg Squadron at RCAF Rivers, Manitoba, in 1953. Tom Patterson, former CO of this unit, recalls doing fighter intercepts against Sabres: "We could take on the Sabres any day and beat the pants off them; in fact we nearly killed a few Sabre drivers at Ottawa. At altitude we could turn inside them. A Sabre would come boiling in, so all you did was start into a tight turn and he's pulling like you just don't believe. All you did was pull your throttle in very rapidly, dump about 15° of flap, set your ailerons back and—Voom!—they went by you. Some of the Sabres tried this at lower altitudes: the slots would pull out and they would go into a spin; a couple spun in at low altitude and scared the living daylights out of their jockeys."** *(Chas Gledhill via Norm Malayney)*

Left: **No 402 Squadron always had colorful markings: yellow and blue rudders and spinners, with the name in yellow on the anti-glare panel. Fred Peterson made a wheels-up landing in 273 in 1956, just before Canada got rid of its Mustangs. The aircraft was sold to a US buyer and is still flying in the USA.** *(Logan Coombs via Dick Phillips)*

Below far left: **The Philippine AF used the F-51 as its primary fighter into the mid-1950s. The type equipped the 6th, 7th and 8th Fighter Squadrons, which sported blue, red and yellow spinners respectively. The large buzz numbers below the cockpit also indicated the squadron: those of the 6th started with 2, the 7th with 3 and the 8th with 4. The F-51Ds were incorporated into the 5th Fighter Wing. These Mustangs were photographed at Manila on 14 December 1957.** *(Merle Olmsted)*

Below centre: **Wg Cdr E. S. Casabar's F-51 sits with 8th Squadron aircraft at Clark Field in the mid-1950s.** *(Merle Olmsted)*

Below: **The PAF alert flight at Nichols Field in the 1950s. By 1959 the last of the F-51s had been retired to make way for F-86F Sabres.** *(Merle Olmsted)*